T0382224

Twilight of the West

Twilight of the West

Christopher Coker

Copyright © 1998 by Westview Press, A Division of HarperCollins Publishers, Inc.

Published in 1998 in the United States of America by Westview Press, 5500 Central Avenue, Boulder, Colorado 80301-2877, and in the United Kingdom by Westview Press, 12 Hid's Copse Road, Cumnor Hill, Oxford OX2 9JJ

Library of Congress Cataloging-in-Publication Data
Coker, Christopher.
Twilight of the West / Christopher Coker.
p. cm.
Includes bibliographical references and index.
ISBN 0-8133-3368-3
1. Europe—Politics and government. 2. Europe—Relations—
United States. 3. United States—Relations—Europe. 4. World
politics—20th century. 5. Liberalism. 6. Ethics. I. Title.
D1053.C63 1998
909.82'04—dc21   98-21245
                                                              CIP

The paper used in this publication meets the requirements of the American National Standard for Permanence of Paper for Printed Library Materials Z39.48-1984.

10   9   8   7   6   5   4   3   2   1

Westview Press
A Division of HarperCollins*Publishers*

Copyright © 1998 by Westview Press, A Division of HarperCollins Publishers, Inc.

Published in 1998 in the United States of America by Westview Press, 5500 Central Avenue, Boulder, Colorado 80301-2877, and in the United Kingdom by Westview Press, 12 Hid's Copse Road, Cumnor Hill, Oxford OX2 9JJ

Library of Congress Cataloging-in-Publication Data
Coker, Christopher.
    Twilight of the West/Christopher Coker.
      p. cm.
    Includes bibliographical references (p.   ) and index.
    ISBN 0-8133-3368-7
    1. History, Modern—1945- —Philosophy. 2. Europe—Relations—
United States. 3. United States—Relations—Europe. 4. North
Atlantic Treaty Organization. I. Title.
D842.C585 1998
909.82'5—dc21   97-31015
                                                                              CIP

The paper used in this publication meets the requirements of the American National Standard for Permanence of Paper for Printed Library Materials Z39.48-1984.

10   9   8   7   6   5   4   3   2   1

Contents

Preface

The political "West" was not a natural construct but a highly artificial one. It took the presence of a life-threatening, overtly hostile "East" to bring it into existence. It is extremely doubtful whether it can survive the disappearance of that enemy.

—Owen Harries, 'The Collapse of "the West",'
Foreign Affairs (September/October 1993)

During the Cold War it was not unusual for people to be asked where they were on the day they heard that John F. Kennedy had been assassinated. These days one is asked where one was when the Berlin Wall had been breached. I happen to remember the day quite clearly. I was in Galveston, Texas, to address the World Affairs Council. The subject of my talk was 'The Cold War: The Next Twenty Years'. Imagine my discomfort, just an hour before I was due to speak, watching live, on the television in my hotel room, the people of East Berlin spilling out onto the Alexanderplatz, intent on ending the division of the city.

Many of my colleagues were taken by surprise by the end of the Cold War. Few predicted that it would end when it did, and fewer still anticipated the manner of its passing. I can lay claim to no greater insight myself. But since then I have given a great deal of thought to why my profession failed the public so completely, despite the support it received from foundations (most of them American), which had invested large sums of money commissioning reports and convening conferences on Cold War themes. Is it inevitable that we cannot predict events, that history can never be decoded? Or is there something intrinsically wrong with the way the profession looks at the world?

One of the reasons I have written this book is that I believe that the subject of international relations requires a much broader frame of reference. Specialists tend to focus too narrowly on specific problems. They tend to ignore the broad sweep of events, the wider picture. Accordingly, I have attempted to extend the enquiry beyond the usual range of subjects into literary and philosophical ideas. I have sought in this book to ask why 'the West', as we call the Western world in its political incarnation, has lost a sense of purpose in recent years, why it is riven by divisions within its own ranks, and why it seems to have entered its twilight years.

If I have deliberately eschewed economic and social science analysis, that
is not because I dispute their importance. Far from it. It is because I wanted
to look at the future of the West from another perspective. I have tried to
anticipate its impending demise by locating its origins in the self-
questioning that is still the defining mark of its own civilisation, its discourse about itself. Whether I have done so convincingly is something that
my readers must judge for themselves.

I have divided this book into three parts. In the first I will look at the circumstances in which the Western community emerged: that unique series of
what the poet W. H. Auden called 'mind-events' of the twentieth century
that brought the United States and Western Europe together for a brief moment in history. Nowhere were these events of more import than in the
Anglo-American imagination. If the alliance was, as I shall contend, the
product of a unique set of circumstances, there is no reason, of course, why
it should outlive the preconditions of its birth.

In the second part of this study I will look at the emergence of another
community, the European Union, and explain why its development, while
running parallel to that of the West, made it impossible to construct an
Atlantic Community as the founding fathers of NATO had planned. As a
political force, Atlanticism never appealed to the French or the Germans,
and neither Britain nor the United States had the will or the energy to push it
forward. Ironically, with the end of the Cold War the Europe that the French
tried to construct has begun to unravel. Europe is being transformed in new
and exciting ways but ones that run against the grain of what is still left of a
Western sensibility. But then the United States too is being transformed under the pressure of demographic changes and social realignments at home.
Both the Old World and the New are in the process of evolving into multicultural communities, a development that has begun to undermine the cultural essentialism on which the Western project was grounded.

In the last part of the book I shall ask whether the new challenges that
the Western world faces, in particular those of Islamic revivalism and the
resurgence of Asia, are in themselves threatening enough to justify a renewal of the Western alliance, or what Nietzsche would call its 'revaluation'. Using this concept I will argue not only that these threats are overdrawn but also that even if they were not, the alliance would find it next to
impossible to find a basis for collective action.

It is almost impossible to imagine a sequence of events that would lead to
a recommissioning of the Western community in the future. The task before
all the major world cultures in the twenty-first century will be the same: to
forge a world civilisation for the first time as the international community
confronts the next challenge of modernity—together.

The idea behind 'the West', of course, has long been that its members will
not long survive the travails and storms to come if they fail to hold to-

gether. It can also be argued, however, that the Western powers urgently need to engage in a dialogue with the non-Western world rather than to retreat into a fortress, so clogged with narrow thinking that it will offer them not a dynamic community but rather a refuge from the future.

Perhaps I owe my English-speaking readers a word of explanation about the 'style' of this book. It may well be a touch too 'metaphysical' for many, with its discussion of historical movements and the importance of the social imagination. Such themes have been accorded very little importance in the English-speaking world. Culture has never been considered a significant factor in international relations. The English, more than the Americans, have traditionally been thought to have had little regard for abstract ideas.

This was not always the case. It is wrong to suggest that Hegelian thinking, for example, has never been regarded very highly in England. There was a strong idealist school that found a voice at the end of the nineteenth century in the work of the neo-Hegelians Bosanquet, Green, and Bradley. Only the onset of the First World War discredited Hegelian thinking and allowed the empiricists Ayer, Wittgenstein, and Russell to sweep all before them. The Cambridge school of Whitehead, Broad, and G. E. Moore considered that the mark of a 'civilised' man was a distrust of any abstractions that could not be proved to be 'real'. As Keynes wrote subsequently, his generation was imbued with 'Moorism'—the notion that sound ideas needed to be constructed in a language shorn of metaphysical conceits.[1]

While it is undoubtedly true that the Germans paid a high price for their preoccupation with philosophical abstractions, the English and the Americans suffered from the overempirical nature of their thinking. In an era when philosophy occupied a central place in the European imagination the devaluation of metaphysics impoverished the political language of liberalism. Karl Popper was the first to attack the Hegelian mentality, in his seminal work *The Open Society and Its Enemies* (1945), but he was also particularly critical of the decline of interest in the great problems, the concentration upon 'minutiae' or 'puzzles', and especially upon the meaning of words—in brief the 'scholasticism' of liberal thinking that made its own contribution to the closing of the European mind.[2]

Today we are confronted with a different problem. In our postmodern world we have no historical ground on which to stand because we have no common idiom in which to express our aspirations. This is a serious predicament, for the future will only be made in a way that favours liberal values if we have a purpose in mind, if we can find some meaning in history. That purpose can no longer be what it was when the Western world came together in 1949—the 'reification' of freedom in a Cold War alliance. It is more likely to lie in what the historian Arnold Toynbee called for: the 'reconsecration' of freedom. That will require a new language of philosophy to suit the times.

In that sense this is not a pessimistic work (on a continental rather than an Anglo-American reading of its title). The twilight of the West is a moment in the continuing history of the Western world. It offers a moment of reflection before we embark on the next phase of history, in which the Western powers are likely to find themselves engaged in a debate with others rather than among themselves.

Let me add one other word. This book has had a long gestation. Oscar Wilde expected to be met at the gates of Heaven by a flustered St. Peter bearing an armful of his unwritten works. This book has taken longer to write than I had hoped. At times I feared that it would never see the light of day. For its final completion I owe a particular debt of gratitude to Armand Clesse, without whose encouragement and initial interest in the topic the book would never have been completed. His Institute for European and International Studies in Luxembourg sponsored a one-day seminar in London to discuss the first draft of the manuscript. I would like to record my thanks to those who took part: Josef Joffe, John Gray, Philip Windsor, Ken Minogue, Fred Halliday, James Mayall, Susan Strange, Mark Almond, James Sherr, Gerald Frost, Donald Cameron Watt and Adrian Hyde-Price. All the questionable judgments and other faults of this work are, of course, entirely my own.

Christopher Coker
London

Twilight of the West

1

The Birth of the West

One world embracing all mankind we shall not see in our time. But what we may
see, if we have the vision and the energy, is the formation of a great Western community, at least a confederation of European and American nations determined to
give the lie to those who say that our civilisation is doomed.

—Walter Lippmann (1948)

"It would have been inconceivable", wrote Henry Kissinger in his most recent book, *Diplomacy* (1994), "that the architects of NATO would have
seen, as the end result of victory in the Cold War, greater disunity within
the alliance." It should not have surprised him, least of all, for he predicted
such an outcome when he was secretary of state in the 1970s. Twenty-five
years ago Kissinger had no illusions that once the Europeans were free from
their fear of the Soviet Union they would also be unwilling to subordinate
themselves to the United States. The fault lines that ran through the alliance
have been evident for years, even if it has taken the end of the Cold War to
expose them in their rawest form.

After a forty-year struggle the West has emerged victorious. Yet what is
most striking is that its demands of history have been quite modest. Its
hopes for the future are tinged not with complacency or a quiet self-
confidence but rather a sense of the overwhelming difficulties that lie ahead
and the burden of obligations that will bear no extension. As the twentieth
century draws to a close, the Western powers show little enthusiasm for
constructing a new world order.

Even within the alliance there are many competing pressures, which are
beginning to pull it apart. Differences over policy in Bosnia created the
most serious rift since the Suez crisis in 1956. The alliance of course is looking for ways to reinvent itself—including internal reform (bringing France
back into NATO's integrated military command) and external revision,
welcoming new members into its ranks.

1

Both miss the point. NATO is only as strong as the larger grouping to which it answers: the Atlantic Alliance, or the Western community, though generically it is most widely known as 'the West'. The West is an elusive term, of course. It is sometimes deemed to include Japan, a country that is in it but not *of* it, and which anyway as a close ally has never figured very prominently in American thinking. Indeed, long before the Cold War came to an end it had displaced the Soviet Union as Public Enemy No. 1 in the popular imagination.

Other countries such as Australia and New Zealand are definingly 'Western' even if they have been outside the institutions that have defined the Western community. Even here there are notable changes in the offing as the Australasian world is forced to respond to the demographic challenge of Asian immigration as it is transformed into a multicultural world in which the European element is gradually being displaced. One day Australia may find that even the epithet 'Western' will lose its emotional appeal.

And what of Latin America, that neglected continent in the Western Hemisphere that lives in the U.S. imagination as much as the United States lives in its own? Is Latin America part of the Western world? Clearly it belongs to it by virtue of its two chief languages, Spanish and Portuguese. Its political and economic institutions are European in inspiration. Brazil even sent a division to Italy to fight fascism in 1943. But if Latin America's roots are European, its horizon is the land and history of the United States: an America that is quite different from the one that exists in the European consciousness, an elusive 'other' that lives within the Spanish-speaking imagination—an 'other' that the Latin Americans have to meet individually or together as a reproach of what they are or a challenge to be themselves.

The West, as it is understood by its members, is a political community that includes only Canada, the United States and Western Europe. It is a cultural construct or it is nothing. It is a dialogue between the Old World and the New. It is a dialogue that is breaking down rapidly. As it does so it is casting both worlds into a political no-man's-land in which they find themselves engaged in continual skirmishing. To understand what has happened we have to go back to the beginning, to that moment in history when the United States and Western Europe discovered each other. We must begin with the debate between two of the most important thinkers of the nineteenth century: Hegel and Goethe. We must begin our enquiries into the state of the West with the philosophical quarrel to which it owes its conception.

Goethe and Hegel Glimpse the World Spirit

What do cannonballs sound like? "The humming of tops, the gurgling of water and the whistling of birds", according to Goethe. On 20 September 1792 he made these observations on the wooded hills of the Argonne, in the same place where the first U.S. Expeditionary Force to Europe would fight 120 years later. Goethe's patron, the Duke of Weimar, had been given command of a regiment of the Prussian army, and when it began the invasion of France Goethe went along out of curiosity. He found himself present at the Battle of Valmy, in which the most professional army in Europe was beaten in a few hours by peasants inspired by the doctrines of the French Revolution. He at once saw its significance. Late at night sitting with the soldiers, he was asked what he made of the battle. "From this place and this time forth", he replied, "commences a new era in world history and you can all say that you were present at its birth".[1]

Goethe's life was transformed by the revolution. He wrote three plays, all now forgotten, about its implications for modern life. "What preoccupied me internally kept appearing to me in dramatic form." In one of his poems he tells us that he strove "to show how the great moments and changes which were taking place on the great stage of the world were reflected in a small mirror". It was a mirror that reflected back an unappealing future. In the very last verse Goethe warned his countrymen "not to propagate the terrible movement . . . we must hold firm and last".[2]

Goethe saw in revolutionary France the representative of a new historical force, that of transcendentalism: the wish to transform political life, to go beyond the present, to turn the Frenchman from a subject into a revolutionary citizen imbued with a sense of mission. He remained hostile towards all forms of transcendental philosophy until the end of his life, for he feared that reason allied to transcendental ambition would construct a world too large for man to live in, let alone to love. In the political realm reason, in seeking to 'reengineer' mankind, would treat man as the material out of which a better kind of humanity could be fashioned.

What we lose in transcendence is the state of balance that Goethe held most dear: between what man is and what he can do. Politics, as Bismarck told us, is about the art of the possible. It involves, or should involve, recognising the limits of political action. What concerned Goethe most was the effect of transcendentalism on his own countrymen. In an aphorism composed in 1826 he expressed his innate distrust of such thinking: "It is now about twenty years since the whole race of the Germans began to 'transcend'. Should they ever awake they will seem very odd to themselves". As Erich Heller adds: "The Germans were indeed to look odd to themselves once they woke up to their real status after all the transcending had been done, as odd, one might add, as a scientist confronted by the all but demonic unmanageability of the results of his analytical radicalism."[3]

Goethe did not believe that a nation like revolutionary France could ever be the expression of a 'great idea'. Great projects made it impossible to value differences of opinion or different points of view. "The question to ask", he wrote, "is not whether we are perfectly agreed but whether we are proceeding from a common basis of sentiment. . . . Men's philosophies are grounded in their innate differences and therefore a thoroughgoing uniformity of conviction is impossible. A man has done enough when he knows *on what ground* he stands and at what particular place on this ground. Once he knows that, he can afford to be calm as far as he is concerned, as well as fair towards others".[4]

Being calm meant enjoying peace of mind, without which there could be no peace in the modern era. Fairness demanded fairness towards others. That is why Goethe believed that America might be the only country that would remain at peace with itself. Indeed, he ended his life firmly convinced that the New World would one day offer a refuge against European transcendentalism. Nearly everyone in his novel *Wilhelm Meister* emigrates in the end. That is why Napoleon criticised him for writing it. He objected to its pessimism. He was not the last dictator to find fault in the creative artists of the day for their lack of faith in the future.

What Goethe saw in the United States was a chance to change "the grounds of history in which life had to be led". By his sixtieth year, he told his friend Eckermann, he had come to realise that both as a man and a citizen, the good, the noble and the aesthetic were properly "of no particular province and no permanent land".[5] In later life the New World seemed to him to encapsulate freedom for precisely that reason. It was a land of immigrants, a land of opportunity, a land in which a man could be 'patriotic' while belonging to the whole world at the same time.

This was not an idea that met with much sympathy in the mind of Goethe's contemporary Hegel, the other great German voice of the early nineteenth century. Fifteen years after Goethe witnessed the Battle of Valmy, Hegel at the age of thirty-seven published his first major work, *The Phenomenology of Spirit*. It was completed in a time of great turmoil. The previous year Napoleon had entered Jena, where Hegel had been teaching. The philosopher had been forced to flee with half the manuscript and little else.

Yet it was on the battlefield of Jena that he caught sight of Napoleon for the first time, Napoleon as the representative of a new philosophical spirit— 'the revolution on horseback'. Like Goethe, he recognised that he had been witness to the birth of a new force in history: that of self-determining man. It was an era that might be said, perhaps, to have come to an end two hundred years later with the collapse of communism in 1989. It was a period marked by war and political violence, or what Hegel was to call "the self-destroying reality of history", "the sheer terror of the negative", the bloody dialectic of war and revolution that history had become.[6]

Although Hegel ascribed the power of modern states especially to economic power, he remained consistent to the end in his view that history was *political* history—the history of ideas realised through political action. The industrial age might transform people's lives but it could do so only to the extent that its power was harnessed for a particular purpose. The course of history, in other words, would be determined by a people growing conscious of their power and their freedom of self-determination. History, he added, would be increasingly determined by whether they had the will to use the power or not, whether, in the highly Hegelian idiom of one German writer in the 1920s, "they had the will to assert themselves historically".[7]

With the defeat of Napoleon, Hegel believed that history had passed into other hands. Nothing more could be expected of France, and even less from the other Catholic powers of Europe, the Austrian Empire in particular, which remained a ramshackle assemblage of people untouched by the idea of freedom. Even though the Russians had defeated Napoleon, they remained on the margins of Western reason and in no way constituted a constituent element of the appearance of reason in the world. As for the English, who had opposed the World Spirit in the person of Napoleon and finally condemned him to a lonely death in exile on the island of St. Helena, in their practical lives and their philosophy they were rooted in the empirical particularity of experience, their own rather than anyone else's.[8]

Hegel had no doubt that it would devolve upon the Germans to determine the Western world's fate. He would have been confirmed in this thinking by what happened subsequently. The Germans, after all, produced Marx, who took Hegel's theory of the dialectic and used it for his own ends. They later facilitated Lenin's trip from Zurich to Petrograd in February 1917 where the Russian Revolution was launched. They even provided the majority of immigrants to the United States in the nineteenth century. (In the 1990 census 59 million Americans claimed to be of German descent, 25 million more than those claiming English ancestry).

It was no less important that Germany furnished that extraordinary migration of European émigrés who found refuge in the United States on the eve of the Second World War. 'Das Land der unbegrenzten Möglichkeiten'—the land of endless possibilities, the German generals called it in the Second World War, the land to which the refugees fled. All of these themes will be discussed at length in the pages that follow.

The history of the twentieth century, of course, would be unimaginable without German ideas, including many that I shall discuss in the course of this work—the ideas of Nietzsche, Heidegger and Husserl, all of whom were conscious of belonging to a single German tradition. Of the members of that tradition none figured more prominently in the Anglo-American imagination than Hegel. Long before the philosopher Karl Popper identified him as the principal enemy of the open society, the philosopher L. T. Hobhouse had reached an important conclusion. He had been annotating Hegel's *Philosophy of Right,* he tells us in the preface to his own book *The Metaphysical Theory of the State,* when he heard the first German bombs falling on London. His first impulse had been to throw away what he had written, despairing of the importance of philosophy to modern political life. His second impulse, however, was the kind of realisation that also influenced Popper: that if Hegel had never lived the bombs might not be falling.[9]

Twenty-five years later, after the Germans had been co-opted by the West, Ralf Dahrendorf informed his readers that they need look no further back than Hegel for an explanation of the unfortunate German unwillingness to live with ambiguity or doubt. Instead they had searched for an ultimate truth by trying to synthesise two opposing ideas. In that respect they were an intensely dialectical people, for all their institutions were characterised by an attempt to evade conflict or to abolish it altogether in superior authorities and institutions. "What the consequences of such an approach are", he added, "German history of the last hundred years has demonstrated" all too clearly.[10] As Nietzsche once put it, "Even if there had never been a Hegel, we Germans would be Hegelians in as much as we [in contrast to the Latin races] instinctively accord a deeper sense and greater worth to that which becomes and evolves rather than to that which is".[11]

In retrospect we can see that Goethe and Hegel agreed on the fact that they had witnessed a change of historical consciousness in their lifetime. Where Goethe differed from Hegel was in his belief that mankind could not have an insight into the end of history and therefore could not attempt to anticipate it in advance. "We must not seek to be anything but to become everything" he insisted. In this he was himself a transcendentalist, a typical German. But he was very un-Hegelian in his insistence that there was no such thing as arrival. Man cannot control his destiny. So important was this theme in his work that he used an extract from his drama *Egmont* to close his autobiographical account *Dichtung und Wahrheit*: "Where are we headed? Who knows. We hardly recall when we came."[12]

For Hegel, by contrast, the end was knowable; the point of arrival could be grasped. The meaning of history could be comprehended in advance. Hegel's world knew where it was going because it knew where it had been. It was burdened by an excessive historical consciousness. If Goethe accepted that the future could be glimpsed in the present (as he had seen at Valmy), Hegel believed the end of history could be too—as he had seen at Jena. Thus the present could be made significant for the next generation. It was this critical difference between them that would lead the liberal democracies into a terminal conflict with the systematising regimes of the next century. The democracies wanted to build the future from the bottom up, the totalitarian world from the top down.

The importance of Goethe's vision was that he recognised intuitively rather than on the basis of any sustained analysis that the Americans would be the master builders of the Western world. Hegel, it must be added, did not ignore the New World entirely. In a footnote in 1826–1827 in his *Lectures on the Philosophy of History*, he agreed with Goethe that it was "clearly the land of the future which is still in the process of becoming". It was a land of desire "for all those who were weary of the historical lumber room of old Europe". America, he remarked, was a land in which the burden of world history would eventually reveal itself. One day America might abandon "the ground on which hitherto the history of the world had developed" and reconstruct the ground of history anew.

As a land of the long-term future, however, it had no immediate interest for him. Even in his own day he did not consider the young republic to be a real state. It could not call upon a spirit of sacrifice on the part of its citizens, for there were too many 'private interests' that devoted themselves to the community only for their own advantage. He was, as ever, opposed to any attempt to extol the interest-group model of politics in which political life was seen primarily to involve balancing competing interests. He feared that this would destroy the cohesion of the state and engender a lack of civic virtue on the part of its citizens.

In America, he added, the state existed as "merely something external for the protection of property". Perhaps the problem lay in its original rebellion against Britain, a taxpayers' revolt against the imposition of taxes for which they had not voted. He also believed that America's westward expansion largely rendered unnecessary political reflection, the ground that properly constituted political action. If the settlers disliked the government, they had merely to venture west beyond the state's reach. For all these reasons Hegel dismissed the United States as "a happy country without a history", one that for the foreseeable future would exert little influence on European affairs.

He was not alone in reaching this conclusion. Many of his later compatriots shared his opinion of this 'happy country'. Spengler claimed that the United States was not a country at all, only a field of opportunity in which people could get rich. "All we know", he wrote in one of his last books, *The Hour of Decision* (1930), "is that so far there is neither a real nation nor a real state. The American does not talk of state or mother country . . . but of *this* country. Actually, what it amounts to is a barren field and a population of trappers drifting from town to town on the dollar hunt".

The Russians were equally critical of American materialism. Even in Hegel's day one Russian writer was moved to call the country "a trading company", not a state. In the Soviet era such thinking became even more pronounced. Marxists (with a few significant exceptions) tended to dismiss the United States for its soulless materialism, which made it impossible for it to engage in history. As the writer Walter Benjamin told his friend Theodor Adorno in 1938, the reason he could not leave Paris for America was that the New World had not yet entered history. France, by contrast, was fighting to remain inside. "There are still positions here to defend".[13]

Even an English writer, Wyndham Lewis, writing in the 1920s from the perspective of the Right, complained that the Americans had vulgarised the zeitgeist in their obsession with material well-being. "Moving in millionaire circles," the zeitgeist had become a salon spirit, the spirit of fashion. Even the revolutionaries of his own time, he added, were "expected to call the *Zeitgeist* by his Christian name".[14]

Such thinking explains why even states that were materially inferior to America believed that they could prevail in any military encounter with it, provided they had what it obviously lacked: a political will. In that sense Hegel can be said to have set the frame of reference in which America's twentieth-century enemies thought and acted.

Goethe, by contrast, intuitively recognised that the situation was quite different: that what distinguished the United States from every other nation was the scope of its historical ambition. In *Wilhelm Meister* a character says, "Since we come together so miraculously, let us not lead a trivial life: let us together become active in a noble manner". The Americans began thinking of themselves in similar terms as early as the 1820s.

What distinguished the United States most from Europe in Hegel's last years was more than its growing economic power. More important was the tendency of its leaders to use a language of international politics that had not been heard before. It was given formal expression in John Quincy Adams's opening address to Congress in 1825: "The spirit of improvement is abroad upon the earth. . . . Let us not be unmindful that liberty is power: that the nation blessed with the largest portion of liberty must . . . be the most powerful nation . . . that the tenure of power by man . . . is to improve the condition of himself and his fellow men".[15]

For America not to use that power, Adams added, would be a great betrayal "of the most sacred of trusts". What he signified in his speech was a peculiarly modern idea, the use of political power to make a better world. The United States of course had to wait almost another century to achieve that end, to realise its national purpose when its Expeditionary Force engaged the German army in 1918, in the same Argonne Forest through which Goethe had travelled in the 1790s.

The twentieth century was to be dominated by these two themes: Would the New World step in to rescue the Old from itself, or would it lose contact with the Old World altogether? When the Europeans began to debate the question in earnest it was notable that, following Hegel's lead, the Germans, unlike the English and the French, tended to leave the United States out of the account.

Writing in 1853, the neo-Hegelian theologian Bruno Bauer was the first person to conceive of the need for an alignment of West European states against a common threat—Russian autocracy. Hegel, he regretted in his book *Russia and the Germanic World*, had been the last philosopher of note who could interpret politics in an exclusively Western orientation without taking into account Russia, a nation that he dismissed because of its lack of a philosophical tradition. One of the very few Russian philosophers of note, Pytor Chaadayev, agreed with him: "We have lived, as it were, outside of History," he wrote in his *First Philosophical Letter,* "and have remained untouched by the universal education of the human race. ... Isolated from the world we have given or taught nothing to the world; we have added no thoughts to the sum of human ideas; we have in no way collaborated in the progress of Reason. ..."[16]

After Hegel's death, however, Russia's power had grown alarmingly. What made it particularly threatening was the absence of ideas in Russia. As a country it was distinguished by intellectual pauperism. A people who were concerned with the conquest of nature needed engineers, not philosophers. Standing armies, not ideas, had become its chief philosophical school. The future, Bauer warned, would decide the question: Europe or Russia?

Although the most influential German philosopher after Hegel, Nietzsche, does not seem to have known Bauer's book, the two men were nonetheless in substantial agreement. Commenting on a leading article that Bauer had written for a newspaper in 1882, Nietzsche suggested that his call for a supranational Europe to meet the challenge of Russian authoritarianism might be his own. Like Bauer he believed that the West needed to overcome the petty nationalism that divided it. A European alliance would, of necessity, have to be based on "the annihilation of nationalities".

With the unification of Germany Nietzsche believed that Russia was not fated to dominate European life. The West could defend itself successfully, provided it had the will to do so. His vision of a united Europe was very much a voluntarist one. He had little interest in a United States of Europe and even less for its forceful unification by one of the Great Powers— which, it was obvious even then, would probably have been Germany. But he was interested in a spiritually united Europe, a Europe united behind a big idea. He believed that only a political force could successfully engage another force such as tsarist authoritarianism. He was equally convinced that only a kind of ideological internationalism (such as an alliance united in a common purpose) could save the Europeans from their own murderous instincts.

Like many other writers at the time, Nietzsche was quite mistaken in his interpretation of Russia. The tsarist system was relatively weak compared with the totalitarian system that succeeded it. But he was right to anticipate that there were in the contemporary Russian scene ideas at work that history might one day discover, as it did in 1917. As Nietzsche recognised quite clearly, there was a dimension of the Russian psyche that, in certain circumstances, could predispose its rulers to act as ruthlessly as Lenin and his successors. Here, he wrote, was a people close to barbarism with the generosity of youth and genuine willpower. It was a people with "a long breath". Like the Church, Russia could wait.[17]

Unlike most other writers Nietzsche's genius was also to detect similar forces at work in Germany after its victory over France in 1871. He had no regard for Bismarckian *realpolitik,* which he dismissed as 'little politics' in order to expose the abyss that separated it from the Great Politics that it pretended to be. Why should a statesman be called great who had inflicted such misfortune on his own people? "Let us hope that Europe will soon produce a *great* statesman and that he who is celebrated as the 'great realist' [a reference to Bismarck] in this petty age of plebeian shortsightedness, will be revealed as *small*".[18]

What is most notable, however, about Nietzsche's position was his total disregard of the United States. The failure of the 'Atlantic' powers—France and England—to engage in the coming conflict with Russia, he concluded, might leave Germany to face it alone—a task in which, he was quite convinced, Germany could not succeed. If Germany succumbed, then France, which had no ideas of its own and was suffering from 'metaphysical exhaustion,' would too.

England's fate would be different. It would be forced to join an Anglo-American world and thus become a member of a larger American commonwealth, losing a lot in the process. It would pay a high price for joining the American colossus, for it would cease to be part of the European system of states; it might even have to forswear everything that made it 'European'.

Like so many of Nietzsche's 'predictions' there was an equal measure of acute farsightedness and intellectual perversity in this vision. He was one of the first philosophers of note, however, to grasp that a Western community would probably arise, and that it would be based on an idea: the defence of freedom.

Such ideas were in the air in the 1870s. They were becoming part of the European consciousness. They were the expression of a specific historical moment. The difference between German and French writers was that the French, as internationalists, did not believe it possible or desirable to leave the United States out of account. In the same decade two French historians, Henri Martin and Jules Michelet, warned that unless the Europeans federated they would eventually succumb to Russia. Martin believed that this would leave only the United States to preserve "all the higher elements of human civilisation". Michelet envisaged an 'Atlantic union' of Europe and the United States against a common enemy, tsarist Russia. The Russian writer Aleksandr Herzen agreed with them. "Our classic ignorance of the western European will be productive of a good deal of harm", he wrote in the 1870s, "much hatred and bloody collisions will develop from it later on".

Echoing Michelet's pessimism, he predicted that the conflict would not be over imperial real estate or trade. It would be a debate about two different styles of government, between two different ideas of humanity, and about which of the two would prevail. It would be a conflict, he added, be-

tween "two different forms of culture". Michelet himself even went so far
as to point the finger of blame at what he called 'communism'—not, in this
case, the ideology of Karl Marx but the system of peasant communes that
made Russia unique, even after the abolition of serfdom.[19]

All three writers, in fact, can claim to be the first of note to foresee the
emergence of an Atlantic alliance in which the New World would be
brought in to balance the Old. It was all the more ironic, therefore, that in
both world wars the Western powers found themselves allied briefly with
Russia against an enemy, Germany, that seemed far more relentless and
threatening—and never more so than in the darkest days of the Second
World War when the West and the Soviet Union found themselves fighting
for their life.

The Past as Prologue

To appreciate why 'the West' came into being when it did we must turn first
to the profound difference in the way that the French and the English on
the one hand, and the Germans and the Russians on the other, envisaged
Western civilisation in the period under discussion.

A society institutes itself through its culture and thereby transforms itself
into a state, nation or tribe. Every culture introduces into those units a conceptual view of the world we call its social beliefs and the images that represent those beliefs. Two of the most potent of these that distinguished the
Islamic and Christian civilisations were the Crescent and the Cross. These
images pointed not only to the visible but also to invisible worlds. Societies
are continually engaged in a dialogue with the world of the social imagination. Indeed, as the poet Octavio Paz argues, social imagination is the most
important agent of historical change. In imagining itself other than it is, a
culture engages in a self-colloquy. It speaks to itself and others about its future. All the great works of history are ultimately works of imagination.[20]

The relations between cultures are similar to those of society itself. They
include negative relationships such as war and revolution, and positive relationships such as the interchange of economic goods, arts and religion. In
the case of early modern Europe these were extended to include diplomatic
practices and international law.

Communication between cultures is more complex than within them,
however, for it includes a new determining factor: that of translation. In
translating ideas cultures become members of a wider community—a civilisation. When we talk of European civilisation, in particular, we are implic-
itly referring to ideas or cultural artefacts, such as a universal system of musical notation, or a common artistic style such as the Gothic or Baroque.

Religion is one of the most important factors of all. Even the great schism
between the Catholic and Orthodox faiths did not undermine the images

and symbols that East and West Europe shared where it counted most, in their collective imagination. By contrast, Asia has had no similar tradition of communication. In different societies Confucianism, Buddhism, Taoism and Islam have jostled for position for centuries. Asia's religious traditions are still extremely diverse, and their development has been singularly different from the experience of Europe. In the twelfth and thirteenth centuries Japan spawned a version of Buddhism very similar to evangelical Christianity, and another very similar to militant Islam. Neither, however, was exported overseas.[21]

China may have exported its laws and art forms, but they did not take root elsewhere. They never progressed beyond mimicry. A civilisation is not imported or imposed. It derives its influence from an intermix of people and beliefs. No such chemistry was at work behind China's Great Wall, or in Japan, which chose to isolate itself from the world, including that of its immediate neighbours, until the end of the nineteenth century.[22]

If an Asian consciousness exists at all it has its roots, paradoxically, in the struggle against the West. Sheltering in a bunker in 1941 during a raid on the capital of Nationalist China, Chungking, the American writer Owen Lattimore was intrigued to overhear a conversation between two Chinese officials—not about the existing war with Japan but about the coming war with the United States. America was a far more formidable adversary in Chinese eyes because of its ambition to 'Americanise' a world much older than itself.[23]

No sooner had the Americans stolen into Asia's consciousness, however, than the phenomenon of Asian nationalism began to delineate sharply what made some Asian societies different from the rest. The threat of Westernisation challenged Asian societies not to unite in face of a common danger but to rediscover themselves—to rediscover, for example, what made them uniquely Chinese. Western imperialism may have succumbed in the end to nationalism, but the Shinto patriots and the Boxer rebels, and even Chinese communists, were predisposed to emphasise their diversity, not uniformity. In India the Gandhian nationalists who chose the constitutional path rather than the revolutionary merely succeeded in emphasising the differences between Hindu and Islamic consciousness, and presided over the partition of a subcontinent that the British had united for the first time.

By contrast, the West that emerged in the late nineteenth century was a political construct. As late as 1713 the Treaty of Utrecht referred to Europe as a Christian commonwealth. In the course of the eighteenth century that communication became specifically political in content: it was transmitted in the language of politics and the vernacular of political life. For the first time the Europeans began to consider themselves members of a common 'civilisation'.

The word itself is a hybrid modern Western word composed of a Latin adjectival stem, a French verbal affix and a Latin abstract substantival suffix, indicating not a static condition but a process still going on. It is a word of comparatively recent coinage, however, and a word of French origin. The Europeans did not think of themselves as members of a common civilisation until the mid-eighteenth century. By then the French who invented the word meant something very specific: a community that spoke a lingua franca, French, the language of the European Enlightenment, that ambitious programme to free the individual not only in the narrow economic and political sense but also in a cultural and religious sense. By the eighteenth century the language of Montesquieu and Voltaire had become the language of the court, not only in Paris but in St. Petersburg and in the Berlin of Frederick the Great. Even when the locus of the Enlightenment shifted eastward, the ministers of Joseph II's court in Austria or Catherine's in Russia read the *Encyclopédie* and were familiar with the writings of the *philosophes*.

With the French Revolution the political language of individualism acquired its own vocabulary, associated with the invention of 'ideology', a word coined by the philosopher Antoine Destutt de Tracy. It described a new discipline whose goal was to help people analyse their own ideas. After 1789 the French no longer derived their humanity from being French; they were superior human beings by virtue of subscribing to a universalism that was the legacy of the French Revolution, in particular the Declaration of the Rights of Man (1789). In this respect, the existence of frontiers and different languages, and even conflicts between nations, was negligible in relation to the ideas of the revolution from which the political vernacular of the Western world emerged.

It was a powerful and yet simple ideology. It was expressed particularly forcefully in a letter written by Bakunin in 1867: "Only in those rare moments when a nation really represents the general interest, the right and freedom of all mankind, can a citizen who calls himself a revolutionary be a patriot too. . . . The French patriots of 1793 struggled, fought and triumphed in the name of the freedom of the world; for the future fate of all mankind was identical with the cause of revolutionary France. . . . It was the most integral theory of humanity ever advanced".[24] It consisted of a single principle: the human subject as universal man.

By the early twentieth century the common language changed to English (with the advent of the United States in international political life). Long before then, however, the common political vernacular had become that of Anglo-American liberalism. As Nietzsche complained in *Beyond Good and Evil* (1886), referring by name to the writings of the English school, particularly those of John Stuart Mill, the 'modern ideas' against which the German spirit had a profound distrust were of English origin. The French had become "merely apes and mimes of these ideas". The "Anglomania of 'modern ideas'" had conquered "the *âme française*". The "plebeianism of modern ideas" was "the work of England".

In both Britain and the United States the word 'civilisation' soon became popular as an explanation for those superior accomplishments that were seen to justify the European conquest of the globe. It did not refer to a distinctive mode of existence but to an ideal order of human society. As a general rule what characterised the English and Americans in this period was the absence from their thinking of 'perspectivism'. For the English, the indigenous peoples of the world were merely living through a stage in a unitary scale of progress whose apex was their own 'civilisation'. As Nietzsche complained, they were wont to confuse their own well-being with that of everyone else and to assume that what was necessary for England must be a universal principle discoverable by reason. For a rule to be true for them, it had to be true for everyone.

When Michelet and Martin first envisaged the construction of a Western political community, they did so, as we have seen, in terms of a political union that included Germany against a common enemy: Russia. Yet within a few years of France's defeat by Prussia in 1871, it had become clear to the French that Germany was the immediate enemy of the Western world. After 1871 it was no longer possible for a Frenchman to be neutral about Germany, to see its idealist philosophy and the development of the human sciences, especially history, in universal terms, as reflections of a Western spirit. The sciences of the spirit, as they were called, were German, not French. The war revealed that the 'value orientation' of German development differed from that of France. After 1871, France confronted a power that was not universalist, and not part of its mental world.[25]

For the Germans, a community was a cultural not an ideological construct. "The Germans", wrote Nietzsche in 1888, "were an *irresponsible* race which [had] all the misfortunes of culture on its conscience and at all decisive moments in history were thinking of something else".[26] What Nietzsche meant by irresponsible was that they did not consider themselves to have a responsibility to be other than themselves. They lived in their own imagination, not in that of others. They had no interest in propagating universal truths.

All the Germans could do for the world, wrote the historian Ludwig Dehio, was to protest against the Western concept of civilisation, but they could not speak for the world as could the English or, after 1917, the Americans. That is why so many German writers thought that the Western powers were so dangerous, more dangerous even than the Russian colossus in the East. When Woodrow Wilson took the United States into the First World War he boasted of making the world safe for democracy, but who, asked the philosopher Max Scheler, was going to make democracy safe for the world?[27]

For the Germans, argued the philosopher Carl Schmitt twenty years later, all wars were intrinsically limited. Whatever their geographical scope they were fought for limited ends. All wars for the West, by comparison, were imperial in their intellectual scope. They were wars fought for a purpose: to end war altogether or to make the world safe for democracy. They were total wars, of course, in that they were fought in the name of the future, the future forged in the act of going to war. In the Anglo-American universal order there was no room for nonconformists. The wars they fought, Schmitt concluded, nearly always ended with war crimes tribunals.[28]

Until the First World War the Germans saw the French as their principal adversary. As late as 1918, Thomas Mann still looked to France when he claimed in a celebrated dictum that the Reformation had "immunised" Germany against French revolutionary ideas.[29] What Nietzsche, for his part, disliked most about the Enlightenment was that it had persuaded the French that they were the font of reason, a "self-intoxication" that had erupted into the French Revolution and the revolutionary tradition of the nineteenth century. What was necessary, he maintained, was to reverse the direction of history, "to strangle the revolution at birth, to make it not happen".[30] Echoing that idea (though interpreting it very differently) Hitler was to claim in the 1930s that the political programme of national socialism promised to cancel out the events of 1789. It offered the German people the chance to construct not only a new society but also an 'antihistorical' order.

German particularism remained in the ascendant for a long time. Writing as late as 1917 while in exile in Zurich, Hugo Ball still felt it important to criticise his own country's view of citizenship in terms of two nineteenth-century revolutionary manifestos, one German, the other French:

Bourgeois freedoms, shopkeepers' freedoms: imaginary, godless, levelling freedoms. We just forget that we do not even have these, that the 'humanitarian liberalism of the Western democracies' (America and France) is essentially very different from the fanatical humanism of Herder, Humboldt and Fichte. I recently compared the Declaration of the Rights of Man of 1789 with German Fundamental Rights of 1848 [the respective Bills of Rights adopted by the Constituent Assembly of the French Revolution and by the Frankfurt Parliament of the 1848 Revolution]. The difference is very striking:

1. The Declaration contains a philosophy (of man and of the state); the Fundamental Rights contains nothing of the kind.
2. The Rights of Man establishes a sovereignty of the people over the state in a universal sense and assigns the state only the negative right of watching over such a constitution. The Fundamental Rights, on the other hand, contains no decision in principle on the limitations of the state or even on the dependence of the state on the nation.
3. The French Constituent Assembly establishes certain inalienable rights of the individual (safety, property, equality before the law and the *right of opposition* to suppression of all these laws). The Constitution is guaranteed by

the whole and by each individual. It recognises only human beings (implic-
itly including the proletariat) and addresses itself to those human beings.
The Fundamental Rights, however, speaks only about the rights of the citizen and subject, not about the rights of man.
4. . . . To characterise the Fundamental Rights one must
5. Not forget to mention that it was drawn up half a century after the French
   Revolution, with all the experiences of the interim period and all the results
   of German classicism. In spite of that, there is not much trace in it of
   German humanity and German philosophy. . . .

In a later entry in his diary Ball added: "The Fundamental Rights of 1848
contain a comical paragraph 6 (before Article 1). It runs: 'The state does
not restrict the freedom to emigrate'. That says everything. They want to be
allowed to flee, at least".[31] It is a passage that reminds one of Goethe's
Wilhelm Meister.

It is interesting that Thomas Mann's *Reflections of a Nonpolitical Man,*
from which I quoted earlier, was not translated into English until 1982, a
typical example of Anglo-American provincialism. It is an interesting book,
a spirited defence of German culture against Western civilisation by a man
who was eventually forced to flee from Germany in the 1930s to the security of the New World. On his own reading, a civilisation was essentially
about material progress, which was by definition international. Germany,
by contrast, was a community that valued its social cohesion. Mann was intent on drawing a distinction between a community and a society, as had
Herder two hundred years earlier in protesting against the cosmopolitanism of the Enlightenment. In Mann's case, of course, it took a different
form and this time an antidemocratic bias. As late as 1923 he was to be
found arguing that "to ask [a German] to transfer his allegiance . . . to
what the peoples of Europe call *freedom* would . . . amount to a demand
that he should do violence to his own nature".[32]

By then, however, the Americans had begun to displace the French in the
German imagination. The sociologist Max Weber chose to see the First
World War as a contest between Anglo-American internationalism and
German *kultur.* Before the war there had been a cold war between Britain
and Germany, a 'dry war' or 'latent war' in the words of two different
German observers.[33] By the time the real war came to an end, the United
States had supplanted France in the German consciousness.

Preventing the world from being dominated by 'Americanism', Weber argued, had been Germany's 'cultural task', its historic responsibility.
Although he subsequently came to accept that Germany had misused its
power in the last years of the war, he still felt able to draw some satisfaction
in the wake of its defeat that at least it had prevented Russian control of
Europe, even if it had failed to prevent the Anglo-Saxon dominance of the

world. "American supremacy was as irresistible as that of Ancient Rome after the Punic Wars. It is only to be hoped that they never share it out with the Russians".[34]

This was the great fear of the 1930s, particularly in the eyes of men of the stamp of Heidegger and Spengler. It came to realisation, of course, in the great summit meetings of 1944–1945, in which the Allied powers partitioned Germany between them.

Even then there were many Germans who wanted to remain neutral, to pursue what Mann described in 1926 as the *Idee der Mitte* (the Idea of the Golden Mean). By the late 1940s, however, to remain German was to engage in an uneasy Cold War between the claims of West and East. It was by then a policy of noncommitment. The irony of disengagement was not one that could be sustained in an ideological era. As one of Mann's characters remarks in his most influential book, *The Magic Mountain,* "*beliefs* are not held in the ironic sphere".[35] And the twentieth century put a premium on belief.

The problem with Russia was very different, which is why Michelet and Martin were indeed to be proved right in the long term, if not the short. It is interesting that in his attempt to define Germany Mann should have quoted Dostoyevsky, who once wrote: "It is the *moral* idea" that forms a nation's character. One is first a German and therefore a man. The same could be said of Russia. The Russians too saw themselves as in the West, but not *of* it. A significant gloss on this is provided by Valentin Kiparsky in his study *The English and American Characters in Russian Fiction.* Invoking the Russian practice of regularly introducing foreigners as a foil to the Russians themselves, he adds that "a Russian novel without a West European or, at least, a Polish, Ukrainian, Jewish or Caucasian character is almost as rare as a West European novel containing a Russian character".

When one moves from the world of fiction to that of fact, the balance was in the opposite direction. Western books on Russia were numerous and usually inspired by fear. Russian discourses on the West were relatively few in number before the Cold War and were often preoccupied with expressing emotional and nationalistic issues relevant to their own country rather than engaging in a debate about the nature of society and man.[36] What made Russia different from Germany was that it had not experienced many of the political and cultural travails that were part of the Western consciousness. Germany by comparison had not been 'immunised' against the Renaissance, the Reformation and the Enlightenment. Germany, wrote Mann, was not a nation: it was a meeting place of ideas. Its soul was a battlefield of competing ideologies.

The concept of 'immunisation' is actually quite useful when we look at what distinguished German history in such an intensely ideological age. Max Weber was among the first to appreciate the importance of the liberal tradition in German life. The measure of a nation's success in the twentieth century would be the extent to which it lived in the imagination of others, including its enemies. One reason why the Allies might win the war, he predicted as early as 1915, was that they would be seen, even by the nonbelligerents, to be fighting for the 'right cause': for History, rather than themselves.

A few years later Spengler blamed Germany's defeat on the presence of an *'innere England'* (an 'inner England' or 'fifth column'), the defection of a class that had been contaminated by liberal ideas, a group that welcomed the defeat as a chance to introduce Western parliamentarianism into German political life.[37] Writing in February 1945 in the ruins of Hitler's Reich, Max Weber's brother concluded that the German soul could only be saved after twelve years of Nazism by joining the West, by renouncing its 'Germanness' altogether.[38]

Russia was not so easily converted. It was not part of the Western world in terms that the French understood: belief in the rights of man. Much of its material Westernisation was the result of importing Western technology and techniques. It was not endogenous. Even in the tsarist period the village commune was taken by Michelet as an antonym of everything the Western world was, as a challenge to what distinguished the Western community from every other in its own consciousness at least, its respect for individualism and civic freedom.

Leninism after 1917 further alienated Russia from the West. Economic autarky was one means; the (re)interpretation of Marxism was another. Leninism might use a universal language and even trace its roots to French Jacobinism, but the roots did not run very deep. "With us", complained Chaadayev, "new ideas sweep away the old because they do not spring from them". Communism intensified all that was non-Western about Russia. Lenin was a product of the Russian reaction against the West, not the catalyst of the country's Westernisation. As early as the 1920s Gramsci and later the Frankfurt school began to distinguish a 'Western' Marxist tradition from that practised in the East.

By the 1930s the West lived on in Russia only in the artistic imagination. "We created the art before we had the society", wrote one Russian writer.[39] The tragedy was that before the revolution, art had been ahead of the game. One artist put it perfectly when he added that the new art of constructivism before 1917 had been taken up enthusiastically after the revolution. Very soon, however, the revolutionary regime repudiated the message, and stifled the medium. In Milan Kundera's novel *The Joke* the artist Cerek is sent to a disciplinary regiment because he loves cubist painting. The revolution decides that modern art is its enemy even though the early modernists earnestly wished to serve it. In socialist society art had to serve society, not only reflect it. The change meant not only the transformation of the artist's place in society but also the relationship between reality and culture.

In the 1920s poets like Pasternak and Mandelstam had hoped for an even more Europeanised Russia. By the end of the decade they knew the worst. "In my beggar's memory", Mandelstam declared, "without a guide" he was "a blind man and his guide". This passage, taken from a poem written between arrests in January 1937, tells us about the loss of sound and senses of the Western world. The old Russia had brimmed over with both. The new Soviet state banished them to the memory.[40]

Such was the concept of 'the West' that emerged after 1870. It was a political construct designed to underpin a particular version of civilisation. If civilisational loyalties and influences can be said to have some objective validity as an epistemological device, it does not necessarily follow that the same loyalties and influences will be found operating subjectively as motor forces in the lives of a society and its people. We must be careful not to confuse the general context in which political decisions are made with the contingent particular motives that determine behaviour. It is one thing for the behaviour of societies to be definingly 'Western', quite another for that behaviour to be guided by direct reference to Western civilisation itself. Nevertheless, the West's behaviour was driven in just this way in the period 1917–1991 in the context of a civil war within the Western world: between the liberal and the totalitarian mentalities. The interwar years saw a proliferation of books with titles such as *The War Against the West* (1938), a book by A. Kolnai to which Karl Popper referred in his own account of these times, *The Open Society and Its Enemies* (1945).

This historical perspective was amplified by the intense use of historical analogies in the twentieth century. The chief parallel in this period was the Peloponnesian War, the conflict that the historian Thucydides portrayed so memorably between a definingly 'democratic' Athens and a 'totalitarian' Sparta. Writing in 1948 the historian Arnold Toynbee recounted how on the eve of the First World War he had found the pages of Thucydides' account of the war pregnant with meaning:

> Suddenly my understanding was illuminated. The experience that we were having in our world had been experienced by Thucydides in his world already. . . . Thucydides it now appeared had been over this ground before. He and his generation had been ahead of me and mine in the stages of historical experience we had respectively reached. . . . Whatever chronology might say, Thucydides' world and my world had now proved to be philosophically contemporary.[41]

Toynbee of course took this insight further than his contemporaries. If it was true that the development of Europe in the early twentieth century was, in some senses, running parallel to the historical development of the fifth-century Greek city-states, was this mere accident, or part of a larger parallelism between the whole life course of the two civilisations? And would similar parallels be discovered in the histories of other people? Was there, in short, a plot or rhythm common to civilisation as a whole?

The Western powers did not share Toynbee's perspective on history, but they were given to drawing parallels between their own time and Thucydides' world. In 1915, for example, placards on London buses appeared displaying excerpts from Pericles' funeral speech, intended to remind the 'heirs' of Athenian culture of the values for which they were fighting.[42] In 1940 the future head of scientific intelligence in Britain quoted from the same speech in an official report to illustrate the dangers of too much openness in a great struggle.[43] Even the *Washington Post* once chided Henry Kissinger for seeing the superpower confrontation during the Cold War as a rematch of the struggle between an effete Athens (the democratic West) and a vigorous and disciplined Sparta (the Soviet Union), a struggle that, like the first, might well end in the victory of the stronger and more ruthless side.[44]

What is happening today is that the West's unique discourse with itself has begun to be replaced by a discourse with others. As the twentieth century draws to a close, the Western world faces a particular challenge: whether an increasingly multiethnic society can transform itself into a successful and genuine multicultural one. Confronting that challenge the Western world is beginning to lose its cohesive identity. Its members are beginning to opt for individual strategies of survival.

The West's traditional definition of 'civilisation' is no longer tenable. It was the product of an age when the Western world took itself to be the acme of human achievement as well as the purveyor of value to others—its unique *mission civilisatrice*. At the end of the century it is beginning to recognise that the civilisation of the future will be a discourse between cultures, each different from the other but all of them confronting the challenge of modernity together for the first time.

It is a process that was first addressed by Nietzsche, the philosopher who haunts the pages of this study. As a philosopher he was unusual in being so critical of his own civilisation at the very time the Europeans were establishing themselves over the rest of the world as the 'lords of humankind'. He was not impressed by his own countrymen's pretensions. Geographical Europe appeared to him to be a small peninsula off the Asian landmass. He thought that other people, particularly the Chinese, had more 'stamina' than the Europeans.[45] He tried to disabuse the Europeans of their cultural relativism by insisting that there had been "more thoughtful times and times more distracted by analytic thinking" than their own. He was thinking in particular of Buddhism, which he praised for its 'philosophical clarity'.

What makes Nietzsche's writing so interesting is that he did not choose to value alien cultures because of their alleged close ties to nature or because of their primordiality, as they had been praised by Rousseau in the eighteenth century. He praised them because of their intellectual, artistic and practical superiority.

Nietzsche deliberately wrote about Europe from the perspective of an outsider, from the perspective of one estranged from his own world. In his most compelling book, *Human, All Too Human,* there is an aphorism entitled 'Estranged from the Present' in which he writes that only by venturing out into the ocean can we see the whole 'configuration' of our own culture and thus better understand ourselves.[46] Only by distancing ourselves can we overcome parochialism: "Direct self-observation is not nearly enough to know ourselves. . . . We have to travel to other nations. . . . And especially to where human beings have taken off the garb of Europe or have not yet put it on".[47] If Europe was to revalue its own traditions, he added, it would need a different way of 'seeing'. Only by distancing itself could it see itself as others saw it. That is what he meant by "the pathos of distance", a phrase that appears in one of his last books.[48]

Of course those who constructed the Western Alliance were convinced that they represented the future of the planet. When Edmund Husserl wrote of Europe in his last book, *Philosophy and the Crisis of European Man*, he was not using a geographical expression. For him the word 'Europe' was a "philosophical idea, imminent in its history". Europe, in other words, was a historical as well as geographical concept, a historical epoch as well as a continent.

Today our history has become much more autobiographical. The coordinates of space and time are no longer deemed to intercept so precisely. The Atlantic powers no longer consider their own future likely to be that of everyone else. They have discovered that there is no Atlantic core to modernity. All modern societies must learn from others. That is what modernity is about: it is a communication between cultures. The dialogue between civilisations rather than the clash between them is the only way, if we are fortunate, that the future may be a little less terrible than the past.

Nietzsche and the Revaluation of Values

Many paradoxes. Nietzsche in the air.
—Paul Klee, *Diaries* (1898)

Nietzsche has the dubious distinction of being the only philosopher who has ever been considered a major cause of a world war.[49] If we look at the literature during the two world wars we will find the widely held assumption in the first that it owed much to the "poisonous fallacies of maniacs such as Nietzsche and Treitschke".[50] In the case of the latter, he was seen as the founder of national socialism.[51] In one book written in 1941 Nazism was described as "nothing less than a Nietzschean transvaluation of values . . . the nihilistic revolution that would not stop at smashing countries but would . . . utterly destroy the civilisation of the West".[52]

These days Nietzsche is rarely held responsible for any of the ideologies that appropriated him for their own ends. He is considered, however, to have identified the cause of the general crisis that produced the Western civil war. Writing in 1944, the philosopher Eric Voeglin, who had been forced to flee from Europe to the United States, acknowledged that the crisis through which the West was passing had been caused not by "the transvaluation of values" but by their devaluation by the "despiritualised" animal force of Nazism.[53]

Nietzsche was indeed one of the first philosophers to recognise the forces that would tear the Western world apart. Fortunately, the West was able to revalue itself and thus meet the challenge of modernity with conspicuous success. The Soviet Union and Nazi Germany succumbed because they devalued rather than revived their societies. In retrospect, of course, it is ironic that both of the West's enemies, the Third Reich and the Soviet Union, chose to engage it on grounds of *their* own choosing: on the battlefield in the case of the former, and on the industrial front in the case of the latter. Both believed that they could win by outfighting or outperforming the West. Both failed because they were simply not modern enough. In the Soviet case, the devaluation of political life was so complete that even though the West did not demand its unconditional surrender, it surrendered nevertheless. In the end, its will failed it; it gave up the ghost.

What did Nietzsche mean by the revaluation of values? It was, he held, intrinsic in the nature of modernity itself. As Kierkegaard wrote in 1844, "Formerly a man derived self-importance from being nobly born, rich etc. Today we have grown more liberal, more 'world historical'. Now all of us derive self-importance from being born in the nineteenth century".[54]

What made the modern world 'modern' was its recognition of the importance of historical time. Every value became conditional in the modern era. It was Nietzsche's peculiar insight to recognise more clearly than most of his contemporaries that a society would not survive long if it continued to adhere to values that were no longer creative. Institutions must be replaced or revised. New institutions, in turn, create new values. It was necessary, in short, to eliminate those modes of organising and directing life that, though taken to embody genuine value, in fact operated to diminish real value overall. In proposing that cultures had to be revalued from time to time, Nietzsche believed himself to be expressing a demand of modernity: that we cease to take received estimations of things for granted and question all values that we have held, including those we have most cherished in the past. We must ask, he insisted in *The Genealogy of Morals,* "What value do they themselves possess?"

The second aspect of Nietzsche's concept of revaluation was the emphasis he put on human agency. It is for this reason that he employed the double formula "the will to power: an attempted revaluation of values", both in identifying a major work in progress, of which he speaks in *The Genealogy,* and in formulating a title for it—'The Gospel of the Future'. "Assuming that life itself is the will to power there is nothing to life that has no value except the degree of power". He recognised, in other words, that human agency and modernity were intimately linked. In that sense, revaluation was the task, the will to power, the principle to be employed in carrying it out. Revaluation encourages us to recognise ourselves as sovereign beings who have control over our lives, not as instruments of fate or creatures of circumstance as was the case in the premodern era.

In other words, Nietzsche claimed that the purpose of modernity was to invest life with meaning. If the principal requirement of power is to empower ourselves, the principal requirement of value is to enhance life. "Art, knowledge, morality are *means*", he wrote. The end is to increase the vitality of the subject, to enhance life itself.[55]

This was especially true, of course, at the time that he was writing of the non-Western world, which had to face a unique challenge: the threat of being dispossessed of its own history. Nietzsche was one of the first philosophers of note to criticise colonialism on the grounds that the purpose of revaluing our institutions is to live a more intense life, for what is being valued is the extent to which we experience life at first hand. Life cannot be experienced for us by others.

Many European writers made the mistake of thinking that they could revalue the societies they colonised by reforming their institutions from above, by engaging in a crude form of social engineering. Marx had been among those to make this mistake. Writing in 1853 he congratulated the British for laying "the material foundation of Western society in Asia". Even in that brief moment of British rule, the comforting dichotomies that seemed to illustrate the reason for Britain's success—the clash between tradition and modernity, continuity and change, status and contract, caste and class—existed largely in the European imagination. For all the splendid phrases of Macaulay's minutes on law reform, the British had neither the financial means nor the technical instruments to carry out a development programme. No Western power had the requisite capital or technology to transform the face of any of the societies they colonised.

In the end, writes the historian Eric Stokes, the British could only fit in the Indian social structure as one more endogenous caste.[56] The upshot is that they are now seen by many Indian historians to have been the offspring rather than the progenitors of modern Indian history. Many years ago J. F. Ade Ajayi hammered the same point home with respect to Africa: "In any long-term historical view of African history, European rule becomes just another episode".[57] With each succeeding year this looks less the exaggeration some thought at the time.

We are our own value esteemers, Nietzsche wrote; "Only through valuation is there value. Without evaluation the nut of existence would be hollow".[58] We esteem ourselves by valuing ourselves and that requires free will. We know that Nietzsche read in French translation and approved of

Dostoyevsky's *Notes from the Underground.* In this text we find the remark, "I am not altogether for adversity any more than I am altogether for
prosperity; what I most stand for is my personal free will".[59] What we read
are that prosperity and adversity are not valuable in themselves. What is
important is a man's personal freedom and his will to use it. More important still is direct experience. The world cannot be interpreted for us. Like
Kant, Nietzsche insisted that humanity could never be treated as a means to
an end. A society that revalues its life is one that goes "beyond its past",
that "*extends* its present".[60]

Colonialism created the conditions for revaluation, as well as the need
for it, but it could not revalue life itself, for it denied the colonial subjects
the right to empower themselves, to take responsibility for the present. The
nationalist revolt that swept away the whole imperial edifice in the course
of the twentieth century served that purpose quite significantly.

Nietzsche's third insight was to recognise that the present could be only
as strong as its foundations in the past. He would have had little time for
the view expressed by T. E. Hulme that a sharp distinction had to be drawn
between the mode of thinking of the nineteenth and the twentieth centuries.
The achievement of the nineteenth century, Hulme contended, was "the
elaboration and universal application of the principle of continuity". The
destruction of that principle was "the urgent need of the present".[61]

Nietzsche was the first philosopher of distinction to argue that progress
would lie not in repudiating but in realising the possibilities of tradition, of
unleashing energies that had not yet been tapped, energies that had been
present in society, if dormant, all the time. He did not believe that it was
necessary to invent new values, only to reinterpret old ones.

Consider, for example, his response to the 'death of God', which he proclaimed so famously in 1870. If the Christian world had shattered, leaving
only fragments of belief behind, those fragments were still deeply embedded in the Western imagination. It was his peculiar insight as a genealogist
to recognise that each fragment could attain a new value, not dependent on
its past function but on its contribution to a new form of life. "I walk
among men as fragments of the future", Nietzsche has Zarathustra proclaim in the most lyrical, if difficult, of his books. As much as Western man
might find a fragmented world distressing, he could at least rediscover aspects of it that he had forgotten: "The hybrid European . . . requires history. Again and again a new piece of pre-history or a foreign country is
tried on, put on, taken off, packed away and above all studied: we are the
first age that has truly studied 'costumes'—I mean those of moralities, articles of faith, taste in the arts and religion . . . [We are] prepared like no previous age for a carnival in the grand style".[62]

Nietzsche wanted men to go back to the past as a source of the future,
for he recognised that the past contained the conditions of its own tran-

scendence. It persisted in the rituals, capacities and social interactions of society. It persisted in the imagination. Modernity might shatter a culture's
self-certainty, but if its integrity was maintained it would survive the experience intact. Indeed, in being revalued, its coherence would be reconstituted
anew. The advantage for the contemporary European, he added, was that
"he could enjoy Homer again; he could rediscover possibilities of his existence of which he had previously been unaware."

As the philosopher Paul Ricoeur contends, it is precisely this process of
'reinterpretation' that we should call 'tradition'. It is interesting that
Ricoeur also quotes Homer in making this point. *The Iliad,* as in every interpretation of myth, is a piece of history reworked into a narrative order.
Homer did not invent the story, he merely reinterpreted it. He invented a
new narrative meaning. He had the entire myth of the Trojan War to
choose from; he chose to focus on one story, that of Achilles' wrath. In developing this story he created a new myth. In his meeting with Priam, the
father of Hector, the hero whom he has killed in battle, the warrior's wrath
expires in cathartic reconciliation.[63] Homer's retelling of the tale exempli-
fies a particular meaning: how the vain and meaningless worth of one hero
can be resolved when the hero is reconciled with another whose nobility is
not in question. Here, writes Ricoeur, we have a powerful example of what
it means to create meaning from a common heritage: to take a tradition
and revise it poetically in order to signify something new.

A return to the past may be "a backward look ... but [can] also be a
look into the mirror too". These words are not those of a political scientist
or a historian but of a composer, Igor Stravinsky, a figure of the highest importance in the history of modern culture. Through neoclassicism
Stravinsky hoped to repossess the Western musical tradition more fully. By
composing in a past idiom he hoped to bring the past back into a more
fruitful relationship with the present. In other words, he consciously used
the past to exploit the present, "to make new paths of the world accessible
to feeling". In digging deeper he wanted to make modernity more intelligible to those who lived with it. In this case he wished to make modern music
less alienating for its audience.

Stravinsky's neoclassicism was, in this respect, "both radical and new,
not because his music was 'about the past', nor an attempt to revive it or
extend or transform it. ... The past, in fact, for Stravinsky enjoys the status
of 'an object'—it is the theme of his music".[64] The idea of the past in his
output is an attempt to experience new possibilities in the present and to do
so through a language that reaches much deeper into the Western musical
tradition so that we can communicate with it anew, and so revalue it in our
own lifetime.

All change, in short, is traumatic. A society divided between a minority
for whom traditional ways or beliefs become increasingly meaningless and

a majority for whom any kind of change is a threat, is a society that has lost its cohesive character.

Let me take as a concrete example Meiji Japan. Many Japanese had difficulty adjusting before and after the Meiji Restoration. Many continued to fear that the process of revaluation would further undermine their traditions that prior to the 1850s had made their life humane. As an early Western observer reported after visiting Japan: "Educated Japanese had done with their past. They wanted to be somebody else and something else than what they had been and still are".[65] Their predicament, he claimed, was that they could not be wholly modern in the Western sense, nor wholly themselves in terms of their own tradition. It was an understanding that had created an excessive self-consciousness that was intensely alienating for many.

The Japanese, of course, successfully challenged the idea that revaluation and Westernisation were synonymous. They imported Western techniques but used them selectively. They managed to transform themselves into a modern industrial society. Their success owed much not to the rejection of their past but to the recognition that their past was the solution, not the problem. They did not repudiate their traditions, they rediscovered them. They were among the first people to recognise that a society's traditions are also the source of its transformation.

What Nietzsche feared most was that in revaluing their values the Europeans themselves might break with the past in an attempt to make themselves autonomous of history. Writing in the aftermath of the Spanish Civil War, Ortega y Gasset described the conflict as a response to the clash between tradition and modernity. The war was a phase in that struggle, an apparent decisive round upon whose outcome would depend whether the Spanish people would modernise themselves on their own terms or be modernised by others—a fate that, in a telling word, he called 'Japanisation'.[66]

Nietzsche did not talk, as did those who often appropriated his language, of creating a new culture different from the old. To have attempted, as did Lenin, to develop the blueprint of a model society that was supposed to transcend everything that had gone before would have contradicted his insight that all cultures are historically preconditioned. Those conditions can be described, not prescribed in advance. To do so would be ahistorical.

In addition, any attempt to impose values from the outside would militate against the purpose of revaluation, to make a world in which life had meaning for those who had to live it. What the Japanese attempted with success, the Russians failed miserably. As Gramsci noted at the time, Lenin had compelled the Russian people "to an enforced awakening, skipping several historical stages in the process". That awakening had shallow Russian roots, though it often used Russian arguments and exploited Russian themes. Nevertheless, Lenin's successors chose to force-march the Russian people into history by cutting them off from their past.[67]

Spengler had written in similar terms of an earlier period of Russian history. Peter the Great's overhasty attempts to Westernise his country had, Spengler concluded, not only cut off the Russian people from their history, but truncated it. The Russians had become "a nationality whose destiny should have been to live without a history". Invoking Hegel, he contended that the Russian problem was not that they were a people without a history but that they had been forced into "a false and artificial history" that would never take root.[68]

Why was Lenin's experiment even more dangerous than Peter the Great's? The answer lies in the attempt by late Western man to make himself the subject and not the object of history, a being who, in Nietzsche's words, "feared nothing but his own extinction" and perhaps, in the quest for his own perfectibility, not even that: "It may be that there remains one prodigious idea which might be made to prevail over every other aspiration, which might overcome the most victorious, the idea of humanity sacrificing itself".[69]

Fascism, too, was a particularly vivid example of that process in action. Although it was highly critical of modernity, it had no real answer to alienation. It offered a questionable panacea at a high cost to those who embraced it. When true to their belief in the superiority of the Aryan race the Germans eventually did try to "breed true", the upshot was the Final Solution. The Europeans might be a people with history, but history was now being made of them, not others. They had become its object, not its subject.

Unfortunately in Soviet Russia, the peasants were seen only as "the material of the capitalist epoch from which Soviet man could be fashioned". "The poet of the new epoch will rethink in a new way the thoughts of mankind and refeel its feelings", predicted Trotsky.[70] All that such experiments resulted in, of course, was sending the poets to the gulag.

Nietzsche was possessed, however, by a double fear: not only that men would seek to make themselves autonomous of history but also that they would devalue the past by overvaluing the future. He had little patience with the grand systemizers of his own day who wanted to create future utopias or who were given to devising blueprints for new societies. He was highly critical of men who saw themselves as Ibsen's master builders reforging man anew. He was an unapologetic relativist and what he expected of society was related to the 'now', not to 'tomorrow'.

All interpretations of the world, he wrote, are in part conditional on the nature of 'being', of the man who seeks to know it. "Coming to know means to place oneself in a conditional relationship to something, to feel oneself conditioned by something and oneself to condition it."[71] It followed that the act of revaluating was as important as the values being revalued. Human beings derive their self-respect from taking responsibility for their lives, not by importing new gods or being reformed by others, and certainly not by attempting to change themselves into something they are not.

In short, Nietzsche was fully aware of the danger of attempting to revalue man himself. "One should not want to be a physician to the incurable: thus Zarathustra teaches". On the contrary, what is incurable must be ruthlessly carved out of the body of a culture. Consequently, he warned, revaluation "may well be the most dangerous venture, that is, not for the one who dares to express it but for the one to whom it is addressed".[72]

Unlike Lenin, Nietzsche did not believe that "man is something to be overcome". "Only a jester thinks that man can also be skipped over", he wrote in *Zarathustra*.[73] He accepted that revaluation could not be unconditional. A society that did not recognise limits would pursue limitless objectives far beyond its strength and exhaust itself in the process. A society that sought the impossible would dissipate the intensity of its power and thus would be in danger of rendering itself powerless. A society that tried to forge a new man (e.g., *Homo sovieticus*) would devalue whole sections of society, including entire classes, considered to be hostile to the regeneration of humanity.

It is this argument that brings us back to where we began—the dialogue between Hegel and Goethe. In one of his better known *Atheneum* fragments, Friedrich von Schlegel identified the three defining tendencies of his age as the French Revolution, Fichte's *Wissenschaftslehre* and Goethe's *Wilhelm Meister*. We have already discussed the contributions of two. Fichte, for his part, asserted an absolute human will that rendered God superfluous and thus effectively dead, long before Nietzsche proclaimed his death to the world. He did not equate absolute will to human will or even human will to humanity as a whole. It was his students who depicted the striving to attain such absolute will in their demonic heroes. And though Hegel had serious misgivings about this demonic heroism he compounded the fault in his efforts to constrain it by making it a world historical force.[74]

By contrast, in *Wilhelm Meister* Goethe captured the sensibility of the liberal West in the aphorism "thought broadens but lames; action enlivens but limits". We cannot attain the impossible, he argued, as a true understanding of the world would tell us. We experience true freedom only through action, not thought, but in acting we also encounter the limits of what is possible. It was the recognition that a future age would not accept this understanding that led to his 'social pessimism', for which he was criticised by Napoleon. At the end of his novel everyone commits suicide in frustration or emigrates to the New World. What he did not foresee, of course, was a third alternative, something else entirely: that the fate of both the Old World and the New might be linked, that Europe and the United States might encounter each other in an Atlantic community.

2

The Anglo-American
Imagination

The Forging of the Atlantic Charter, 1941

In August 1941 a British warship, the *Prince of Wales,* escorted by several destroyers, carried Winston Churchill across the Atlantic to a rendezvous in Placentia Bay, Newfoundland. It was the first meeting between a British prime minister and an American president since Woodrow Wilson's visit to Europe in 1919. In the course of their meeting a somewhat tenuous relationship between the two leading Western powers was forged into something quite different, a closer, more ambitious political alliance that in time came to be known as the Western Alliance.

Placentia Bay was a symbolic meeting place, a U.S. naval base leased from a British dominion, Canada. It was a symbolic meeting too, especially for Churchill. In the early days of the Russian civil war, in the 1920s, he had spoken of the need for the West to unite in a new struggle. Rather than allow the alliance with the United States to lapse, he had wanted to retain the Western coalition in the face of an enemy obsessed with usurping history in the name of its own recondite understanding of its meaning. On another occasion he had defined Western military intervention against the new Soviet government as "a point of concentration" for the "strong and dominant forces in our national life", which only a coalition locked in another war could provide.[1]

Perhaps Churchill recalled these earlier thoughts as he crossed the Atlantic. In 1941 a new world was about to be forged. Roosevelt's thoughts were more pragmatic. Although the United States had taken on more and more of the defence of the North Atlantic against German U-boats, it was not at war with Germany and there was no prospect that the U.S. Congress would allow it to be. The attack on Pearl Harbor was still four months off.

Churchill brought with him a delegation that included Alexander Cadogan, the permanent undersecretary at the Foreign Office, and the three service chiefs. Roosevelt's team included the three American chiefs of staff, General George Marshall, Admiral Harold Stark and General Henry Arnold. Within a year such meetings were to become commonplace. The Allied Joint Chiefs of Staff would establish an unprecedented tradition of concerted strategic planning that foreshadowed the eventual creation of the Atlantic Alliance.

On the following Sunday, Churchill and Roosevelt attended a church parade. "We sang the sailors' hymn, 'For Those in Peril'," Churchill later reported to the British people:

> We sang 'Onward Christian Soldiers' and indeed, I felt that this was no vain presumption but that we had the right to feel that we were serving a cause for the sake of which a trumpet had sounded from on high. When I looked upon that densely packed congregation of the fighting men of the same language, of the same faith, of the same ideals, and to a large extent of the same interests, and certainly in different degrees facing the same dangers, it swept across me that here was the only hope, but also the sure hope of saving the world from merciless degradation.[2]

Even Roosevelt was not unmoved by the symbolic nature of the meeting. "We live by symbols", one of the American negotiators wrote to the president (in a letter that was subsequently released and published by the press), "and you two in that ocean . . . in the setting of that Sunday service, gave meaning to the conflict between civilisation and an arrogant, brute challenge".[3]

If both leaders were conscious of the historical significance of their meeting, they were more conscious still of the immediate need to keep Britain in the war against Germany. In the course of the staff talks between the generals the Americans accepted that should the United States enter the war, even if attacked by Japan, the defeat of Germany must be their first priority. They also agreed on the manner in which the war should be conducted. Neither side wished to witness a repetition of the trench warfare of the Great War or send their men ever again to die on the 'killing ground' of the western front.

History, however, remembers their meeting at Placentia not for the staff talks between the two nations but for its immediate outcome: the Atlantic Charter. In origin little more than a mimeographed press release, it was one of the most articulate expressions of the values the principal Western powers held in common.

What place those values would have in the new world order was one of the principal issues on Churchill's agenda. Of the charter's eight clauses one pledged the two countries to eschew any form of 'aggrandisement' for themselves. It set their face against any territorial changes inspired by undemocratic means. In another the two leaders pledged themselves to "respect the right of all peoples to choose the form of government under which they will live", a reference not only to German aggression but also to Russia's forceful incorporation of the Baltic states the year before.

The force of the draft was clear enough and its ambition remarkable. As Churchill pointed out to the War Cabinet when submitting the declaration for its approval, "the President undoubtedly contemplated the disarmament of the guilty nations, coupled with the maintenance of strong, united British and American armaments both by sea and air for a long, indefinite period".[4]

The two leaders agreed that the peace of the world in future should be policed by the United States and Britain. The aggressor states would be disarmed and the postwar world placed under the supervision of the United Nations. A reference to such an organisation, which was intended to succeed the bankrupt League of Nations, was struck out at the last minute because of its presumed unpopularity with the U.S. Congress.

Roosevelt would later assert that there was no formally signed copy of the Atlantic Charter; indeed that there was no official text, only a press release that declared some guiding principles. Yet its eight points had as persistent an appeal as Woodrow Wilson's Fourteen Points in 1918, with one significant difference. The charter was not a unilateral declaration by the United States but a joint statement by the two principal Western powers, which Britain explicitly signed on behalf of all but one of the European governments then in exile in London. The exception, a significant one, France, did not sign the Charter until 26 December 1944, in the closing months of the war.

If in later years Churchill called the charter both in substance and spirit "a British production cast in my own words",[5] the Americans had pressed for it far more than the British. Roosevelt recognised at once that the war was a historical turning point that had drawn the United States and Europe inexorably into closer contact with each other. In a sense Churchill eavesdropped on a private conversation in 1941, a debate among the Americans themselves about their historical purpose. Their failure to work with Europe in the interwar years was an embarrassing reminder to Roosevelt, beset as he was at home by isolationist or openly pro-German forces.

The idea of a permanent Western alliance was out of step with mainstream American thinking. It had to be expressed imaginatively or not at all if it were ever to be realised. In that sense the 'West' was an *idea* as much as an alliance, and it is as an idea that I shall treat it in the pages that follow.

A Change of Consciousness

What had occurred by 1941 was a change of consciousness, a change of perspective, an acknowledgement, often unconscious to be sure, that the Western powers had discovered each other at a critical moment in their history. The Western Alliance presented them with an opportunity to reformulate their ambitions and ideas. It produced a heightened consciousness of the values of Western civilisation. It reminded them in the most compelling terms of what they shared in common. As André Malraux averred at the time, every generation has its own unique way of looking at the world. "The modern age ... shows us with simple clarity and insistence the continuous development of certain principles of life which were defined for the first time at a certain date. That date is a decisive one in a series of dates which make up the modern era".[6]

What Malraux believed he had witnessed was the emergence of an Atlantic community that would link the United States and Western Europe, two cultures that hitherto had been divided by emigration, by the escape of the politically oppressed and economically disadvantaged immigrants fleeing from the Old World to the New. In 1945 the two worlds were finally reunited in a struggle against a common foe.

It is of course difficult for any age to understand its own birth. Those who live through great changes are often the last to understand them. As the Argentinean writer Jorge Luis Borges once remarked, men are usually confronted by the "modesty of history". In plying their trade historians work to identify historic turning points and to date them precisely. Real history, however, is more modest. Its essential dates remain secret for a long time. Nevertheless, Borges wrote, on learning of the liberation of Paris on 23 August 1944, he also recognised that he had been present at a definingly important moment in history, one that had witnessed the birth of a Western community of nations.[7]

Of course if the British had had their way the alliance would have been consummated much earlier. They had tried hard, in fact, during the First World War to create an enduring partnership between themselves and the United States. As early as 1916, Lord Grey, the British foreign secretary, had proposed forming a 'League of Nations' in which the United States would play a principal role. If another war was to be avoided in the future, he had written to Wilson's secretary of state, America would have to have a hand in the peace. "Germany is the peril today, but the peril will recur every century in Europe if Europe is left to itself". This was one of the first references to an Anglo-American security role in the world at large, one that would be designed to deal with what Grey called "the larger conditions of peace" in the postwar world.[8]

All such efforts of course were frustrated by Woodrow Wilson, who was more interested in constructing a universal order than an Atlantic confederation of states. His indifference was informed by his belief that the United States and Western Europe differed significantly in the importance they attached to an open society. At best, Britain and France could be considered imperfect democracies, 'associates', not allies—a word he refused to use.

Although they might be partners in a common cause, they were something less than members of a common community.

Even the *New York Tribune,* which was inclined to denounce Germany, claimed as late as November 1916: "Despite widespread sympathy for France and a well-defined affection for Great Britain in a limited circle of Americans there has been no acceptance of the allied point of view as to the war ... the thing that the British have failed to get before the American people is the belief that the war is one in which the question of humanity and civilisation is uppermost for the British themselves".[9]

Wilson's Peace Note on 18 December 1916, his abortive initiative to persuade the European powers to end the war, latched onto the hollowness of British official rhetoric: "The leaders and several belligerents have ... stated their objects in general terms. But, stated in general terms, they seem the same on both sides. Never yet have the authoritative spokesmen of either side averred the precise objects which would, if attained, satisfy them and their people". Wilson watched the unfolding conflict with increasing dismay. A few months before he took the United States into it he told his closest adviser, Colonel House, that America's involvement "would be a crime against civilisation".[10] The implication that there was no real difference between Britain and Germany was not well received in London. In the aftermath of Wilson's Note, it would have seemed incredible to imagine that within five months the United States would enter the war on Britain's side.

What had transpired in the interwar period was a profound change of consciousness in the way in which the Western powers regarded each other. By the time Churchill and Roosevelt signed the Atlantic Charter both the British and the seven governments in exile that were also signatories to it considered themselves members of a larger community in the making.

It was a community that transcended without denying the idea of the nation-state. It was one based on the recognition that the world had moved into an era of blocs, or coalitions informed by ideology. If we look back at the First World War we will see the beginning of that consciousness, as yet unrealised, a promise that history had yet to discover. It was then that a number of English writers began to talk of the need for a 'democratic internationalism'—an internationalism, wrote Norman Angell, that might not be necessary for Germany but would most certainly be necessary for the British themselves.[11]

Aristotelian thinking was very much to the fore for the British governing class in the early twentieth century. "In my day," a colonial civil servant in the 1920s told an American visitor, "we had not all forgotten Aristotle. I was continually asking 'what is the end or object of this endeavour?'. But no one could, or would, give me an answer".[12] They might not have been able to provide an answer for the British Empire—that unique if short-lived commonwealth of people whom the British had united at the end of the nineteenth century—but they could for the West, and began doing so with vigour after 1917.

Another writer of the time, the influential philosopher Bernard Bosanquet, had seen the state before the war in highly Aristotelian terms, as the expression of 'an ethical idea'. And as an ethical idea it had to have a faith or sense of purpose. It followed that even if the unity of mankind as a whole was not possible, this was not true for those societies whose members lived the same version of the good life, who were in broad agreement with the values that, in their eyes, made life worth living.

Writing after the Treaty of Versailles, Bosanquet concluded that Britain could never go back to what it had been before the war. It had fought with France and the United States to defend a principle on which its political identity was based. What it meant to be British in the twentieth century was to be true to a democratic idea. To be true to that idea they could no longer consider themselves only subjects of the king. They were also members of a Western community of nations. Nationalism and internationalism were, on these terms, not incompatible but linked.[13]

Echoing this view thirty-five years later, George E.G. Catlin talked of an internationalism founded on an 'Anglo-Saxon' tradition—the title of one of his many books; he wrote another that was subtitled 'the foundation of Anglo-Saxony'. In it he referred to Gilbert Murray's claim in the 1930s that "sovereignty could only be pooled by those who share[d] values". The postwar world saw the proliferation of many similar works, including one by the presidential candidate Wendell Willkie entitled *One Anglo-American Nation*.

Important though such books were, the alliance derived its deepest impulse from the great speeches that Churchill made in 1938 outlining the strategy of a new European alliance directed not simply against the two totalitarian systems but against any and all regimes that endangered the existence of civilisation itself. What he grasped, in particular, was that freedom would not survive or peace be kept "unless a very large majority of mankind unite together to defend them and show themselves possessed of a *constabulary* power before which barbaric and atavistic forces will stand in awe".[14]

It took the Second World War to translate this vague commitment to democratic internationalism into the defining raison d'être of the Western powers. In 1941 both the British and the Americans wanted an alliance that would, in the words of the émigré German philosopher Karl Mannheim, writing at the time that the Atlantic Charter was signed, create a democratic order. Such a system, he argued, would "differ from the relativist *laissez-faire* of the previous age, as it will have the courage to agree on some basic values which are acceptable to everyone who shares the traditions of civilisation". Unconsciously echoing Churchill's plea for a new constabulary power, Mannheim referred to his own vision as 'a new militant democracy,' a doctrine armed and prepared to defend itself through war.[15]

If Mannheim was rather vague about the values the United States and Britain shared, he had no doubt that in future they would be the two countries charged by history to promote them. Writing in the closing months of the war, the novelist V. S. Pritchett was equally insistent that the two democracies should work together in the future: "We felt that our war is a war to defend civilisation even when we are not reading official propaganda, and we have felt this *not because we are especially clear about what our civilisation is,* but because we have thought that this war and this kind of society that produced it was a conspiracy against man".[16]

One of the most profound changes in Western consciousness in this period, in fact, was a belief, perhaps dimly expressed at the time, that the West would have to accomplish something of importance if it was ever to redeem itself for its failure to stand up to the dictators in the 1930s. In future it would have to promote the democratic cause in the face of those who were implacably opposed to it, the new barbarians.

Barbarians of course are usually so called by others; they do not call or consider themselves 'barbarous'. What was novel about the twentieth century was that for the first time certain Europeans undertook to describe themselves as barbarians in a critique of what they considered to be the decadent or racially impure cultures that had grown up in the West in the intervening years. The Third Reich, for example, regularly enjoined its people to celebrate the barbarous sentiments of "violence, youth and catastrophism", and the constant testing of all three in battle.[17]

Russia of course had been considered barbarous much earlier than Germany. "In our attitude to the Europeans", wrote Aleksandr Herzen, "there are points of resemblance to the attitude of the Germans to the Romans. In spite of our exterior we are still barbarians". This view became more marked after the October Revolution. Stalin was particularly dismissive of the 'civilised' values that Churchill held so dear—tolerance, rationalism and the rule of law. One of the first poems of the Bolshevik period, 'The Scythians', published by the otherwise humanistic Aleksandr Blok, celebrated the barbaric qualities of the new rulers in Moscow. Blok later recorded that when writing it he had been deliberately targeting the decadent Europeans from the vantage point of a Russia renewed by a return to its earlier barbarism.

> Yes, we are Scythians. Yes we are Asiatics
> With slanted and avid eyes. . . .
> For the last time, come to your senses Old World.

Later, in 1919, Blok gave a lecture at the newly founded Free Academy of Philosophy. He entitled it 'The Crumbling of Humanism'. In that celebrated text he proclaimed the end of the age of humanism, the end of the concept of ethical man.[18] No wonder that as he lay dying two years later he said that he could hear "the stormwinds of history blowing overhead".

What made both fascism and Marxism so dangerous was their appeal to the sensibilities of the West's own citizens. Subversion from within was feared as much as attack from outside. Many Western politicians were all too aware that the barbarians not only were hammering outside the gates but also were already to be found within, attempting to break out. The idea of barbarism was not the product of a fevered imagination. It was symbolic of all the forces at work in interwar Europe. It was a metaphor of the time for the negative forces that lurked beneath the political fabric. It was a metaphor for a ferocious energy that was directed largely against itself.

The British Vision: Forging an Atlantic Community

It would be quite wrong to conclude that every British observer, even those most implacable in their opposition to totalitarianism, shared Churchill's vision. At the end of the Great Nuclear War in Orwell's nightmare vision of the future, *1984,* the world is divided into three large power units or super-states. Oceania was the name given to the empire comprising the United States and Britain. The centre of authority was probably but not certainly North America, though the ideology that united its territories had been developed by British intellectuals and was known as English socialism or INGSOC. Britain itself was renamed Airstrip One, a neutral designation that was not intended to be contemptuous. As for the other superstates, continental Europe formed part of Eurasia, a vast bloc united and run by the former Soviet Union.

It was to avoid that fate, or something similar, that Orwell had called in 1947, in the pages of the *Partisan Review,* for Europe to unite in a power bloc independent of the two superpowers that had saved it. Such a bloc, committed to democratic socialism, might stand as 'a third world' different from, if not opposed to, the worlds of American capitalism and Soviet communism.[19]

The idea of a third force, however, had little appeal even to Orwell's fellow socialists, and certainly not those who formed the first postwar Labour government. They were committed to a quite different vision, an Atlantic community that would effectively perpetuate the wartime coalition against Germany and, in the process, transform America into a European power. As early as March 1946 Clement Attlee recognised that "it may be that we shall have to consider the British Isles as an easterly extension of a strategic [arch] the centre of which is the American continent".[20]

Such a vision was not without its appeal even in France. Although, wrote Malraux, the Americans did not have "all the essentials of a European past", nonetheless everything that was essential for them was bound to Europe. "American culture . . . is still purely and simply the invention of Europeans".[21] Even fascist dictators who survived the war, like Franco, hoped to join that community, or something very like it. A more scholarly equivalent of Churchill's *History of the English-Speaking Peoples,* the collaborative *Historia de España y de America,* was planned in the 1950s by the Catalan historian Jaime Vicens Vives. He was no friend of Franco, but the project suited the Spanish dictator's policy of cultivating an Atlantic-Hispanic identity. Franco's unrealised ambition was a good example of the development of an Atlantic rim society that was linked across the seas by exchanges of personnel and trade.[22] In the immediate postwar years the desire for Atlantic unity was so great that it even transcended the political divisions within the Western world.

Nevertheless, the idea of the West was most vivid in the Anglo-American imagination. The idea of an Atlantic world had been formulated in the British mind long before American and British soldiers found themselves huddled in the trenches of the Anzio beachhead or pinned down on the Normandy beaches. The idea of a partnership with the United States had been in the imagination for some time, awaiting only its historical moment of realisation.

For Britain the decisive moment in the twentieth century was 1940, the moment perhaps when it last spoke for the world. It was the year that saw the 'miracle of Dunkirk', an event that for the duration of the century defined Britain's view of itself as the only Western power that had stood against Nazism from the beginning of the war to the very end. Like so much else in its history, the real events of 1940 did not form part of the Dunkirk myth. However we interpret that myth, however, it seems inconceivable that Britain might have taken a different road from the one that it chose to travel for the next forty years.

The only attempt to chart a different course into the future came in the closing days of the fall of France, when, in an attempt to stiffen French morale, Churchill offered the prospect of an Anglo-French union that would persist into the peace as well. In fact, thinking along these lines had been evident five months earlier in a memorandum written by Sir Orme Sarjent, the assistant undersecretary of state to the Foreign Office, in which he had suggested that after the war the United Kingdom and France would have to enter some form of political union if they were ever again to deter Germany from going to war. Sarjent acknowledged that such a proposal would represent "an alarming and dangerous surrender of British sovereignty", but he maintained that it might be a necessary one.

The idea won the support of Neville Chamberlain and his Foreign Secretary, Lord Halifax. The Board of Education even planned to produce a new set of history textbooks in which British children would discover that France had always been their country's 'natural' ally, even if that reality had not been appreciated at the time.[23] Such aspirations, although expressed less forcefully, met with some French support as well. In an article in *Le Figaro,* Wladimir D'Ormesson saw Churchill's offer of an Anglo-French union as a historic step indeed, one that would mark Britain's irrevocable commitment to a European future. "England is now in Europe", he wrote—in the event prematurely.[24] The fall of France a few weeks later not only led to an immediate shift in the balance of power: Britain found itself at war with an entire continent. Its only hope appeared to lie in an association not with a European ally but across the Atlantic with the United States.

The 'miracle of Dunkirk', the eight days from May 29 to June 4, during which the bulk of the British Expeditionary Force was successfully evacuated from the continent, finally laid to rest these European ambitions. By July Halifax was to be found writing that instead of a closer union with France, the cabinet was considering 'a special association' with the United States, an association that quite soon would become, in British thinking at least, 'a special relationship'. It was an idea, he added triumphantly, that would finally discredit the promise of "an Anglo-French union among the various plans we make for the future". Indeed, Churchill's cabinet was relieved that the very idea of a union seemed to be one whose time had passed. "It is almost a relief to be thrown back on the resources of the Empire", wrote Sir Maurice Hankey, who had reluctantly chaired the committee to examine plans for closer Anglo-French cooperation after the war.

If the United Kingdom was ultimately successful, Hankey concluded, its success would "expose the fallacy of the glib statement that Great Britain is no longer an island—we shall have disproved the strategical theories on which our policy has been based in recent years". Foremost among them, he noted, was the idea that an association with France was essential to Britain's future security. As Lord Beaverbrook put it in the summer of 1940: "We are all splendid isolationists now".[25]

Hankey was mistaken, of course. The United Kingdom fell back not on the resources of the empire but on the United States. The British suspected that they would be able to maintain their independence even if the rest of Europe fell under the domination of a single power, at least until the United States came into the war. No less important, perhaps, they hoped that they might win at comparatively little cost in lives *because* they had no European allies who would force them to fight another continental war.

The fall of France, in short, confirmed the British in their long-standing faith in the superiority of the Anglo-American tradition, in the distinctiveness of Britain and the United States as nations. In the early months of the war this crucial difference also entered the American consciousness. The first American to call for an Atlantic union, Clarence Streit, in a widely read book published in 1939 entitled *Union Now,* proposed setting up a federal union of Atlantic democracies patterned on the federation of the

United States. What he looked forward to was the birth of a common security system, one that in the first instance would be restricted to the seven English-speaking democracies.[26]

Streit laboured tirelessly on behalf of his cause. *Union Now* sold 10,000 copies in its first year of publication. It sold 300,000 in all. He spent most of 1941 crisscrossing the country to preach the cause. When France fell he spent $2,000 on an advertisement in the *New York Times* proposing a provisional union of the United States and the British Commonwealth. Then, after the United States entered the war, he revised his plea for a democratic union as the only means of assuring a durable peace.[27]

In 1943 George Catlin put forward similar proposals in a pamphlet entitled *Anglo-American Union as a Nucleus of World Federation*. Sixteen years later he was still to be found arguing that the U.S.-Canada-British area of the Atlantic would form "the substantial nucleus" of an Atlantic world grounded on ideas that the English-speaking democracies shared in common, and that some of their continental European allies did not. The relationship between America and Britain, Catlin maintained, would always remain "the bridge" of the Atlantic world, in the theatre where it mattered most, in the imagination of the two countries.[28]

Both Streit and Catlin were typical representatives of their age. Both men wanted a piecemeal approach beginning with a democratic union in which the world's democracies would preserve their independence by acting collectively in a common cause. Their federalism went no further than that of the *Federalist Papers*. In the end even that proved too much for the Atlantic nations themselves. As we shall see in the next chapter, the idea of an Atlantic federation was doomed from the beginning.

Anglo-American Atlanticism

Britain's association with the United States, in short, was more than just an unresolved transaction, the promise of an alliance that had not been consummated in 1919. The alliance between the two countries was brought about not only by the war. Its roots ran much deeper. In retrospect, we may see both peoples in 1941 as members of an unrecorded community that history was about to discover. It was a community anchored to three principal themes.

The first theme was the 'universalism' they shared. It differed from that of the French in one crucial respect. As Paz writes, their universalism enabled them 'to be' in the world, while at the same time to exclude the world next to them—Latin America in the case of the United States, continental Europe in the case of Britain. Both societies represented that branch of Western life that was most 'democratic', at least in terms of its commitment to individualism.[29]

The British aversion to 'continentalism' was of long standing. Long before the Second World War it had become part of the accepted national wisdom that they were quite distinctive from their European neighbours, in both the spirit and the nature of their institutions. They were distinct from them in particular because they had escaped what Carlyle described in the 1840s as "the continental nuisance called bureaucracy". Instead of being harassed by *douaniers* and *gendarmes,* the English saw themselves as citizens of a country that permitted them to do broadly what they wanted. Of all the differences that distinguished the English from other Europeans, even in American eyes, none was deemed as significant as that which was presumed to exist between a corporate Europe and a noncorporate England.

The Americans displayed a similar disregard for their Latin American neighbours, whom they dismissed as an exotic and indeed fairly disreputable people with a taste for military coups. In that sense, adds Paz, neither of the two Anglo-Saxon powers was interested in a dialogue with the 'other', only with each other. Both were censorious of their neighbours for representing 'error'. A historical dialogue with the rest of the world was acutely difficult for both countries because it always assumed "the form of a judgment, a trial or a contract". What distinguishes Britain's view of Europe even today is that it is still censorious of what the Europeans believe makes them definingly themselves.

It is interesting that this was also the case with America's relationship with continental Europe. Even for the writers of the 1930s, such as Hemingway, Stein, Miller and Fitzgerald who lived and worked in Paris, Europe remained alien, not their own. They may have developed an attachment to European city life but none became assimilated. None lost altogether that residual habit of mind, which, for want of a precise term might be called 'American'. Many of their works were about place and identity. Others were about an imaginary Europe in which they still found themselves displaced. In the end their identity stemmed from the fact that the United States was not a country as, say, was France. Reflecting on his return from Europe the poet Archibald MacLeish called his country "neither a place nor a blood-line" but a project, a social experiment. In that way, at least, it was quintessentially un-European.[30]

It was not, however, quintessentially un-English. What divided the United States and Britain from their neighbours brought them together in the Atlantic world. The Anglo-American relationship helped to make sense of a dangerous world. It offered a partnership that many writers thought necessary if the twentieth century was to be survived.

Let me take as an example two exiles, T. S. Eliot from the United States, and W. H. Auden from England, the two greatest twentieth-century poets of the English-speaking world. In New York, removed from the immediate fighting and the experience of air-raid alerts, Auden found a perspective from which to look back on the 1930s, the decade that he had left behind. He still saw himself rooted in a world that permitted him to be its historian, or what he called 'his generation's generaliser'. It was appropriate that he should have written the very first war poem ('September 1, 1939'), an important work set in a bar on Fifty-second Street, New York, which was concerned not with the war itself so much as its deeper and more profound moral meaning.

Years later Auden expressed in a poem written in memory of Louis MacNeice the desire to "become if possible a minor *Atlantic* Goethe". It was a significant admission, the crucial word being not 'Goethe' but 'Atlantic'. At a very early point in his poetic career Auden recognised that the English language was not unique to England, but transatlantic in its appeal. Just as Latin had sustained the largest of all European empires, the English language might sustain a larger community still. Indeed, speculates Joseph Brodsky, one of the reasons Auden decided to leave England for America was his belief that he was not leaving England at all.[31]

In similar fashion, T. S. Eliot was also intent on settling in the one country, England, that allowed him, as an American, to escape into a wider community without entirely repudiating his American heritage. As Edmund Wilson noted at the time, Eliot saw himself in these early years not as an Englishman but as an Atlanticist. What Eliot was escaping from was a nation that in the 1920s was obsessed with discovering what it meant to be 'American'. What he found most discouraging of all was his country's pursuit of 'Americanness' in the interwar years. It represented more than just a cultural footnote to isolationism. The 1920s saw the publication of studies entitled *The Rise of American Civilization* and *The Rise of the Common Man*. As late as the eve of the Second World War, into which the United States was dragged reluctantly, James Truslow Adams wrote an essay about his own country in the *New York Times* significantly entitled 'A Nation Rises'.[32]

It was this 'Americanism' that represented such a marked departure from the past, at least for many intellectuals who wanted to find an inspiration deeper than that provided by the old ideas and missions. By becoming English, wrote Edmund Wilson, Eliot became not a European, but an Atlanticist. In his own person he represented "the growth of American internationalism".[33]

In 1940, of course, Eliot was able to place England at the centre of world history. His great patriotic poem 'The Four Quartets' remains as preoccupied with the ways in which he was not English as the ways in which he was, and this in the texture and cadence of the verse as much as in the memories of earlier shores, the rocky Massachusetts sea of 'Dry Salvages' and its hint of an earlier and other creation.

In his poem 'Little Gidding' he talked of a people of "no immediate kin" who were nonetheless touched by "a common genius . . . united in the strife which divides them". It is a sentence that inserts peculiarity, difference and strife into the idea of a transatlantic community as a necessary basis of it. Eliot did not make light of the differences that still divided America and Britain. But he also observed with an acute eye the values that united them. He saw himself as a 'spirit' "between two worlds much like each other", between two countries, that, for a brief moment in time, discovered that they were members of the same community.

The second theme that distinguished the Anglo-American discourse was their attitude to history. The early twentieth century was self-conscious in a way no other century had been before. Many societies believed that the logic of history could be grasped and exploited and that their future depended on whether they kept in step with that logic or not.

The philosopher Maurice Merleau-Ponty in his interpretation of Marx called the logic of history a form of 'historical selection'. History set problems that social structures such as societies or classes had to solve as best they could. He spoke of Marx's work as a 'perception of history' in order to emphasise the cognitive relationship that Marx was able to establish with his subject matter. It was a relationship that was only possible because the problem-solution dialectic gave history a discernible structure. It was the dialectic that created the two vantage points from which the structural meaning of history could be grasped. A society that grasped the fact that it was the force of history was a society in tune with the logic of the times.[34]

This was not just an idea confined to Marxism. In 1940 many intellectuals believed that Germany had tapped that power in a way that the democracies had not. "In the face of Hitler, Mussolini, Stalin", wrote the Jesuit-scientist Pierre Teilhard de Chardin in a letter from Peking: "Don't you see that Churchill and Roosevelt are grotesquely antiquated. Personally I stick to my idea that we are watching the birth, more than the death of a world. . . . The world is bound to belong to its most active elements . . . just now the Germans deserve to win because, however bad or mixed is their spirit, they have more spirit than the rest of the world".[35]

The French writer Pierre Drieu La Rochelle agreed with him: "How can you believe that the winner of this war would be an empire of which every part is an anachronism from the past? Someone who today believes in the victory of England is like someone who in 1900 had prophesied the victory of China with its Mandarins and pig-tails and jade buttons over the European empires with their motors and cannons".[36]

These were not isolated voices. In the 1930s it was a received opinion even in the United States that Germany was the more dynamic of the two powers. In one of his short stories, 'Mosby's memoirs', Saul Bellow addresses this theme in the person of a very forward-thinking American bureaucrat. The chapter contents of his memoirs reveal him to be very much a twentieth-century man—a man of *ideas:*

Fundamentalist Family in Missouri – Father a successful builder – Early school-
ing – the State University – Rhodes Scholarship – Intellectual Friendships –
What I learned from Professor Collingwood – Empire and the mental vigor of
Britain – My unorthodox interpretation of John Locke – I worked for William
R. Hearst of Spain – The personality of General Franco – Radical friendships in
New York – Wartime service with the OSS – Limited vision of FDR – Comte,
Proudhon and Marx revisited – de Tocqueville once again.

In Bellow's story Mosby, for all his erudition, or perhaps because of it,
makes a terrible career mistake, which explains his frustration that his life
has not lived up to its promise. He makes the great mistake of misreading
history. He had foolishly embraced the Burnham school of management,
"declaring, during the war, that the Nazis were winning because they had
made their managerial positions first. No allied combination could conquer
with its obsolete individualism, a nation which had reached a new state of
history and tapped the power of the inevitable".[37]

Mosby of course is a man of his time. The melancholy figure of Guy
Crouchback, who appears in Evelyn Waugh's trilogy *Sword of Honour*, captures a picture of an England that was behind the times, one for whom the
real enemy was not Germany but "the modern age in arms". Waugh did not
of course consider America to be unmodern. Far from it. But he feared that
it had become Britain's fate to be dragged along by its stronger ally. The new
relationship of client and patron is caught vividly in the picture of Ritchie-
Hook, who goes to his death with an American press photographer in atten-
dance "like a pet dwarf privileged to tumble about the heels of a prince of
the Renaissance". After the war, of course, the roles had been reversed. That
is the main reason we are told by Ritchie-Hook's batman that he never
wished to go home. "More than once he said to me, Dawkins, I wish those
bastards would shoot better. I don't want to go home".[38] What was there to
go home to in 1945 for those who imagined that Britain had become an ageing, sclerotic nation that had totally exhausted its cultural élan?

What is striking about Waugh's trilogy is its unconscious Hegelianism—
the complaint that Britain had entered an age in which it would have difficulty keeping up. In falling behind it would soon become historically irrele-
vant, a mere caricature of itself. In that sense Waugh's profound misgiving
about the nature of Britain's victory in 1945 reflected a historical consciousness that prevailed for most of the twentieth century, the idea that nations rise and fall, that in the end their good fortune runs out.

Mosby and Ritchie-Hook, however, were both wrong. The English and
the Americans might be dismissed by others as historyless; at times the
English feared that this was the case themselves. But the countries that in
the end rendered themselves historyless were those that broke with the
past, those that devalued it. What distinguished the United States and
Britain from their adversaries was that they remained in touch with history.

In the end what made England more modern than Germany was that like the United States it was a society in touch with its past.

It had been the Swiss historian Jacob Burckhardt who had foreseen in the late nineteenth century a disturbing new trend in the making, a barbarism of 'radical contemporaneity', a wish to transform society without reference to the past, without regard for what was being destroyed or constructed, a systematic and sustained rejection of history.[39] Both the Nazi and the Soviet regimes promised a break with the past. The United States and England did not. The former could lay claim to being the oldest modern state, with the oldest written constitution and the oldest political parties. England ran a close second.

It was this peculiar sensibility for the past as a mark of the truly modern mind that prompted Ortega y Gasset to call England, of all European countries, the most fortunate because "it always reached the future first". It was the most modern because it had not repudiated the past but experienced it anew from day to day. "From a future that we have not reached they show us a past in full force". Ortega went on to congratulate the English for what they valued most in themselves, an acceptance that the modern was the continuity between past and present rather than a radical break of the kind that had left other countries 'deformed' or 'stunted'. The English had rejected the 'revolutionary method' in their modernism—the rewriting of history and the devaluation of the past that characterised the irrational, unmodern trends in the political life of the 1930s.

He considered the English to be the most modern European country because they were at ease with their past, because they were "able to continue one's yesterday today without thereby ceasing to live for tomorrow, to live in the real present since the present is only the presence of the past or future, the place where the past or future actually exist".[40] In retrospect, it is remarkable that so original a thinker should have seen England in the light that many Englishmen, such as Waugh, did not always see themselves. It is all the more remarkable that he should have grasped that if the United States was the country of the future, the English were the first Europeans to have arrived there.

The third theme that defined the Anglo-American discourse was the fact that it was conducted in a common language. Bismarck had predicted that this would become one of the most significant political facts of history. It was not merely a question of volume, of the number of immigrants who arrived from Britain. Much more important were the skills they brought with them. They came from the country that had the highest per capita income in the world, where they had been trained for jobs that demanded high skills. Within a generation many of them became members of the political elite. Unlike most other migrants, including those from Germany, the British were not 'pushed' but 'pulled'. They were drawn not by economic hardship at home but by the prospect of greater opportunities abroad. In the forty-year period before the First World War, 75 percent of British immigrants were skilled workers. Given these circumstances it is ironic that Americans of English descent have never been studied by historians of immigration as a distinct ethnic group.

After the First World War the British were concerned that their political capital might run out once the English majority was marginalised in Washington by the new non-English immigrants flooding into the continent. The white Commonwealth dominions of the Pacific were fearful of what it might portend as early as the Imperial Conference of 1921. The New Zealand prime minister, William Massey, considered the future of America itself to be the major problem facing the English-speaking world: "No one can look at all those mixed races in the United States: 13 million negroes and millions of people from southern Europe, northern Europe, all sorts and conditions of men and women without wondering what the population will be like in another forty or fifty years from now."[41] Twenty-five years later in a much neglected but rewarding book, *America and Cosmic Man,* Wyndham Lewis forecast that America's involvement in Asia might produce an 'Asiatic element' in American life that would compete with whites of English descent as the most significant ethnic group in the United States.[42]

In the event, Britain's problems with ethnic America were not with the Asians but with the two largest *white* ethnic groups: an Irish community that still saw England as the traditional enemy, and a German-American community that wanted to keep its country out of the two world wars. For seventy years after Massey's somewhat hysterical warning, the British had to contend not with what he called 'the mongrelised races' from Asia and southern Europe but with the white middle-class professionals whose parents and grandparents had emigrated from Germany and Ireland.

Fortunately for the British, the English-speaking majority managed to maintain its iron grasp on foreign policy until the late 1960s. When Wilson accused the German community in the 1916 presidential campaign of dividing the American nation, it responded that it did not wish to Germanise America, only to de-Anglicise it, to make it more American. Two Democratic administrations were able to defeat the demand that 'neutrality' in the two world wars meant precisely that, rather than a guise under which Wilson and Roosevelt were able to connive at arms sales to the United Kingdom and ensure effective British command of the seas.

At the end of the war the British government once again voiced its fears that non-European immigrants might weaken America's cultural ties with Europe. In 1949 the Permanent Undersecretary's Committee warned that the ethnic minorities in the United States and their influence in American elections might endanger Britain's position as America's closest ally.[43] In the event, there was no lack of support for the containment of the Soviet Union

among the Slovaks and the Poles, the groups that had been less than enthu-
siastic about the war against Germany. To the end they remained persistently anti-Russian. Even the Jewish intelligentsia who were more inclined
to give the Soviet Union the benefit of the doubt shifted markedly to the
right in the 1950s.

There are two aspects, of course, to any language. One I discussed in the
previous chapter—the medium itself is all-important: in this case, that of the
Anglo-American empirical tradition. The British and Americans spoke the
same language. They were both positivists, heirs to a liberal tradition that
put an emphasis on reason and an empirically verifiable view of the world.
Neither was unhappy with the challenges of the modern world. Both confronted their fears head-on and resolved them to their own satisfaction.

Even in the arts British and American writers took a self-consciously different view of themselves from that of their German or French counterparts. Even the adjective 'modern' was used differently in the Anglo-
American world than in continental Europe. The continental expressionists,
for example, went out of their way to declare how unmodern they were.
Not so their British and American counterparts. "The very moment of
German repudiation of the modern as a valid term", adds Malcolm
Bradbury, "marks the start of Anglo-American modernism as it is currently
understood".

Of course, Bradbury concedes, the links between German and Anglo-
Saxon culture were still strong. He cites the impact of Nietzsche, and the
links between D. H. Lawrence and German expressionism, and he notes the
strong European elements in the works of writers as diverse as John Dos
Passos and Eugene O'Neill. The Anglo-American community also had its
heretics, like William Carlos Williams and Hart Crane, who were critical of
Eliot, and Ezra Pound, who fled the United States to Italy and fascism.

Nonetheless, Bradbury contends, the Anglo-Americans' vision of modernity was peculiar to themselves, with its juxtaposition of opposites for reso-
lution. Both insisted on objectifying the subjective, rationalising the irrational; conventionalising the extraordinary; intellectualising the emotional
and secularising the spiritual. This was what made the Anglo-American tradition so modern as well as unique—its acceptance that there were no con-
clusive answers to the exigencies of political life, that "uncertainty [was]
the only certain thing".[44]

It was that particular quality that marked their contribution to the age.
The English and the American schools of philosophy followed the same
path. They were both intent on demystifying politics. They both challenged
the existence of the 'world spirits' or 'historical absolutes' that inspired
their totalitarian adversaries. Neither was inclined to take seriously the
more arcane notions of the German idealists or the metaphysical speculations of Husserl and Heidegger. Both were critical of the Germans for taking their thoughts for realities.

The American Vision:
The Forging of the American Century

Without the Second World War, of course, the alliance might never have come into existence. History depends on the contingent as well as the profound, on chance as well as the tectonic forces that historians identify as 'phases', much as economists talk of price cycles distinguished by their length, by short-term fluctuations or secular trends. It is the profound forces, however, that I have been discussing in this chapter. I shall conclude with one of the most important of these, the tendency of the Americans to see themselves after 1941 in grand historical terms.

In February 1947, Auden asked an important question: "Why don't the communists model themselves after Virgil? He's wonderful for the business about the historical mission for the special race. Aeneas isn't just a private person".[45] In fact it became quite common in the 1950s for American politicians to compare the American empire with the Roman, to see the United States itself as a new Rome. A suitable twentieth-century text could have been drawn from Virgil's *Aeneid*. *"Tantae molis erat Romanam condere gentem"*, wrote Virgil in the first book of his epic poem. "It was a thing of so much weight to found the Roman race". Aeneas can only leave Troy by carrying his aged father on his shoulders. He is condemned, to quote Sartre, to carry the past on his back all his life. The United States ventured into the second half of the twentieth century like Aeneas bearing the aged Anchises on his flight from Troy, "those invisible parents astride their sons all their life".

In Virgil's epic, of course, Anchises is more than Aeneas's father. He is the burden of Rome's destiny. And that burden was easier to bear if the bearer himself was permitted an occasional glimpse into its meaning, as Aeneas himself is in the sixth book of the poem, in which he descends into the underworld. *"Bella, horrida bella"* (wars, hideous wars), the sibyl tells him when he questions her about Rome's future. To the end of the poem Aeneas remains burdened by the suspicion that there will be no end to his labours. Nor for that matter will there be an end to Rome's. The new world he plants when laying the foundation of the new Rome will know no universal peace, only a universal striving. In the 1950s America's fate seemed to be similar to that of Ancient Rome. The weight of mission for both could not be avoided. Both were denied an individual voice. Both were offered a historical role by their respective founding fathers, a role that could only be realised through involvement in war.

War was the key to political life for much of the twentieth century. "At this stage of history war is inevitable", complained Orwell in 1944.[46] It was the means by which a nation could stamp its imprint on history, or coin history in its own currency. "We were convinced that this was Germany's

Century," declares a character in the novel *Doctor Faustus* (1943–1947), Thomas Mann's great enquiry into what had gone wrong with Germany in his own lifetime. "We were certain that it was our turn to put our stamp on the world . . . that the twentieth century was ours".[47] All that attempt resulted in, of course, was the near destruction of Germany as a country and of its people as a moral force in the world. Standing in the rubble of Berlin in May 1945, the Soviet propagandist Ilya Ehrenburg declared that the twentieth century would be 'Russia's' after all, that the Soviet Union had fought its way into the history of others as well as its own.[48]

In the event, neither of the West's chief antagonists was able to realise its ambition. The Third Reich collapsed; the Soviet Union was exhausted after the war—perhaps it never really recovered. America's situation was very different. It had doubled its national income during the conflict and doubled it again a few years later. Writing in 1944, a year before the Red Army fought its way into Berlin, Henry Luce, the founder and editor of *Time-Life*, proclaimed that the twentieth century would be the 'American Century' just as the nineteenth had been the British.

Luce himself was an interesting phenomenon. After founding *Time* in the 1920s, he used it as a vehicle for the transformation of urban middle-class values into the lifestyles of mid-twentieth-century America. His genius was to take such traditional values as belief in God, work and personal achievement and translate them into an authentic American idiom, an American creed.

In an era of change Luce held to one constant vision. At a dinner of *Time* editors, he declared: "I regard America as a special dispensation—under Providence . . . my spiritual pastors shake their heads about this view of mine. They say it tends to idolatry—to idolatry of nation".[49] In fact it tended to a greater idolatry still, to a view of the people of the rest of the world as lesser beings, children of a lesser god. Not only was he sure that the United States was the one country in the world that had a destiny, but he also believed that it represented the destiny of others.

Luce's concept of the American Century of course would not have been so compelling had it not also offered a faithful rendering of precisely the ways in which those who lived in the twentieth century understood their own times and the Americans understood the twentieth century. It was the context in which the Western Alliance was forged.

When the world thought in terms of an American Century it did so in three very different respects.

It thought of it first in terms of historical continuity. The twentieth century was continuous with the past—with the century that had preceded it. It was continuous with an interpretation of the past, one that was quintessentially Western, a post-Enlightenment belief in progress. In this respect, it was important that the Americans should have been passed the baton by Britain, the original 'workshop of the world', in a historical race in which the nations of the West believed themselves to be at the head of the field. In that sense the Americans saw the century as a completion of what the British had begun.

When Henry Adams attended the Paris Exposition in 1900 he found himself "lying in the gallery of machines . . . his historical neck broken by the sudden eruption of forces totally new". What dominated the gallery was a forty-foot dynamo, a machine designed to make more and more energy. "Before the end", Adams reported, "one began to pray to it: inherited instinct taught the native expression of man before silent and infinite force". In the new century it would be America's destiny to become either "the child of the new forces or the chance spirit of nature".[50]

Adams was proposing one of the laws of proliferating energy. The dynamo whose avatars he saw in Paris was his image of modern force measured by speed and motion. It led him to propose a dynamic historical theory, a "law of acceleration", the multiplication of force by force leading to the exponential acceleration of history.[51]

America's own experience told it that history was linear: things got better. It went in a straight line from success to success. The Americans had never experienced defeat in the field, or occupation by a foreign enemy, or economic collapse. Progress, in fact, *was* the American philosophy, which explains why there has always been a comparatively weak American philosophical tradition. The Americans have never reflected too much on the human condition. History has not encouraged them to do so.

Other societies have been quite prepared to be dragged into the future on America's coattails. "Reality: that is the lesson of America", concluded the twentieth-century architect Le Corbusier in the 1940s. "It gives our bolder speculations the certainty of imminent birth".[52] Not only was the United States believed to have a future, but it was believed by many to *be* the future, a claim that might at times have been unreal for many but that was for most of the century real enough for those who chose to emigrate to the United States and turn their back on the Old World. Even as late as the 1960s the Irish journalist Conor Cruise O'Brien could write that "when looking at the United States we feel we are looking at ourselves in the process of becoming".

There was of course an alternative vision offered, glimpsed by the American journalist Lincoln Steffens when he visited Russia in 1934 and claimed that he had seen the future at work. What is significant, however, is that even communists like Antonio Gramsci and the Italian novelist Cesare Pavese disagreed with him. "We realised during those years", Pavese wrote in 1947, "that America was not another country, a new departure in history but simply a gigantic theatre in which was played out . . . a drama common to us all".[53] What made this statement particularly challenging on the eve of the Cold War was that Pavese, like Gramsci, was a notable Marxist writer of his day.

Indeed, the United States posed a threat to many Europeans who wished to trace their own lines of advance into the future along socialist lines. It was not without significance that socialism failed to establish itself as a serious political force in America. What frequently troubled European socialists most at the turn of the century, such as Werner Sombart and H. G. Wells, was that if the United States was indeed the most advanced industrial economy, yet at the same time the least inclined to follow the socialist path, might it not follow that the entire experiment was doomed from the very beginning?

Interestingly, in the great conflict between liberalism and communism America's political philosophers had little to contribute. This may appear surprising until we acknowledge that for most Americans there was no need to worry about the question of political value. Progress itself promised to transcend all the divisions of class, caste and race that fed the totalitarian creeds.

Since America believed that its own history presaged the history of others, it followed that there was no real need for it to be other than itself. Its belief that its finger was permanently applied to the fast-forward button of history was one shared by many other nations, including its own allies. For a time it was part of the ideological glue that held the Western Alliance together.

The twentieth century was America's in a second respect, in terms of historical *discontinuity,* for it offered for many the chance for the world to break with history, or more precisely, to make man autonomous of it for the first time. In the course of the twentieth century the United States and the Soviet Union both contended for the right to make history different from everything that had gone before. "The century which we are entering," proclaimed the U.S. vice president, Henry Wallace, during the Second World War, "can and must be the century of the common man". Both superpowers offered that vision. In the end only one of them succeeded in realising it. In this respect, consumerism was more than just an American style. It was a philosophy, one that made few concessions to its critics or detractors. George Steiner put it rather well in his novella *Proofs* when a disillusioned Marxist priest tells his proofreader friend that the United States is the first civilisation to have encouraged "common, fallible, frightened humanity to feel at home in its skin".[54]

It was all the more ironical, therefore, that it was the Europeans who felt most threatened by the rise of consumerism. The main claim against America in the eyes of writers such as Ortega y Gasset was its 'vulgarity' and materialism. "The characteristic of the hour is that the commonplace mind, knowing itself to be commonplace, has the assurance to proclaim rights of the commonplace and to impose them wherever it will". Mass man, Ortega complained, was not ignorant. He was cleverer than earlier generations. The very fact that he was concerned with ideas and values was an indication of his mental alertness. The problem with the common man was not that he glorified idiocy, but that he ignored genius. "The mass crushes beneath it everything that is different . . . individual, qualified and select." "As they say in the United States: 'to be different is to be indecent'".[55] It was to this country of "anti-human reductivism", however, that so many of the dispossessed and disenfranchised of Europe fled.

In the 1930s Carlo Levi, one of the intellectual dissidents of the hour, was banished by Mussolini to Eboli, a remote town in southern Italy. Even here, he discovered, America was dreamed of by those who had never set foot in the New World. It offered them a future, one no less palpable for its being ever out of reach. In the eyes of the Calabrian peasants the United States was the future, for it offered them the chance for the first time to become men rather than beasts of burden, eking out a subsistence living.

Levi found a tenacious affection for the American myth, the vision of a promised land that few would ever visit, an eternal promise or hope, a country forever elusive in a world in which the centuries past and present had been much the same.[56] It was *their* America, of course, in the only way that it could be: a myth. It was nevertheless a powerful myth, one of the most powerful of the twentieth century.

As for the alternative myth, the Marxist variant, it never really caught the imagination of the people as it did that of the middle-class elite who tried to lead them into battle. In the early days of the Soviet experiment the consumer was identified as dangerous. One of the key forms of planning in the Stalinist era was control of consumer demand. Communism was even described as 'power over the consumer' in the economic textbooks of the 1930s. Soviet economists were loud in their praise of one of Stalin's central contributions to socialist economic praxis: the policy of 'the planned shortage'. Keeping consumer demand low was deemed the best way of keeping the citizen fit for war. The Soviet Union was constantly at war with the world and with itself. Its citizens were constantly exhorted to win the battle on the labour front, or the war against waste, or the campaign to increase productivity.

It is true that in the late 1950s Khrushchev abandoned the high ground of ideology and offered the workers of the world what they wanted: to improve their material condition. When he visited the United States in 1959 he threatened to 'bury it' under consumer goods. By 1970, his advisers assured him, the Soviet Union's industrial production would surpass that of the United States by 5 percent. Within another ten years it would be 170 percent as large as America's, by which time the socialist bloc would be in an unassailable position. It was of course a flawed prediction. But it was also, more interestingly, a highly cynical position to take. To make the masses' understanding of the truth dependent on their standard of living was to give proof of a quite unrevolutionary conception of the proletariat, as well as a quite unphilosophical conception of truth.

Third, and finally, the promise of the American Century offered an ultimate twentieth-century vision, that of a century neither continuous nor discontinuous with the past but continuous with itself. It promised the creation for the first time of a universal order.

A hundred years earlier Britain had created an international division of labour. That is what had made the nineteenth century 'British'. Writing in 1940, the American sociologist Robert Park confidently predicted that the United States would take the process further, that the world was moving towards "a common historical life".[57] Of all countries in the course of the twentieth century the United States offered the world a vision, at the two critical moments of its interface with modern history: its entry into the two world wars.

Like the Russians, the Americans were not interested in earthly empires. They were interested in eternity. They were not interested in colonising space but in colonising time. The United States was a construct, wrote Paz, "aimed against history and its disasters, oriented towards the future, that *terra incognita* with which it identified itself so closely".[58] The question was, would the Americans bring history to an end in their attempt to reach the future ahead of everyone else?

Many Europeans were fearful of this outcome, particularly the French. As the journalist Raoul de Rusty predicted during the Second World War, America might demand from its allies not a material but a moral tribute. Rather than seek land or financial recompense, it might demand access to markets previously closed to its goods. It might, in other words, demand that the Europeans accept America's version of the future. It might seek to impose its ideas, export its virtues and consider its intervention "a blessing for lost and suffering humanity".[59]

That is why so many European intellectuals feared the Americans more than they feared the Russians even in the darkest days of the Cold War. The Americans stole into the European consciousness at the same time that the Europeans became aware of their own weakness. "The unparalleled sacrifice of America", complained Thomas Mann shortly before he left California to return to Europe, "to make other people happy. One is not allowed to spurn this love".[60]

Conclusion

In short, the British and the Americans succeeded after the war in creating not so much an Atlantic community as a common world in which both nations could agree on what George Lichtheim called "a mid-Atlantic stand-point".[61] In a sense, in the early Cold War years the rise of 'the West' created, as it could not for the French or the Germans, a sense of sublimation. The British felt that they had been subsumed into a community that had given them at least a role in a larger mission, which compensated them for the loss of their power after the Second World War. Of course for much of the first twenty-five years of the Cold War the Americans paid only lip service to the ideas that animated their British ally. They did not have a vision of a community of English-speaking people, one made famous by Churchill's fierce advocacy of the idea in his six-volume *History of the English-Speaking Peoples*.

The British were not mistaken in their suspicion that without the support of the United States their own power would decline. But they were wrong to think in terms of a special relationship with America. The Americans tried to treat all the Europeans equally, as allies, or junior partners at best. They made their intentions clear enough even before they entered the war. The Lend-Lease Programme to Britain, for example, was universally praised at the time as an act of generosity. But it was not a gift. It was granted on strict conditions. As one of its terms the United Kingdom was stripped of its gold reserves and overseas investments, and its export trade was reduced to almost nothing. Contrast this with the unconditional Mutual Aid Programme granted by Canada, which was a nonrepayable gift, not a loan. Indeed, per head of population the Canadians contributed more to Britain than did the United States, and proportionally more of them fell in battle.

America's 'West' was not Britain's, but it was a version of it as it could not be for the French or for the Germans, whose embrace of the Western idea from the beginning was not sentimental but purely functional. For all their universalism, the French had no conception of a steady march of their history to that cold August day in 1941 when Churchill and Roosevelt signed the Atlantic Charter. Nor did they necessarily share the British belief that they had to make of their history something larger than themselves—the Western Alliance—as if their destiny related not to them but to a historical mandate they had not drawn up, to a purpose at once more public and less personal. For them the great postwar challenge was to construct a European not an Atlantic community.

But before looking at that endeavour we must ask why the Atlantic Community itself never assumed the shape its founding fathers had intended. We must first ask why Atlanticism failed to establish a permanent place in the European imagination.

3

The Rise and Decline
of Atlanticism

In 1947 Henry Luce published an article on the prospects of Western civilisation. It was designed as a discussion of the work of the British historian
Arnold Toynbee, whose magisterial *Study of History* had set out to describe
the way in which a variety of civilisations in the past had responded or
failed to respond to the challenges of their time.

In his cover story Luce claimed that Toynbee was a man who was
uniquely equipped to tell the American people why they should step in
where the United Kingdom could not—a reference to President Truman's
decision earlier in the year, at Britain's request, to provide military assistance to Greece and Turkey. Britain's withdrawal from Greece, Luce wrote,
had sparked off "a crisis in western civilisation itself. . . ."

Time presented Toynbee's vision as a call to arms, a call addressed largely
but not wholly to the United States, the only power capable of matching
the might of the Soviet Union. As Luce confessed, Toynbee's vision of the
West was not his own, for Toynbee saw America as an extension of Europe,
not "as a special dispensation under Providence". Both men, however, were
of the opinion that America and Europe were members of the same community, which it was their duty to defend.

Both men were members of a generation that found themselves in these
early days of the Cold War reaffirming some of the values of Western life, a
belief in progress, in the Christian faith, in the ideals of the democratic order. As *Time* concluded, a reading of Toynbee's book showed that it was
not the materialist but psychic factors that are the decisive factors in history. "The real drama unfolds within the minds of Man. It is determined by
his response to the challenges of life".[1]

In the case of Britain those challenges had been evident at the opening of
the modern era. They had entered the American imagination too, often
subliminally. They were merely waiting to be rediscovered in the Cold War
when both powers were required to respond more decisively than ever.

They were embodied in the North Atlantic Treaty of 1949, which in turn owed much to the thought of Edmund Burke, the leading philosopher of what came to be known as 'Cold War liberalism'.

Edmund Burke and the Cold War

Burke's hour came with the Cold War. From being classed as a liberal utilitarian up to the 1920s, he became a prominent conservative, a natural law theorist. As one of his contemporary biographers writes, the new interpretation fitted a new need in the 1950s: "In reviving the crusader against radicalism it discovered a welcome ideological support for the Cold War crusade against the apprehended threat of Soviet Communism".[2]

Whether Burke was seen at the time as a liberal utilitarian or a conservative natural law theorist, his writings were often invoked to define the idea of the West, a community that began to assume some of the characteristics of a religious belief. The *reification* of the West in the 1950s was far from being an accident. It owed much in both its vocabulary and its content to Burke's ideas.

Burke came into his own because the break with the continent that was occasioned by the French Revolution against which he had fulminated had permanently cut England off from continental thought. The estrangement persisted well into the twentieth century—and it still does. It has not been repaired. The revolution produced two very different forms of nationalism, two diverging sensibilities, two very different philosophical positions. The French were the first people to give currency to the concept of novelty as a value. The English, in contrast, retained their faith in the virtue of continuity.

Burke's importance in the Cold War years stemmed from the fact that the French Revolution and the October Revolution were intimately linked in the eyes of Lenin and Trotsky. Even in France left-wing historiography incorporated the events of 1789 into a macrocosmic Russian revolution, making the former "the mother of a real revolution duly registered in October 1917". The Russian Bolsheviks never—before, during or after the Russian Revolution—lost sight of that affiliation. By the same token the historians of the French Revolution projected into the past their feelings about the October Revolution and tended to highlight those features of it that seemed to presage, indeed anticipate, those of the second.

> At the very moment Russia—for better or worse—took the place of France as the nation in the vanguard of history because it had inherited from France and from nineteenth century thought the idea that a nation is chosen for revolution, the historiographical discourses about the two revolutions became fused and infected each other. The Bolsheviks were given Jacobin ancestors and the Jacobins were made to anticipate the communists.[3]

By contrast, both the United States and Britain could look back to a very different revolutionary tradition. And if the Glorious Revolution was not America's, if the American Revolution had been far more radical, at least it had been invoked by the Americans when they rebelled against the Crown. It was important that they had done so in the name of the rights of Englishmen rather than the Rights of Man.

In the 1950s the Americans were encouraged to see their own revolution as a purely anticolonial struggle, a war of independence that had involved few if any social changes of importance. It was John Quincy Adams who had translated a tract written in 1800 by the Swiss writer Friederich Geertz that had contrasted the American revolt in defence of established rights with the French attempt to assert new ones. The merit of Geertz's essay, wrote Adams in an introduction, was that it rescued "the revolution from the disgraceful imputation of having proceeded from the principles of the French". In 1955 the same essay with its introduction was reprinted for mass distribution with a foreword by Russell Kirk, a publicist of 'the new conservatism'. The fact that the war had been as much a social revolution as a rebellion against Britain was speedily forgotten. In the Cold War years the national consensus depended on eliminating from the national consciousness a once significant element of social dissent.[4]

In the 1950s the two powers chose to engage the Soviet Union on ground that Burke had staked out 150 years earlier. Let me single out three features.

To begin with, Burke had thought that Britain was most fit to lead a Western coalition against France because of *its own* revolutionary experience, a revolution, of course, that was in accordance with the principles of tradition and prerogative. The Glorious Revolution, he argued, had restored a condition that had previously been lost. It had not destroyed the present in the name of the future. Unlike the French Revolution it had not been "a revolt of innovation". It had not been a revolt for "the pretended rights of men" against the "rights of the people".

All social bonds, Burke insisted, depended on sympathies that reach out to persons both living and dead and by extension accord with the habits and culture they have passed on. "Men are not tied to one another by papers and seals", he remarked of political and military coalitions, "they are led to associate by resemblances, by conformities, by sympathies". In a speech in 1790 he contended that the French Revolution wished to abolish the past, to extinguish links uniting the generations, to create a radically antihistorical hatred of existence itself.[5] Burke was one of the first writers to recognise that a society that devalued its history would pose a threat to what Western societies valued as most important in their own life.

We must recall what was so significant about rebelling in the name of the rights of Englishmen rather than the rights of man. The Americans grounded their rebellion on a wish to secure or defend their ancient rights of which they had been dispossessed by a tyrannical government in London. America like Britain was respectful of the past even in the most revolutionary moment in its history. Indeed, in the 1950s it could claim to be older than England: it was the oldest political community in the modern world, with the oldest constitution, the longest unbroken line of government, and the oldest political parties. What it embodied in its own person was a principle of modern life: that a modern society is one that builds its future on deep foundations, for it is the past that gives legitimacy to the future, not, as in the totalitarian world, the other way round. We all crave the future, of course. That we can imagine the world other than it is at present is the mark of modernity. It is history, however, that makes that claim, or the future itself, legitimate.

The only time the Americans came close to devaluing their past was in the McCarthy era, when they were encouraged to define their behaviour in ways that were inconsistent with the role models they had borrowed from the founding fathers. They did so at the risk of turning their country from a 'contract with history' into a decisive break with it, of transforming the American Idea from a 'proposition' into an 'ism'.[6] For the most part, however, American presidents continued to exhort their citizens to fight in the name of the political vision of Washington, Madison or Jefferson. They remained what Dean Acheson once called them, "a nineteenth century people" who acted on the basis of "inherited ideas".[7]

Secondly, Burke had seen the French Revolution from the very first as a great schism that made it almost impossible to distinguish between war and peace. "To talk of the balance of power to the governors of such a country was a jargon that they could not understand even through an interpreter".[8] Peace with such a regime would have all the nations "disarmed, disheartened and truly divided".

He was eager to impress on the British government of the time that war against revolutionary France should not be defended as a war for national independence but as a crusade against the principles of Jacobinism itself. The world had to be made safe not for democracy but for the *ancien régime*. He was beside himself when a war-weary England tried to negotiate peace in 1795. Peace with such a regime, he insisted, would not be peace at all but an 'interlude' in which the enemy would regroup for the next battle.[9]

This was very much American thinking in the early years of the Cold War. 'Waging peace' is what John Foster Dulles, the most outspoken of all secretaries of state, promised the American people. Peace in this period was defined in terms of war, for it was often impossible to tell the difference between them. The 'Long Peace' is what its chief historian, John Lewis Gaddis, calls the Cold War. So it was for those who talked of 'the strategy of peace' (the title of a book by Raymond Aron). Even the U.S. Strategic Bomber Command adopted as its motto "Peace is our profession".

The Europeans adopted the language too. To the end of his life the German scientist Wernher von Braun, who had been brought over to the New World by the American army after the war to work on its missile programme, referred to himself as a 'prisoner of peace'—the long, hard, unforgiving peace of the Cold War.

Finally, for Burke, the French Revolution had heralded a new political age in which nations were only as strong as the consciousness of their missions. The defence of the old order required that one country take the lead. Clearly in the 1790s, Britain could be the only 'directing power' in an anti-French alliance. It was "the soul of the whole confederacy" because of its unique constitution: "The British state is, without question, that which pursues the *greatest variety of ends,* and is the least disposed to sacrifice any one of them to another one or to the whole. It aims at taking in the entire circle of human desires and securing for them their fair enjoyment".[10]

Where the British had led, the Americans followed. "The great advantage of the Americans," de Tocqueville had declared, "is that they have arrived at a state of democracy without having to endure a democratic revolution." This was not true, of course. The American Revolution was indeed revolutionary, however much some writers tried to deny it. The United States likewise never doubted that its own revolutionary tradition made it the West's natural leader. It never questioned its right to lead a coalition of Western states as its most modern and radical member at the same time. Its concept of radicalism, of course, was grounded on the understanding that a true revolution aimed only to free the people, not to remake them. It could only be concerned with political rights rather than social engineering, for in trying to create an egalitarian state it would destroy what made a society worthwhile: political freedom.

The American agenda in the Cold War years was inspired by a wish to persuade the rest of the world not to eschew the revolutionary course but to base it on Locke rather than Marx. Locke had a particular attraction for Americans. "In the beginning all the world was America," Locke had declared in his *Second Treatise.* Lockean liberalism was deeply embedded in American life. As Louis Hartz wrote in the 1950s, American policy was criticised for being too economically driven and imperialist, too moralistic and interventionist, too utilitarian and isolationist. All paradoxically were true, for the concern with wealth, power, status and moral virtue were transformed into a single set of mutually reinforcing values by the paradigm of Lockean liberalism.

In short, Burke set an agenda that the British have followed ever since. They are still opposed in principle to novelty. They are still implacably wedded to a deep suspicion of anything that compromises historical continuity. The irony of course is that the United States has moved on. Cold War liberalism is dead. More serious still for the Atlanticists that the British remain is the fact that the West has no conceptual view of the world, Burkean or otherwise. It has no operational frame of reference with which to look at the world. There is no longer a common idiom in which to express its fears. In such circumstances it is not surprising that the allies are beginning to think of individual strategies of salvation.

Atlanticism and Its Shortcomings

We must of course be careful not to preempt history. Whatever the crisis that confirmed the ties that bound the two nations together, the Americans were always suspicious of Britain. Even the Atlantic Charter was not intended to be a blueprint for an Anglo-American world. It was subsequently ratified by forty-seven nations and confirmed by the Big Four in January 1942.

At times the Americans displayed almost as little sympathy for their principal ally during the Second World War as the British did for the French. Some remarks reported by Roosevelt's son (a not entirely reliable source) reflect his state of mind at Yalta. Even then Roosevelt did not envisage shutting out the Soviet Union. He thought it would devolve upon the United States to act as a mediator between the two other members of the Grand Alliance that had defeated fascism: "Britain is on the decline, China still in the eighteenth century. Russia—suspicious of us and making us suspicious of her. America is the only great power that can make peace in the world stick".

Roosevelt then went on to define what he imagined the function of the United States would be in the postwar world: "to integrate in the future organisation of the United Nations the disparate views of the Empire-minded British and the Communist-minded Russians".[11] As late as 1946 even the usually astute Walter Lippmann expected that America would stand aside in any future conflict between Britain and Russia.[12] Many Americans, indeed, wanted "the strange alliance" with the Russians to continue, to cite the title of a book published in 1947 by an American general who had been stationed in Moscow during the war.[13]

This feeling was especially acute for a generation that had seen Europe running to perdition. Many Americans wanted America to remain true to its own first principles rather than to treat history as a parable in which it continued to draw meaning from serving others rather than itself. Only in June 1948 did the Senate allow the United States to be associated "by constitutional process" with regional self-help organisations that were anti-Soviet in inspiration, in particular the Brussels Pact, which Britain, France and the Benelux countries had entered into earlier in the year. Soon afterwards the U.S. Joint Chiefs of Staff met in Newport, Rhode Island, to discuss the Allied command structure that might be required in the event of a war with Russia.

It was expected even then that the British would take the lead in any peacetime arrangements that might be needed. As late as mid-November the secretary of defence, James Forrestal, was asking whether an implicit military relationship with Britain was really necessary. Was it really essential for the United States to enter into a binding pact with its allies? Only British insistence forced his hand.[14]

The negotiations that finally led to the signing of the North Atlantic Treaty in 1949 and the creation of NATO were tough and uncompromising. But by then something quite new had occurred. The Americans and the Europeans had come to realise, belatedly to be sure, that they had embarked on an attempt to forge a community quite different from any other association of states in the past. In the Senate Foreign Relations Committee's twenty-eight-page report on NATO, the Soviet Union was mentioned only once. The main focus of the report was not the defence of Europe from Soviet aggression, but the continued stability of democracy in Western Europe itself.

The members of the North Atlantic pact, Truman declared at the signing of the North Atlantic Treaty in Washington on 4 April 1949, "were joined by a common heritage, democracy, individual liberty and the rule of law". The pact, declared Paul-Henri Spaak, the Belgian prime minister, was "an act of faith in the destiny of Western civilisation". The Italian prime minister, Carlo Sforza, insisted that its members would fail the spirit of the pact if it belittled its ideological force, if they considered NATO merely "a protective umbrella". At last, proclaimed Britain's Foreign Secretary Ernest Bevin, the Western world had become "a cohesive organism, determined to fulfil its great purpose".[15]

The rhetoric may seem somewhat forced, but it was sincerely meant. Indeed, what characterised the alliance in these early years was the rhetorical nature of the commitment. Its practical commitments, by contrast, were quite modest. Not only did it commit the United States to a nonreciprocal guarantee to its European partners, but also it did so in default of a *casus belli*. Article 5, which provides that an attack on one member would automatically be considered an attack on all, was often taken to represent the indivisibility of the commitment, but it really did nothing of the kind. It was a promissory note that might or might not have been cashed in a crisis.

What made the prospect of its being honoured more likely than not depended very little on the narrow commitments set out in the articles of the treaty. It depended a great deal more on the values set out in its preamble, which articulated a common vision against a common threat. It counted for much that in the early years the threat was internal in nature, that there were few areas of life in the West that were not touched by the all-pervasive threat of communism.

Even in the United States the containment of the Soviet Union in the early days of the Cold War assumed an overtly political form, the translation in the McCarthy era of the American Idea into an 'ism'. Even if the United States was at peace with the Soviet Union the threat of subversion required it to be permanently at war at home. Those who had grown up during the 1930s had experienced an earlier cold war between the democracies and fascism. Many were quite ready to accept the idea that the pursuit of peace at any price would permanently deny the American people peace of mind.

Accordingly, the minds of the politicians who met in Washington in April 1949 were mostly focused on the political and not the military containment of the Soviet Union. Before the outbreak of the Korean War (1950) the United States was still insistent that Europe's economic recovery should come before rearmament. Only postwar growth, it believed, would persuade the people of France and Italy to vote against communist parties, which were almost successful in their bid for power in the 1946 and 1948 elections. As Paul Nitze, the director of Policy Planning, made clear during a visit to London earlier in the year, not even the imminent explosion of the first Soviet atomic bomb had changed the thrust of American thinking.

In the wake of the Korean War, the leaders of the Western world had to engage more and more with a military threat from outside. It was the conflict in Korea, the first in which the American people were conscripted to fight communism, that led to what Charles Bohlen subsequently called "the militarisation of NATO", the conversion of a nonreciprocal guarantee to Europe into the alliance we know today, with its own strategic and military doctrines and parliamentary institutions, an alliance unique in modern history.

Yet the Atlantic Alliance never evolved into what its founding fathers had hoped—a genuine political community. Even as a concept Atlanticism meant increasingly little to the French, and after the early 1960s to the Germans. Even those who continued to use the words 'Atlantic Community', such as Christian Herter, Dulles's successor at the State Department, found that it had little popular appeal. Atlanticism offered Germany a role in the aftermath of the war, but one that could not compete in the imagination with its role in Europe. Twelve years after its foundation, wrote the French writer Claude Delmas, "the Atlantic alliance was dominated by the feeling that it was but a hint of a political organisation in search of its form".[16]

Its failure to progress beyond the narrow terms of the NATO treaty has left the alliance what it is today, an anti-Soviet coalition in a world in which the Soviet Union no longer exists. It was a failure that did not go unremarked even at the time because it made a nonsense of a community of risk in which the United States was most at risk itself, in large part because its European allies could do so little in their own defence.

For a few years, in the period 1959–1962 in fact, there was an attempt to take the Atlantic project much further, in a race to get through a closing door, that of the European Common Market, which offered a different future, another vision. "If we do not draw together quickly", Henry Kissinger predicted at the time, "we shall drift until we are suddenly apart".[17] It was time, he insisted, "to examine carefully the possibility of creating federal institutions comprising the entire North Atlantic community". Without a federal future economic cooperation between the United States and Europe might give way to rivalry. The economic integration of the Atlantic area, he advised the readers of *Foreign Affairs,* would follow, not precede an Atlantic political partnership.[18]

Confronted by the competing process of European integration, American officials tried to drive the alliance itself along the road of integration. Henry Cabot Lodge talked of the need for a political general staff, or steering committee; General Norstadt, NATO's Supreme Allied Commander, called in 1962 for a permanent council elected by the NATO Council of Ministers, a supreme authority with wide discretionary powers, capable of articulating common interests. In 1960 the U.S. Congress voted to name a U.S. Citizens Commission in NATO, inviting other governments to appoint commissioners of their own. The upshot was the Atlantic Convention that met in Paris in 1962. It achieved little of consequence. A year earlier the NATO Parliamentarians Conference had established an Atlantic Institute in Paris. It too, however, never lived up to its promise.

The Americans not only were haunted by the fear of the competing vision of a European union but also were driven by a strong belief that the Soviet system was far superior to that of the West because it was controlled by a country with the will and ruthlessness to act decisively in a crisis. In 1961 Clarence Streit returned to the theme he had addressed twenty years earlier. In *The Struggle Against the Soviet Union* he had insisted that union was the only way of facing a universal threat. On the eve of the Second World War it had been desirable, not necessary. By 1961 there was no alternative to a federal solution.[19]

In the end the Atlanticists lost the argument because in the context of the Atlantic Alliance fear of the enemy within was much greater than fear of the enemy outside. Up to the very end of the Cold War the United States feared the Soviet Union more than it feared its allies. In the case of the French this was never the case. The French feared the Germans more than they did the Russians and devised a European Community to counter that threat. As Walter Hallstein, the president of the European Commission, remarked in 1961 before he left Washington for Brussels, the Europeans no longer envisaged the West as a "collective political personality", only "an Atlantic association based on two pillars, Europe and the United States".[20]

What Hallstein meant, however, was more profound than the Americans recognised at the time. By the end of the 1970s, Europe had become a political force with its own institutional identity. If most Americans did not recognise the distinction that Hallstein drew, this was because they imagined the European commitment to the Atlantic Community was greater than it was. The process of European integration, however, could not be reversed. The process of Atlantic integration could.

For the French in particular the European project was a permanent one; the Atlantic Alliance was not. As Jean Monnet told Konrad Adenauer in May 1950, the purpose of the prospective European Coal and Steel Community was political, even 'moral' in nature. It offered a chance to deal permanently with the problem of Franco-German rivalry that had dogged the Europeans since 1870. Monnet, in fact, ended his memoirs with the claim that the European Community, unlike the Western Alliance, was a long-term commitment to "the organised world of tomorrow". The Cold War was incidental to that project. One day it would come to an end. One day America would slip its moorings; one day the legions would be summoned home. The European Community, by contrast, was not an end in itself. It was a process of change that would continue indefinitely into the future.[21]

The Europeans became increasingly preoccupied with their own messianic possibilities, as prophets with a vision of a new society, one based not on radical reform so much as a radical change of heart, the creation of a European consciousness.

The failure of Atlanticism to establish itself arose from another factor, and in the long run a more worrying one. Those who took Atlanticism seriously did so because they thought of the alliance in existential terms. What defined it in their imagination was its understanding of a common destiny to which both Europe and America were committed. As an American historian had written in 1941, the most fundamental issue of the hour was not the present but "the future contained in the present". In that sense, the war against communism, like that against fascism, was a total war, for it involved the past, present and future. Put another way, war and peace were comprehended as simultaneous occurrences, for the vision of peace was part of the war effort.[22]

What made the superpowers definingly twentieth-century states was that they both preferred to live for the future. The basis of economic planning, after all, both in the form of Roosevelt's New Deal and Stalin's five-year plans, was predicated on projecting economic growth and political development into the future. The emphasis was not on the exact sciences, with their inferential methods and logical and mathematical premises, but on the inexact sciences whose inductive and deductive methods of research were more informal. These were preferred in social planning precisely because they dealt with the cultural, social and historical laws of evolution. And it was the inexact sciences that formed the basis for all economic planning, particularly in the United States, where Herbert Hoover became the first president to bring social scientists into his immediate circle of advisers.

By the 1960s it had become strikingly clear that Europe's vision of the future was not America's. Not only would its European allies not do more to defend themselves, but also they had begun to fight shy of being pulled along in America's historical undertow. Towards the end of the Cold War the United States began to blame the Europeans for persistently criticising American policy in the world at large while doing little themselves to maintain Western interests beyond Europe. In 1982 the *Wall Street Journal* suggested that the mere possibility of an American withdrawal from Europe might compel the Europeans to decide finally "where they stood". The *Washington Post* found it "impossible to justify the deployment of [U.S. ground forces] on behalf of rich, indolent allies", a picture that conjured up the existence of a 'risk aversive' society that was far more interested in marginal increments in social welfare than in playing a significant role in world affairs.[23]

This criticism was not voiced only by conservatives. Many liberal democrats, including the former presidential candidate Eugene McCarthy, were strongly of the opinion that the United States had "few if any true allies", only client states that it maintained at great cost to itself in an unsatisfactory and contentious dependency relationship.[24] Even if America's allies could help to defend its national interests, rather than solely their own, more narrowly defined, interests, their help would be so general as to afford little or no assistance. Amid so many voices of dissent the Atlantic Alliance began to look somewhat anachronistic. It had been designed for a world that had changed radically.

America's increasing interest in the world after 1960 was not just a phenomenon of the hour. Nor was it dictated entirely by the Soviet Union's gradual emergence as a world power whose influence was no longer confined to Eurasia. The Europeans might continually challenge whether America's interest in the 'free world' was as important as its interest in defending Western Europe, but it was the free world that became increasingly important in American thinking.[25]

From early on, as far back as 1919, the Americans had been critical of their allies for their truncated perspectives, for their narrow understanding of the wider world. At Versailles the Europeans were alarmed by Wilson's vision of the future in part because he took the notion of civilisation much further than they were willing to do themselves. Edward Grey had hoped that the United States would finally see sense and accept that the 'civilised world', or the Allied powers, would have to police the rest of the globe on indefinite contract to history. This was not the world order that Wilson envisaged. His understanding of the 'civilised world' was inclusive rather than exclusive.

In the Cold War the United States was always loath to limit its perspective to the Atlantic. It tended to look beyond the closed frontiers and narrow perspectives of its European partners, that lancet window through which the British and the French traditionally viewed world affairs. Although in the Second World War Roosevelt initially favoured a four-policemen scheme for the policing of the next world order, he was quick to explain to Britain's Foreign Secretary Anthony Eden that "the only appeal which would be likely to carry weight with the US public . . . would be one based on a world wide conception".[26]

The defence of the free world was an intrinsic part of the security regime the Americans tried to establish after 1947. It was central to their understanding of the American Century, and it was part of the national mythology. It was symbolic that the only time the American people were conscripted to fight communism on the battlefield was in Asia—in Indochina and Korea. What is significant is that on both occasions they answered the call. The 'silent majority' prevailed. To the very end a majority of Americans were willing to pay the price to keep Vietnam out of the communist orbit long after it had become clear that the American political class no longer considered the price worth paying.

Europe's increasing reluctance to see the Cold War in global terms seriously undermined the commitment to the future in one other respect. Europeans began to interpret history in a very different way. The common history that Europe and the United States had shared in the 1950s gave way to a more exclusive reading of events.

In El Salvador, for example, the French and Dutch governments chose to recognise the leading guerrilla movements in 1983 in defiance of American wishes and did so in terms of the need to "come to terms with history".[27] The deputy chairman of the German Social Democratic Party, addressing an audience in Princeton in 1982, insisted that Europe could no longer afford to join the United States in defending "outmoded social structures".[28] Another Social Democratic Party leader urged the United States to come to terms with the forces of armed struggle instead of vainly attempting to oppose them. In the face of this manifest sympathy for quasi-Marxist movements a commission appointed by President Ronald Reagan came to the conclusion in 1983 that the United States could not possibly grant its allies a veto over American policy simply because of their fascination with allegedly "benevolent revolutions".[29]

It would be wrong to conclude that the Europeans had any more affection for Third World revolutionaries than did their American friends. What largely distinguished the two Western powers was the modesty of Europe's ambition. In Europe's understanding of history, as in Flaubert's description of the realist novel, there were *"pas de monstres, et pas de héros"*. It was a world in which radical regimes could be suborned or socialised by economic assistance, a world in which the line of least resistance was likely to promise the highest return. It was a world where history was best responded to, not made, even at the risk of rendering itself 'historyless'.

The Post–Cold War World

As long as the Cold War persisted, of course, these divisions could be effectively, if not always successfully, disguised. The divisions within the alliance, the political fissures that ran through it, could be accommodated—just. After 1989 with the end of the Cold War, and even more following the Soviet Union's disappearance from the map, the fault lines that ran through the alliance could no longer be obscured by repainting its walls and papering over its cracks.

The first casualty of the victory was President George Bush's attempt to hold the Western Alliance together by constructing a 'New World Order'. What the United States promised, in the words of Robert Gates, the president's deputy national security adviser, was a new era of peace constructed "on the ruins of the great despotic empires and discredited ideologies", just as fifty years earlier it had constructed the old world order on the ruins of the Third Reich and the discredited ideology of national socialism.[30]

The war in Bosnia that broke out in 1992 did not, unfortunately, find the West united in the construction of a new order, or even in the defence of the old. Instead it found it divided and at odds, in a way that devalued its collective association in the eyes of its most important member.

Nothing, in fact, confirmed fears about the viability of the alliance than the failure of Western resolve where it counted most: in the heart of Europe. Either the alliance should go into the Balkans, wrote the widely syndicated columnist William Safire, "or shut up shop". Nothing short of "the credibility of western power in the world at large", added another respected liberal voice, Anthony Lewis, rested on the fate of the Bosnian Muslims.[31] Invoking the language of the Cold War, Safire proclaimed that whenever brutality was inflicted on millions of people America's place would always be in "the vanguard of marshalling civilization's response".[32]

Safire and Lewis were liberals, but they were also Americans. They were both heirs to the redemptive tradition in American politics. When they looked at the world, they looked at it with a redemptionist eye. They looked behind problems, not so much at them, and found deeper causes for Bosnia's condition in the cowardice or moral cynicism of the Europeans. What distressed them most was the West's apparent loss of faith in its own beliefs, its spiritual timidity. As Americans they probably could have endured a world without order more than a world without belief.

History has moved on, however. Both Europe and the United States have changed significantly. The Europeans no longer think in terms of international orders. And the Americans are more cynical about them. In the speeches of Bush's secretary of state, James Baker, we can find a more pragmatic vision of the order, one confined to the industrial democracies, to the First World rather than the Third, together with the countries of the former Second World, which had only just escaped from the shadow of communism.

The second attempt to avoid the possibility of a future conflict of interests between the United States and its allies was the Bush administration's attempt to construct a new "Euro-Atlantic community" that would take account of the East European nations as well as Japan. These were the goals of an administration desperately anxious to preserve "a European-Atlantic outlook", or what Baker, in a revealing phrase, referred to as a community based on "the Enlightenment spirit".[33]

That spirit was the spirit of the eighteenth-century philosophes whose own writings were so essential to what the American founding fathers had wanted their new creation to become. It was a Western outlook by definition. It was one that Baker clearly believed should persist if the world was to adopt what he referred to as a new concept of security. "Cooperative security" entailed less a vision of cooperation between the West and the rump of the old Soviet empire than of a continued cooperation among the Western powers themselves. In short, the new world order, like the old, was intended to contain the centrifugal tendencies that were dividing the Western powers. It was intended to ensure that new security architectures would box America's allies into arrangements in which the United States would remain central—to ensure that now that they were free from fear of the Soviet Union they would not convert their former subordination to Washington into insubordination instead.

Ironically, Baker's conviction was very much that of Britain's Foreign Secretary Ernest Bevin, who fifty years earlier had worked hard to bind together the fate of Europe and the United States. The connection between the two men, in fact, went back a long way. In 1952, while an undergraduate studying at Princeton University, Baker had submitted an impressive 150-page thesis in praise of Bevin's diplomatic skills. Bevin, the young Baker concluded, had been an "expert negotiator who always sought concrete advantages" for the country he served as Foreign Secretary in the last years of his life. "Bevin never became lost in the idealistic. He was always practical".

Baker knew that the United States after 1989 faced challenges similar to those with which the British had to contend forty-five years earlier. Bevin's genius had been to fight a rearguard stand that had masked the extent of Britain's decline as a global power through membership in alliances such as NATO and financial institutions such as the International Monetary Fund. For forty years the United Kingdom had been locked into a leading role in the postwar political and economic system, one that long outlasted its real weight in affairs. In Baker's mind the United States faced a similar task: that of adapting an overstretched and economically faltering superpower to a new world that was beginning to look just as menacing as the old.[34]

The mood in Washington changed markedly after Bill Clinton entered the White House. The United States is much less willing to concede that it is in decline, or fighting with its back to the wall. But the renewed sense of optimism has not been translated into a willingness to pursue a more active policy overseas. Instead Clinton has redefined the goal of American policy in the post–Cold War world from the containment of communism to the promotion of free trade. It is by no means clear that it can ever have the same moral force or produce the same sense of purpose, let alone figure so prominently in our imagination, as the containment policy.

If this is true, it is a symptom of a much more significant change in the fortunes of the Atlantic Alliance. Most of the rules of engagement that had helped to define it as a community of values have begun to disappear, leaving nothing behind but the hollow rhetoric of unity. None of the challenges that Baker and his successors identified, including the growth of Islamic fundamentalism, has proved fearful enough to persuade the alliance to reinvent itself. The one issue on which the allies are agreed—that NATO should be enlarged to include Central Europe—is (as I shall explain in a later chapter) something that will change the centre of gravity in Europe but will not bring America and Europe closer together.

There is almost no demand in the United States for what the British have called for: a new Atlantic community based on what Defence Secretary Malcolm Rifkind called its members' "shared destiny". A sense of 'destiny' is precisely what seems to be lacking and has been for some time. "An Atlantic community", he added, "would prevent the European Union and the United States from becoming inward looking. . . . It would be a historic and appropriate initiative as we approach a new century and the third millennium".[35] It is precisely the introspection of both partners, however, that is such a marked feature of Atlantic life in the last years of the twentieth century. The allies do have interests in common. They also share values that make them natural allies in a way in which, for example, the United States and Japan are not.

But the allies no longer think in terms of destiny. We are living in a phase of history that can be defined by the prefix 'post'—postmodern, post-Marxist, post-ideological. We are drawn to the dangers and opportunities of a pluralistic world in which each of us may have a different destiny. No new tasks challenge the Western world's imagination. For a brief period in their history the Atlantic states did indeed share a common experience. Their moral needs and preoccupations were reflected in the substance of their common endeavours. A historical situation was turned into a myth, and incorporated into the structures of their national past. They invented an Atlantic history that led 'inexorably' to that historic meeting between Churchill and Roosevelt in 1941. The intellectual force of the Anglo-American heritage in turn translated the immediate needs of both countries into an Atlantic sensibility. The attempt to create an Atlantic community was a courageous challenge to the reality that Europe and America had been divided for two centuries, and that they were continuing to grow apart. It was symbolic of the need of the moment. It could not be sustained beyond it. The moment has passed.

4

France and
the European Vision

In Paris I have often noticed that the Germans, yesterday's oppressors are less hated than the Americans, the liberators. That says nothing at all about oppression or liberation as such. It is, I believe, an expression simply of this disquiet: the Germans, in spite of everything, were Europeans. There was probably the same sort of feeling between the Athenians and Alexander the Great when he ruled the world. It never occurred to the Athenians to fight to the last drop against this world domination. Why should they? It was enough for them to know that all the good things the young Alexander was spreading were the fruits of the Greek spirit.

—Max Frisch, *Journals* (July 1948)

Every society consciously names itself in order to distinguish itself from, or identify itself with, other societies.[1] The French tried hard to 'name' Europe after the Second World War, to transform it into a community with its own language, French, and its own agenda, the forging of a permanent friendship between the German and the French people. By 1989 they had come close to realising that aim. As the eminent American columnist William Pfaff reminded his readers, Europe had become something very different from the United States. Its thoughts were no longer American, any more than were its imaginings and ambitions:

The West European nations have less in common with the United States than forty years of slogans about . . . Atlantic civilisation suggest. There are crucial values held in common but the general, largely unanalysed assumption made since the Second World War that all societies are going in the same direction, towards the same goal, led by the United States must be challenged. There is much that the Atlantic nations have in common but there is much they do not and the differences have grown larger.[2]

As in Britain, the lessons drawn from the events of 1940 were critical in forming French attitudes in the Cold War era—much more so, in fact, than

the onset of the Cold War itself. The British were confirmed in their view of
Western civilisation as a facsimile of the Atlantic world. The French, by
contrast, turned their back on the revolutionary universalism of the early
twentieth century and began to think in more culturally specific terms.
They began to talk less of the defence of Western civilisation than of the
survival of European culture; they became what the Germans had been before 1945: cultural relativists. In time they became an intensely self-
referential nation whose leaders chose to devote most of their energies to
the construction of a European rather than an Atlantic community. To understand why, we must look a little more closely at the lessons that their
leading thinkers drew from the catastrophe of 1940.

France and the Lessons of 1940

At a conference in Geneva in 1946 that was convened to discuss 'the
European mind' the French writer Maurice Druon declared that he had
known two Europes during the war. One was the Nazi empire in which the
sun had risen in the Caucasus and set in the Atlantic; the other, with its seat
in London, had been made up of European exiles who belonged to Europe
not only by birth but also by virtue of engaging in a common struggle. In
the end, the second had prevailed.[3]

It is not surprising that the idea of European unity should have been
given forceful expression in the war by the resistance movements that
sprang up in the countries occupied by Germany after 1940. In 1944 the
representatives of nine such movements drew up a federalist draft declaration of European unity. It was much influenced by British federalist writing,
a fact acknowledged by the Italian Resistance leader, Altiero Spinelli, whose
own declaration of European unity, the *Ventotene Manifesto,* was published in July 1941. Many years later Spinelli had the opportunity to realise
at least part of this vision when he became a member of the European
Commission.[4]

What the resistance leaders had in common was a vision of Europe—one
that was totally different, of course, from that of Hitler's New Order.
Hitler's other opponents, among them Robert Schuman, Alcide De Gasperi
and Konrad Adenauer, also had in common the fact that they were
Christian Democrats. They were also all 'border men' in terms of their geographical background, and all speakers of German. Two of them had also
experienced a change of nationality produced by the fortunes of war, in this
case the redrawing of borders. The war predisposed them to think in terms
of changing identities in a way that it did not for the British.

The British, in fact, shared no common idiom at all with the founders of
the European movement after the war. They came from different back-
grounds, indeed different political traditions. Some of them also suspected

the European idea of being too closely associated not with the resistance movements but with those who had collaborated with Germany after 1940. "Unless we take account of these bitter memories", wrote the young Max Beloff in a report written for the European Study Group in 1957, "we may fail to understand why some people find the ideal of European unity so equivocal". Fifteen years earlier, many 'Europeans' had simply been 'collaborators'.[5]

Interestingly, there were many Europeans who might have agreed with him, while drawing very different conclusions from the experience. The philosopher Maurice Merleau-Ponty, in the first article he wrote for *Le Temps Moderne*, cautioned his readers that the resistance campaign had been unrepresentative as a political experience and was therefore of only limited historical significance. In making too much of it the French risked distorting the central meaning of the war—the occupation.

The year 1940 had carried a defining moment in European history, one of those in which "the traditional ground of society collapses and man . . . must reconstruct human relations".[6] Merleau-Ponty conceded that the collaborators had wished to forge a 'life-world' with the enemy and thus to share a single history. They had been right to recognise that choices had to be made, that a life-world had to be forged. The term 'life-world', an invention of Edmund Husserl, meant a world in which experience was not derived from pure subjectivity but rather from a mode of being with others.

The collaborators' mistake had not been to abandon the universalism that had served France so well in the past but to have embraced an unacceptable political philosophy, one on which a united Europe could not be built. A political creed that insisted that there was only one option offered a world that was not worth living in—indeed, the defining value of a life-world was choice freely entered into. That is why Merleau-Ponty saw the trials of the collaborators in 1945 not as much in terms of the confirmation of individual freedom as of a community's affirmation of its ethical identity, the forging of a life-world on terms of its own choosing. By restoring the reciprocity between victim and accused their punishment affirmed "a single history", one that in due course would include the Germans as well.[7]

The occupation, Merleau-Ponty argued, was important precisely because the French could draw from it a lesson that their two other allies, Britain and the United States, could not. He contrasted the terrible but lived reality of occupation with that of war fighting. "We cannot think of war because we do not make war. . . . France does not await its self-deliverance".[8] In 1940 the Germans had had their own view of France's future. The Allies also had a vision of what the postwar order might look like and in its name had fought their way through to Berlin. "We are unable to preview our destiny and even less, it seems, to make it", he regretted, because France had been liberated by others.[9] After 1945 the only experience from which it could learn was one that had brought it into closer contact with the more abrasive realities of the twentieth century.

Looking back on the war, Merleau-Ponty portrayed the occupation as an educative experience that had moved men closer to an understanding of the terms on which history had to be lived. The first lesson the French had learned from their defeat in 1940 was that people did not choose their fate; instead their fate was determined by history. Some time before the war the French had begun to feel themselves, in Sartre's words, "abruptly situated". In his memoirs the writer Jean-Pierre Maxence echoed this feeling of history closing in when he wrote that "events came to seek us out".[10]

In an age when Europe's historical consciousness was more pronounced than ever, this sudden awakening to the fact that history was becoming distinctly dangerous had a profound impact on a significant number of French thinkers. Perhaps never before in French literary history had so many writers been possessed of what Paul Nizan (quoting Dostoyevsky) called "a passion for the present".[11] It was a passion that was informed by the terrible suspicion that the French no longer controlled events, that their future was about to be determined by other people, in particular the Germans.

To quote Merleau-Ponty, the Europeans could no longer allow history to be determined by the 'meaning' one country wished to give it. Its meaning would have to be determined in cooperation with others: "Looking for the world's essence is not looking for what it is as an idea once it has been reduced to a theme of discourse. . . . The world is not what I think it is, but what I live through".[12]

The second truth of the occupation was that history could no longer be judged as it had previously been on the grounds of 'right action'. Before the war humanity had been judged largely on the goals it sought rather than on the consequences of pursuing them. After the war men had to consider the consequences of their actions.

What we find here is a practical expression of Edmund Husserl's concept of the life-world. "Man is within the world; it is in the world that he recognises himself".[13] No unilateral line of thinking could ever again be allowed. The life-world was one that the French and the Germans would have to live together.

The third lesson that Merleau-Ponty drew from the war was that the Europeans had become the unconscious agents of historical action rather than the willing initiators of it. They had inherited their social roles. The old Franco-German animosity had made France a prisoner of history. In the postwar world it would be necessary to find a "middle ground between the voluntary actions of some and the passive obedience of others". History would demand a political programme. In the early 1950s that programme was to become the European project, the attempt to create a European community.

The grounds of historicity were a grand theme, one common to some of the most influential French thinkers after the war. If I have taken Eliot and Auden as the voice of Atlanticism, let me take two very different writers, Albert Camus and Jean-Paul Sartre, as the voice of Europeanism.

In an unsigned article that appeared in the resistance paper *Combat* on 21 August 1944, a time when Paris was in the throes of the popular insurrection that preceded its liberation, Camus wrote that the war had imposed on the French a specific moral and political obligation to create a political order in which war would never break out again. "In 1940 they had only faith; in 1944 they have a policy." In the present state of affairs, he added, it was a commitment that was truly "revolutionary".[14]

Perhaps this was true, but it was not the revolutionary tradition that Thomas Mann had written about after Germany's defeat in 1918. Faith in universalism gave way to a more qualified internationalism: a responsibility to Europe, not to the world. It was a smaller, less ambitious enterprise, and perhaps a more realistic one. It was also one against which the Germans had not 'immunised' themselves. Indeed, it appealed to their communitarian values much more than did Britain's attempt to bring the New World into a permanent association with the Old.

As one critic wrote, during the years of occupation Camus's primary concern had shifted from "the situation of the lone individual to that of the community." Perhaps it would be more accurate to say that Camus had become less interested in the community at large than in the problem of the individual committed to serving that community.[15] This change in focus reflected the position of many French intellectuals in the early postwar years: a belief that France's responsibility was no longer to mankind but to Europe in this most critical moment in European history: its division between two non-European powers.

History was also the key to Sartre's understanding of the events of 1940. "If a man is to have a history", he wrote in 1952, "it is necessary that he change, that the world should change him as it changed and that he may be changed in turn as he changed the world". Movement and change were built into his image of historically conscious man. In that respect the events of 1940 were as critical for Sartre as they were for Merleau-Ponty. "It was the war which made the obsolete frames of thought explode", he later recorded; "the war, occupation, resistance, the years that followed". Sartre himself emphasised two major features of that change. One, personal, stemmed from his experience as a prisoner of war; the other, intellectual, derived from his confrontation with history.[16]

As a prisoner he had learned that the French people would have to forge a life-world of their own if they were to live together harmoniously. It was only when he found himself interned with his countrymen in a German prisoner-of-war camp that, as an intellectual, he had come upon them for

the first time. Only then did he discover a language in which he could speak
to his fellow inmates, the workers and peasants who were interned with
him. Before the war he had seen France in terms of divisive social categories. In the prison camp, he shared with his fellow Frenchmen an awareness of their common predicament. In the course of captivity they had ob-
jectified their predicament and transcended it, and in the process had
discovered that they were Frenchmen.

This discovery did not make them excessively nationalistic. Far from it.
Sartre's experience of occupation, after his release from prison in 1941, was
critically important in this respect: "We were never so free as under the
German occupation. We had lost our rights and with it the right to speak . . .
we were deported en masse as workers, Jews, political prisoners".[17] As
Germaine Brée points out, Sartre himself was none of these. Nor was he
silent. He wrote three of his most important works, *Flies, No Exit,* and *Being
and Nothingness* in these years, and it was during this time that he came to
prominence as a writer. But he now acknowledged that the survivors needed
to identify with those who had fallen victim to the brutality of others.

As a victim France lived in three worlds—in the world of a momentous
historical struggle that had been played out at its expense; in its own imagination as a victim of the brutality of the occupation; and in a metaphorical
world as a symbol of truth: as a witness to freedom. To still have a history
would it not have to become something other than itself?

Sartre's idea that man is free and defines himself by what he does was
one that was widely shared after the war. His philosophy was an invitation
to leave the past behind and look to the future. In Sartre's hands Husserl's
"every consciousness is consciousness of something" became "every consciousness is consciousness of something to be done". What was to be done
after 1940 was to become European.

In short, long before the events of 1940 the French had begun to lose
faith in universalism. In light of their Pyrrhic victory in 1918 they had rediscovered a European agenda instead that had been transformed in the
late 1930s into an unhealthy pacifism. Instead of the revolutionary tradition and the Rights of Man, writes Louis Dumont, they found refuge in a
more introspective response to history.[18]

During the 1950s they came to recognise that they lived in the same
Lebenswelt as the Germans, a world grounded in a common experience,
with its own cultural terms of reference, its own historical heritage and its
own distinct personality. It was a world that had also appealed to an earlier
generation of German writers such as Max Weber and Max Scheler, who
had struggled to find something that could be rescued from the wreckage of
the Great War. By comparison, the Atlantic world that the British and the
Americans sought to forge appeared to offer nothing but an economic
space, with growth its only value.

It helped, of course, that many French and German intellectuals had lived for some time in an intellectual community. As Merleau-Ponty wrote in 1945, many of them on reading Husserl or Heidegger for the first time had the impression of recognising "what they had been waiting for". Their ideas were part of the fabric of modern thought.[19]

Existentialists like Sartre and Merleau-Ponty served in the war. Both were taken prisoner, although Sartre was released early on the instigation of Pierre Drieu La Rochelle. Even those who later broke with the phenomenological tradition found themselves engaged in the great struggles of the century. One of the most influential contemporary philosophers, Emmanuel Levinas, was taken prisoner by the Germans while serving as an interpreter with the army and spent the next five years as a forced labourer in a forestry unit for Jewish prisoners of war.

Phenomenology (from which existentialism arose), with its emphasis on 'being' and its insistence that consciousness must be understood as intentional (or transitive), was quite consistent with the inquiry into what made Europe 'European'. It was quite in the spirit of the day—the concern that unless Europe united it might never again recover for itself, in the memorable words of Sartre's great antagonist Raymond Aron, the status of a "subject in history".

Like Husserl, Sartre and the existentialists of the 1950s believed that to think was no longer to contemplate but to commit oneself. How could they have judged otherwise in so intensely a political age when not to commit oneself could lead to disaster? As existentialists they insisted that people create themselves through the choices they make. One is not born with an essential human nature that determines how one takes major decisions. Rather, as Sartre said, "existence precedes essence". Of course there are historical constraints that narrow the range of choice, but within these constraints people are "condemned to be free". Even if a person can live without taking responsibility for choice, or even deny the need to take responsibility, one does so at great risk. For one will have to live in 'bad faith' with oneself and the world.

Like Heidegger, the existentialists were interested in the emphasis on universal 'being' though less convinced that there were a few persons, such as Friedrich Hölderlin, of exceptional imaginative power whose destiny it was to bring the German people into contact with it. Both Merleau-Ponty and Sartre were critical of Husserl for not going far enough, for arguing that the goal of all thought is simply knowledge. They were also critical of Heidegger for eliminating all individuality from the realm of 'being' and thus all responsibility of the individual for others. As existentialists, they were more interested in the destiny of Europe than they were in that of France.

It also helped, of course, that as philosophers they had lived in one another's world before the war. Writing of his arrival at the University of

Tübingen in July 1946, the novelist Michel Tournier spun a compelling tale of a Franco-German world waiting only to be rediscovered. Here, he wrote, was the heart of German culture, where students saw the halls in which Hegel and Schelling had studied, and Zimmer's low tower where Hölderlin had spent thirty-five years in the darkness of insanity: "Tübingen exhilarated me. French and German students stared at one another incredulously, dazzled by the sight. . . . We were 20. Had fate really given us this incredible gift, to live and work together on tasks requiring intelligence, to create freely without fear of the stupidity of war? *We belonged to ourselves at last*".[20] Even now it is a striking phrase, one that essentialised the fact that to be born on one of the great border regions of Europe was to be born a European as well as a German or Frenchman.

Even so avowed an Atlanticist as Raymond Aron found a similar peace of mind in Tübingen when he lectured there in 1953. He had first encountered German students there in 1931 when lecturing on the philosophy of Joseph de Maistre, the poetry of Paul Claudel and the novels of François Mauriac. Twenty years later he discovered that his postwar students, though different, were not entirely unlike their predecessors: "as un-Hitlerian and un-nationalistic as possible. They loudly agreed when I improvised this definition of world history—*die Weltgeschichte diese Mischung von Heldentum und Blodsinn* (world history, a mixture of heroism and stupidity)".[21]

As Aron made clear in his memoirs, it was German culture rather than the German people that had first captured his imagination. What he found so compelling was the richness of its ideas—the ideas of Husserl and Heidegger, and those of the neo-Kantians in the person of Max Weber.

After 1945 it had devolved upon the French to seize the intellectual high ground in Europe, in the persons of existentialists like Merleau-Ponty and Sartre, hermeneutic phenomenologists like Paul Ricoeur, critics of ideology like Levinas, André Breton and Jacques Derrida. Some, like Levinas, had studied with Heidegger and Husserl in Freiburg; others, like Ricoeur, had begun their careers by publishing critical commentaries on Husserl and Karl Jaspers. What Aron makes clear in his memoirs is the remarkable degree of engagement between French and German intellectuals in these years, one that had no parallel between the continental and Anglo-American schools, or for that matter within the Anglo-American tradition. In a telling phrase, Aron tells us that what he discovered in 1946 was that history had offered the French a second chance, that the "cunning of Reason" offered it a second opportunity for the dream of his youth, that of Franco-German reconciliation.

The Forging of a European Consciousness

Let me illustrate the slow but steady growth of a European consciousness by invoking the work of one of the great French historians of the twentieth century, Fernand Braudel, one of the key figures of the *Annales* school, a group of historians who sought to broaden the scope of historiography by introducing social and economic concerns alongside what had traditionally been taught until then—political and diplomatic history.

While Churchill and Roosevelt were meeting in Placentia Bay the young Braudel was working on his magnum opus, a study of the Mediterranean world in the reign of Philip II. As he languished in a German prisoner-of-war camp he wrote the 600,000 words of text from memory. Of this time he was to write, "We the defeated . . . represented the lost France. . . . The real France, the France held in reserve, *la France profonde,* remained behind us".[22] If there was something heroic in Braudel's scholarly use of his enforced sequestration, he admitted that the work to which he had applied himself so assiduously required a deliberate distancing from the day-to-day horrors and eventual excitements of the war. "I had to believe", he wrote, "that history, destiny, was written at a much more profound level".[23]

The *Annales* journal that Braudel edited in the middle years of his life was the most significant organ of three generations of historical giants, beginning with its founders Marc Bloch and Lucien Febvre. It rejected narrative in favour of a history informed by economics, sociology and anthropology, history distilled into a single *"science de l'homme"*, a phrase that encapsulated the "new history", as it came to be known in the Anglo-Saxon world. Although the *Annales* journal was founded in 1929, its governing ideas were set forth by sociologists like Emile Durkheim who shared a determination to find in their subjects the 'deeper', 'essential' features that could not be deduced from the 'mere description' of events.

The *Annales* school was a dynamic one. What made it so influential was its association with the main philosophical movements of the first half of the twentieth century—Marxism, existentialism and anthropological structuralism. "I am by temperament a structuralist", wrote Braudel, "little tempted by the event or even by the short-term conjecture".[24] Indeed, Braudel thought "the history of events" dangerous. Even if it were "the most exciting of all, the richest in human interest", he wrote, "we must learn to distrust this history and its burning passions, as it was felt and described by contemporaries whose lives were as short and as *short-sighted* as our own".

How could his own countrymen at least limit their short-sightedness? How would they know when one historical period had ended and another begun? Only by understanding the permanent features of their own civilisation, the "structures of history"—the constraints imposed by geography, the collective psychology of a people as well as the economic forces that govern its actions—"all profound forces, barely recognisable at first, especially by contemporaries, all taken for granted if thought of at all".[25]

These are the structures that give every civilisation its outline as well as its meaning in the eyes of others. Those structures persist over time. Indeed we can only approach them, Braudel argued, in the *longue durée,* from the long-term perspective. But though they persist through the centuries the form they take differs from period to period. That is what he called "periodicity", or the "structure of history".

The history of events—in short, the events in which we ourselves take part, or what Paul Lacombe called *l'histoire évènementielle*—must be seen as periods that come and go, leaving civilisations themselves intact. Every civilisation passes through certain periods, each with its own themes and preferences, its own historical styles. It is studying the point at which one generation gives way to another that helps to make sense of exceptional events.

In invoking Braudel I am aware that his reputation among historians at the end of the century is being revised, that the limitations of his approach to history present some serious problems in any attempt to use it as an aid to understanding the European consciousness in 1945. Braudel showed throughout his life, particularly in his preoccupation with long- and medium-term patterns and cycles, a systematic disregard for the actions of politicians. What was the European project, after all, if not the creation of its founding fathers, Jean Monnet and Robert Schuman, Paul-Henri Spaak and Alcide De Gasperi?

But Braudel's description of the Mediterranean world and the broad sweep of his work in the 1940s were also quintessentially European—in this, perhaps, the last grand moment in Europe's intellectual history. At the time that he wrote, his themes were uniquely European, and his concepts must be judged as such—uniquely European, not Atlanticist. From the beginning the commitment that the French and the Germans made to the European idea was much greater than the commitment that the Americans and the British were willing to make in constructing an Atlantic community. For the French in particular the pursuit of a united Europe had the force of what the philosophers of the time called an *existential* choice. There are some moments in life when the choices that have to be confronted are life determining. However one chooses, the results of one's choice will determine the kind of moral person one becomes and the way one will live.

The European idea in France was driven by a wish not only to preserve its own culture but also to do more, to forge a distinctive European personality in the face of the threat of 'Americanisation' by ensuring that it did not become subsumed in a wider Atlantic identity instead. As Jean Monnet explained in April 1949, Western Europe was in a vacuum on either side of which were the two great dynamic forces of communism and American capitalism. It was, he felt, a vacuum that could be filled either by one of the two outside forces or by the development of a third force, a distinctive "West European way of life".[26]

It was not a vision that inspired the British. It did, however, inspire Monnet's own countrymen. It was also consistent with a new mood that dominated French intellectual life in this period. It was an idea that, so to speak, discovered the French, or found them out. As Nietzsche once said, the great changes of consciousness in history are always "inaudible". They creep up on a society unsuspected. In the case of France and Germany the European idea had been creeping up on them for some time. It was to be found at the heart of three contemporary historical forces.

The Anti-American Tradition

The first of Braudel's measurements of civilisation was geography. In the course of the twentieth century, geographers began to redefine the concept of geography in terms of cultural zones in which humanity itself was transformed. As the historian Jules Michelet had written at the end of the nineteenth century, each cultural zone witnessed "the decisive shaping of self by self".[27]

This understanding of geography can be found in the later work of Edmund Husserl. For him the very word 'Europe' was not a territorial expression but a spiritual principle, for it designated the unity of a creative activity that stamped on those engaged in it a unifying character. In that sense Europe was a "philosophic idea imminent in its history". It was a theatre of activity. It was a historical concept as well as a geographical one, an epoch as well as a continent, for it lived "in the free fashioning of its being and its historical life—one forged by the ends it seeks and the tasks it undertakes".[28]

Husserl, in fact, consciously used geographical terms to define Europe in the 1930s. The Europeans were distinguished from others by their metaphysical aspirations. Though they might live in a finite part of the world, their horizons were infinite, for they wanted to Europeanise the world, to reduce it to their own image. In that sense he saw Europe as a "spiritual territory" as well as a geographical one.

In 1945 the Europeans emerged from the war to find themselves divided between two non-European powers. At this critical juncture the French in particular became conscious of a more demanding challenge: the construction of a European rather than an Atlantic community. Europe was now threatened on two sides. Of the two threats, communism and capitalism, the latter was considered by some to be far more powerful, and far more insidious. They also knew of it at first hand.

This was also true of many of the refugees who had fled from Germany on the eve of the war. The experience of living among a foreign people can often alter an individual's sense of self, producing important changes in self-perception and consciousness. In his book *Invisible Cities* the novelist Italo Calvino depicts the situation of the wandering expatriate in paradoxical terms: "Arriving at each new city, the traveller finds again a past of his that he did not know he had: the foreignness of what you no longer are or no longer possess lies in wait for you in foreign unpossessed places". Many

German exiles who had fled to the United States in the 1930s discovered this for themselves. In 1947 Thomas Mann and Bertolt Brecht returned to Europe from their wartime exile in California thoroughly convinced (in Mann's words) that they were fundamentally different from the "gentle barbarians" among whom they had lived amicably enough, but at a distance.

A new generation, and with it a new European elite, came of age during the war. If the events of 1940 made the British conscious of their Atlantic identity, the collapse of France made the French conscious of their European identity. What makes a generation aware of itself as a collective entity depends on two things: consciousness of a unique shared experience, and a sense that that experience distinguishes those who share it from those who do not.[29] For the Europeans in the immediate postwar years this self-consciousness was all the sharper for loss of self-esteem brought on by perhaps the gravest blow of all, the division of Europe between the two superpowers. The irony of course was that the injury to European pride came less of its partition by the Soviet Union than of its subordination to the United States. The Soviet Union clearly posed a threat to Europe's security, but so, in a different way, did the United States, with the threat of modernity itself—a threat to European *culture*.

The American threat had a longer history than that, however. "They are all being subjugated to American taste", complained Herbert Ihering one day in the 1920s on seeing his countrymen flocking to a cinema. "They are standardising, made uniform. The American cinema is the new international militarism. It is advancing. It is more dangerous than Prussianism. It is swallowing up not just individuals but the personality of a whole people".[30] In the eyes of many German intellectuals, Americanism became a catchword for untrammelled modernity.

It was the Anglo-American axis that they feared most at the end of the First World War, much more, for example, than they feared communism. Writing on the eve of Germany's defeat, twenty years before he fled to the New World, Mann had warned that the union of Russia and Germany would be a political and spiritual necessity "in case the Anglo-American alliance should endure".[31] In the following summer the journalist Ludwig Quessel added that the peoples of continental Europe, both victims and vanquished alike, had been left "in danger of being enslaved by the two great Anglo-Saxon world powers".[32]

Like the Americans, Spengler claimed, the English saw the world only as a source of booty rather than a theatre of action. Both countries were not real nations, only fields of opportunity in which people grubbed around to make themselves as rich as possible in the shortest possible time. If either country led the West, then Western man would end up worshipping technology for its power to transform the world for its own sake rather than for any particular end.[33]

By comparison, anti-Americanism in France was very different in character. "We are all being Americanised", warned the de Goncourt brothers as early as 1857.[34] They feared that history had become merely the entropic product of violent social change, of modernity run rampant. Though the French were free they were constantly reminded of the inadequate grounds of their own existence. As Heidegger later wrote of their defeat in 1940, they had become so Americanised that they lacked "the metaphysics equal to their own being", and had paid the ultimate price in military defeat.[35]

As in Germany, warnings had sounded in France in the 1920s by writers such as Henri Dubreuil, who had warned that unless Europe united it would not be able to withstand American power. "Cries of alarm are multiplying all over Europe", wrote Lucien Lourat in 1929. "In every language one and the same outcry is endlessly repeated: the colossus across the Atlantic is menacing us. . . . It will soon be a real and serious threat".[36]

We can find such thinking still strong thirty years later in the writings of two very different characters, Sartre and Charles de Gaulle. General de Gaulle's critical stance towards the United States can be traced to the sentiments he shared with an earlier generation of Frenchmen who had rejected Anglo-American materialism in favour of an idealised French-European order. One day, he hoped, France would be able to offer the world a model of industrial civilisation based on European, not American values. In the defence not of France but of Europe, de Gaulle found the ultimate defence against what he called *'mondialisation'*, a buzzword for the evils of a homogenised West dominated by the United States.

From the first, the French saw their culture as the main instrument in creating a single European identity. In a text that refers to the "European cultural construction", the French Foreign Office reaffirmed as recently as the late 1980s that it was the task of French culture to impose a feeling of European unity. The paper went on to chart the "determining role" that France could still play in "the collective coming to awareness" of European man in the face of the United States.[37]

The United States, in fact, came to assume an allegorical function. Those who visited New York (or, like François Mauriac, refused to go there on the grounds that French culture had already been transformed in America's image) did so to confirm their own prejudices. America was treated not as a living reality so much as a countermyth. The survival of France required its blanket condemnation.

Anti-Americanism in these years was compounded by a tenacious belief that the French Revolution, not the American, was the "crucible of modernity" (in Simon Schama's vivid phrase). As such, at least in its Jacobin phase, it represented "a common tradition" that could accommodate both Robespierre and Lenin. Given this perspective America was the more dangerous of the two superpowers, for it threatened to dispossess the French people of their revolutionary heritage. Sartre expressed a conviction shared by many of his countrymen that the world of the European and that of the Anglo-Saxon imaginations were, and always had been, in competition not only as alternative ways of life but also as alternative promises of the future.

Later Sartre went much further, denouncing the attempt to 'Americanise' France as a strategy little different in ideological terms from the despairing conclusion that men like Drieu La Rochelle had reached in the 1930s, which was that only by espousing fascism could France escape German aggression. "If you do not succeed in making fascism the victor in your countries," the eponymous hero of Drieu's novel *Gilles* (1939) tells two foreigners, "you will bear the burden of the terrible consequences of your weakness".[38] In Sartre's eyes, a similar fear had informed the French commitment to American capitalism, a commitment that was equivalent to collaborating with the enemy, to selling France short. It was America, not the Soviet Union, that he had in mind when, at a congress in Moscow in the summer of 1972, he called for "the demilitarisation of European culture".[39]

Sartre became increasingly ridiculous in his old age as he struggled, with a singular lack of success, to integrate the insights of existentialism into a Marxist framework and show how choice can play within the constraints of economically and historically determined situations. Even today, however, the voices of protest against Anglo-Saxon values still make themselves heard. In the battle to sign the General Agreement on Tariffs and Trade (GATT) French politicians began referring to *"la delocalisation"*, an odd term that was meant to describe the transfer of capital to high-return markets and the invasion of products that might deprive French workers of their jobs.

With the collapse of communism the debate about Americanism has become even more heated. Alain Duhamel, an influential commentator, warns that France's refusal to assert its own cultural independence would mean "the triumph of the Anglo-Saxon market, integration in a transatlantic society and the burial of the European personality".[40] In 1995, *Le Monde* called the strikes that crippled the public services "the first popular revolt against globalisation"—all the more important because globalism and American 'commodification' are often thought to be the same. Philippe Seguin, who had become speaker of the French National Assembly two years earlier, went so far as to accuse the French Government of conniving in another act of appeasement, "a social Munich", by putting open markets ahead of the need to preserve jobs.[41] It is a striking phrase, its significance deriving from the fact that no British politician would use the term—even now. That the British are still blind to the American 'threat', argued Jacques Toubon, the Gaullist culture minister, was to be expected of a country that had allowed itself to become a branch of the American home market.[42] It is a threat that has become intimately linked with a second force behind European integration, the creation of a social market economy. This is the second of Braudel's themes—the fact that every culture is defined by a specific personality, which in the case of Europe is a social democratic sensibility.

The Social Market Economy

In addition to anti-Americanism, another theme that emerged from France's experience of defeat in 1940 was the need to challenge an Anglo-Saxon model of capitalism that allegedly paid little attention to social needs. In this mission the Europeans succeeded beyond their own imagining. Indeed what strikes one most in retrospect about European society after 1960 is the almost complete absence of class conflict, together with the disappearance of extreme left- and right-wing radicalism.

The postwar politicians of the francophone countries France and Belgium saw the need to form greater national cohesion by making the present worth defending. In 1940 those who had rallied to the flag had done so in the name of the past, in particular of France's historic, even heroic role in history. The Resistance in the early days was largely a conservative, bourgeois phenomenon that had little grassroots support in the industrial cities. Joseph Goebbels, perceptive as always, professed himself most anxious about the conservative opposition, "the reactionary opposition" he called it, on which not only the English but also Stalin had to rely in 1941.[43]

The 'past' had not been strong enough to unite the French people in 1940. Indeed, what had started as a national defeat by an external enemy quickly became a civil conflict between a variety of internal adversaries who showed remarkable ill-feeling towards each other. For the communists the enemy was the capitalist class. For the trade unions it was the old 'yellow unions' instigated by their employers during the occupation, and the corporatist unions organised by the state in Vichy France. A patriot in 1940 was not only a man who refused to accept the terms of the armistice. It was one who refused to abandon the syndicalist movement, who continued to engage in communist activities, who protested for more food, who tried to escape conscription in the ever growing labour force required to man Germany's expanding armaments industry. Resistance was most effective where the movement leaders recognised that there was not one enemy, Germany, but several, nearly all of them French.[44]

Pan-Europeanism, in other words, was as much a response to France's class divisions as it was to the vision of Franco-German reconciliation. During the war Emmanuel Mounier, no collaborator but a man imprisoned for a while by the Vichy government, wrote that Europe, "divided against itself [was] giving birth to a new order, not only perhaps for Europe but for the whole world". Many of the sentiments that Mounier expressed in a text written five months after France's defeat help to explain the ambiguity that existed even among members of the Resistance in their response to the events of June 1940:

> It is nevertheless true that pre-war France needed some muscle and a bit of savagery: put together socialism, religion and a virile spirit, as one of Drieu's spokesmen stated. . . .
>
> Indeed, if the point of this war were to return, once the dangers had passed, to the charms of an age recently gone by, and to revive waltzing Vienna, slum-ridden Naples, baroque Munich and glittering Paris, we should very soon lose face. "Turn fascism against Italy and Germany" remains an ambiguous, ill-balanced formula but yes—turn against the monstrosities of fascism the virtues of fascism and whatever living history it has given birth to in aberration and terror, and there can be no more durable victory, adapted to the world as it is, without such integration.[45]

In Belgium many of those who chose to work with the Germans looked to a future in which the social market economy would be secure. Germany's victory seemed to provide the only basis for social democracy, insisted the erstwhile socialist leader Henri de Man in a manifesto addressed to socialist activists throughout Europe. France's defeat, he assured them, could become the starting point for the construction of a new world:

> For the labouring classes and for socialism, the collapse of a decrepit world, far from being a disaster, has been a deliverance.
>
> Despite all the setbacks, sufferings and disillusionment we have experienced, the way is clear for the two causes that embody the aspirations of the people: European peace and social justice.[46]

For years de Man had developed a critical ideology that in nearly all respects was already fascist. His position represented neither a rupture nor an aberration in the ideological development of a whole school of socialism in the French-speaking world. During those years de Man was not just an isolated socialist revisionist but the leader of a great socialist party that was at the heart of mainstream Belgian life. Several years later, in April 1944, while the country was still under German occupation, the leaders of the trade unions and the main employer organisations signed a social pact that brought such measures as health insurance, the promise of full employment, the provision of old-age pensions and child benefits under the rubric of a social security system for the first time, a few years before the United Kingdom constructed the first welfare state.[47]

Even in Germany the origin of the social market can be traced to the Second World War. By its end foreign labour, 7 million strong, made up a quarter of the workforce. Many German employees found themselves elevated to the position of overseers and foremen, enjoying a degree of social mobility and an experience of authority that was significant, even lasting. For a number of reasons the interest of labour and the employers moved closer together. Both had an interest in protecting workers from conscription. If the war discredited Nazism as a political philosophy, it confirmed one of the movement's social priorities by encouraging employers to invest in social policy provisions.

Indeed, in the words of one of the new generation of German historians:

> The mood of *Wirtschaftswunder* and take-off now benefited from the very destruction of tradition and recasting of standards of behaviour brought about by the Third Reich. Part and parcel of the changes were the new type of workers, achievement-orientated, individualistic and prepared to trade high productivity for high wages: the modern nuclear family, isolated in its private life, satisfying its social needs in the market place.[48]

In short, during the Second World War the principle of cooperation between employers and employees was extended from the sphere of industrial relations to that of social provision. As one of the architects of European unity, Robert Marjolin, later revealed in his memoirs, the French were keen from the very beginning of the European Coal and Steel Community to ensure that the social provisions of French workers were not threatened by the market. They originally wanted a mandatory provision for social insurance and a minimum wage, an ambition that was finally achieved in the social chapter of the Maastricht Treaty (1991).[49]

The need for a social contract, a lesson learned from the interclass conflicts that had weakened Europe's democracies in the run-up to the Second World War, accounts to some extent for a form of capitalism that is still intrinsically different from its original Anglo-American model. The German government, for example, at both the state and the federal levels, has more shares in more industries than any other government. It has a socially financed apprenticeship system and social welfare policies that are not usually seen as a necessary part of the market economy mechanism. In the German model (unlike the American) a centralised level of control is considered preferable to decentralised power. Central controls are deemed necessary to prevent irresponsible fiscal policies encouraging high interest rates and high inflation.[50] As the century draws to a close, however, the social market model is under increasing challenge. As labour costs have risen (European workers are now the most highly paid in the world) the European economy has become less competitive. If they are to continue to pay themselves high wages the Europeans may have to think in increasingly protectionist terms, as they continue to preach the virtues of competitiveness without applying them at home. "If those increasingly costly social market provisions are to be sustained", noted Jacques Delors in an unguarded remark in 1993, "Europe might have to retreat behind high tariff walls—to lock out the rest of the world, America included".[51]

France itself still provides a vivid illustration of Europe's democratic challenge. Can it combine growth and social security with low inflation and low unemployment? Can solutions be found that will be acceptable to a still rigid corporatist society? Can it negotiate a new social contract given the fact that the last attempt provoked the only real political rebellions in the postwar era, or what the newspapers called somewhat euphemistically *"les mouvements sociales"*—the student revolt of 1968 and the strikes that brought Paris to a standstill twenty-eight years later?

Even the history of the social market concept is being revised by contemporary historians. An increasing number now believe that its origins lie not in an altruistic sacrifice of the better off but in the anxiety of the middle classes, who were anxious to secure state insurance after their experiences in the interwar years. At the same time, the influential public choice school of economists and political scientists has begun to challenge the belief that Europe's bureaucrats—the *"Enarques"* (graduates of ENA, Ecole Nationale d'Administration) in Paris or the civil servants who worked within the welfare sector—consciously operated in the public interest. Instead they are seen to be primarily self-interested, seeking power through increasing the size and adjusting the shape of their budgets. They are increasingly being seen not as high-minded professionals concerned with the welfare of their clients but as bureaucrats anxious to retain their own income, status and working conditions.

Whatever the social market concept's origins, trying to reform the system without imposing unacceptably high costs on the national consensus may be impossible. The welfare system in France has traditionally focused not on the child or the struggling mother, as in America, nor on a guaranteed level of wages, as in Britain, but on a broadly accepted defence of the family as the basic social unit. The social unrest that has been such a marked feature of French political life in recent years may have to do with the misgivings the French people have for the government's stated aim of dismantling a universally accepted welfare system that has deep roots in the consciousness of politicians on both the Right and the Left. These roots are older than those of socialism itself—and will not be uprooted easily.

The United States, by comparison, though suffering from many of the same social ills, has outpaced both Europe and Japan. At the end of the century it has pulled ahead economically by a decisive margin. It employs more of its population, enjoys lower inflation, and has an internal market that is the largest and the least regulated in the world. It taxes its citizens less. Even demographically it is set to remain the youngest society in the industrial world, and will thus escape the ageing of the population that is already creating in Europe an almost irresistible pressure for even higher social provisions.

As Europe continues to languish, the arguments over protectionism will grow more insistent, notably in Germany, where the economic problems are structurally worse than those of France. The fear of the Atlantic free

traders is that Germany will be drawn into a pact with the social democratic protectionists of France, with the Jacques Attalis rather than their
more menacing populist cousins like Jean-Marie Le Pen. What many in the
former camp want is a social Europe regulated and protected culturally, socially and economically. It would seem that the price to be paid for trying
to retain the social market model may be the end of a liberal dream, that of
a free trading, deregulated European economy, linked with the United
States in a transatlantic free trade area, an idea that is at the heart of the
U.S. attempt to anchor its post–Cold War policy not to the containment of
communism but to the promotion of free trade.

European Economic Unity

We can even trace the European single market to the year 1940. In an entry
in his diary on 10 July, John Colville, one of Churchill's private secretaries,
recorded his employer's concern that the Germans, recently victorious in
their war against France, might attempt to construct a European economic
community. Such an idea, had it been debated before the war, would have
met with little sympathy in London. The idea of a European community,
Colville wrote, preoccupied Churchill precisely because of its superficial attraction to a war-weary Europe eager for peace, even if the price was
German economic domination.[52]

It was not an idle threat. If British propaganda during the Second World
War seldom mentioned a united Europe, German propagandists frequently
did. In June 1940 a former Dutch prime minister called for a European federation led by Germany. The secretary-general of economic affairs in
Belgium also spoke of "a positive willingness to contribute to the making of
a new order in Europe", a theme that was taken up by a former French foreign minister later that year.[53]

Clearly such writers had been thinking about the future for some time. If
the perception of their own position led the British to think instead in terms
of an English-speaking alliance, the prospect of national decline prompted
many French intellectuals, particularly on the Right, to think of a German-
led European union. "Ideological variations come and go", added the
writer Alfred Fabre-Luce the following year, "the function of Europe remains the theme of the twentieth century". Hitler agreed with him. As he
told his foreign minister a few months later, the war "was no longer a matter of Germany and England, but a common pan-European interest within
the European economic area".[54]

The German business community took the idea seriously. In 1942 the
Berlin Union of Businessmen and Industrialists organised a colloquium entitled 'The European Economic Community', in which the inaugural lecture
was delivered by the minister of economics, Walter Funk. Stressing the need
to control inflation and outlining plans for a social market economy ("the

people of Europe will rightly demand a sense of social responsibility from their leaders after the war"), Funk emphasised the role that an economic union would play in consolidating European integration. "A stronger sense of economic solidarity must be fostered among the people of Europe", he demanded, "by means of cooperation in all areas of economic policy".[55]

The British and the Americans consulted each other in the summer of 1940 to see how they might successfully counter the idea of such a community, long before the majority of Europeans gave it serious thought. They were inclined to portray the concept as a cynical German attempt to harness Europe's wealth in its own interests. "At the same time", Colville wrote, "it was proposed that we ourselves should make some positive suggestions defining the advantages of the international economic structure which we and the United States wished to see emerge as part of a peace settlement". The idea, he added, was "to break down the artificial barriers to trade which impede any general rise in the standard of living".[56]

The idea the War Cabinet eventually came up with was that of a free-trade bloc binding the United States and Europe after the war, an Atlantic economic union rather than a European one, a definingly Western construct. Displaying typical British pragmatism, Colville added, "we prefer to do things because reason tells us they are worth doing, not because we fear the sanctions attaching to failure to do them".

Consistently from the beginning the British blocked every attempt after the war to create an economic union, including the argument for a European League for Economic Cooperation proposed by the former Belgian prime minister Paul van Zeeland in May 1946; the call in February 1947 by the Socialist Movement for a United States of Europe; Didault's call in The Hague the following August for a customs and economic union and a consultative European assembly. Throughout his tenure at the Foreign Office, Bevin railed against "the European idea" for its "appeal to the mind" rather than "its genuine echo to the heart". It was a revealing phrase that illustrates how little enthusiasm the British, engaged as they were in the Atlantic project, had for anything European. Eighteen years later, after Britain's refusal to enter the European Common Market, Harold Macmillan revived the idea of an Atlantic Free Trade Area in a belated attempt to arrest rather than reverse the course of European integration.[57]

The French, for their part, were reconciled to the European project even before the war came to an end. In 1943, Monnet wrote that "the solution of the European problem is important to the life of France. . . . France is bound to Europe. She cannot escape". He made clear to Robert Schuman that unless France was bolted into some kind of union, "Malthusianism" (the economic and demographic pressures of the future) would "efface her".[58]

Like most of his countrymen after the war, Monnet was obsessed less with shaping the future than with escaping the nightmare of the past. What influenced him most was the threat of a resurgent Germany, the fear that sooner rather than later it would recover and once again be in a position to depress the fast-forward button of history.

"History does not normally provide second chances," the historian Fritz Stern has noted. Unfortunately, the history of Germany seemed to be the exception. A few days after the finalisation of the Schuman Plan Monnet drafted a background paper in which he expressed his fears that unless Germany was tied to France its economic recovery would be as dangerous for its neighbours as it had been in the 1930s. When under Allied pressure the dismantling of German industry in the French zone stopped in 1949, the next best thing was to secure access to German coal and a voice in the control of the German steel industry. The Schuman Plan for the integration of Europe's coal and steel industries was vital to France's future, and it got it on terms of its own devising, as the memoirs of Belgian Foreign Minister Paul-Henri Spaak make clear.[59]

It was for this reason that the instrument of European integration was a sectoral one. We must remember that coal was Europe's main source of energy at the time and that oil accounted for less than 8 percent of Europe's fuel needs. Control of coal gave France a decisive voice in the continent's postwar recovery. It is not clear still whether Schuman was taken in by Monnet or whether Monnet really did have a wider agenda. The point is that the European Coal and Steel Community (ECSC) that was set up in 1952 was a French interest dictated by a French geopolitical concern.

Initially the Germans did not see any necessary antagonism between membership in the European Common Market five years later (a logical extension of the ECSC) and the Atlantic Alliance. In 1958 Ludwig Erhard, who was at the time the German minister of economic affairs, insisted that the "dogma of European unification" should not prevent the Europeans from accepting that, of the two institutions, the Atlantic Alliance would remain the stronger, for it was the only one that met the twin challenges of East-West competition and the potential conflict between the rich world and the underdeveloped world. Schuman also insisted that the Europeans should "reaffirm their Atlantic convictions at a time when the tasks confronting Europe are greater than ever".[60]

In the event, of course, the Germans were swept into a closer French embrace than either Erhard or even Adenauer had originally contemplated. In the early 1960s they were confronted with a changing of the guard in Paris when Monnet's vision of Europe was displaced by de Gaulle's. Like de Gaulle, Monnet believed that, once established, an integrated Europe would be strong enough to stand up to the United States. But to precipitate a breach with the United States, to weaken NATO as de Gaulle actually did when he took France out of its integrated military command in 1966, would be to put an undue strain on the working relationship between Paris and Bonn. It would also precipitate a breach with Britain and thus keep the British out of the task of reconstructing Europe.

In reality de Gaulle merely took Monnet's vision to its logical conclusion. From the beginning he saw that Atlanticism and Europeanism were conflicting ideas. All this makes it even more surprising that the Americans did not share British suspicions that the creation of a customs union or a European Bank (an institution that the Dutch proposed as early as the late 1940s) might one day create a movement that would be incompatible with Western unity. Instead the Americans were impressed by Monnet's arguments that although the Bretton Woods system might restore minimum trading volumes, it would not expand trade decisively. The economies of Europe were not strong enough to compete as individual units. Dynamic growth, Monnet argued, could be obtained only through some form of integration.

Few American commentators at the time recognised that European integration might be based on principles very different from those of American capitalism. The American passion for European unity, argues A. W. DePorte, "owes much of its strength to the conviction of its proponents . . . that what looked like a step away from fundamental American goals was in fact a step towards them".[61] As Michael Hogan suggests, many Americans saw European unification as the best way to "rescue the vision" of a multilateral trading area, which the emerging Cold War had begun to undermine.[62]

The United States supported the European idea in the mistaken assumption that what it created, it could later control. It would seem that Monnet was able to reassure the Americans on this point. When he threw his energies into supporting a European Atomic Community he was supporting America's claims to control Europe's military and much of its civil nuclear power. While Harold Macmillan was stumbling towards his doomed application to join the European Community, George Ball, the American official in charge of European affairs, was talking with Monnet on how best to force the British into Europe while denying them many of the exemptions from the Treaty of Rome that Macmillan wanted.

Indeed, except in the smallest details, everything Monnet advocated for Europe was what his contacts in Washington wanted. When he retired from public service it was to found the unofficial Action Committee for the United States of Europe. In the late 1950s the committee was one of the two programmes that took most of the funds of another organisation, the American Committee on the United Europe. The chairman of that organisation was the famous wartime American intelligence chief, Bill Donovan, and his deputy was the wartime spy Alan Dulles; both were closely connected to the U.S. Central Intelligence Agency (CIA), the latter of course as deputy director and director. As Alan Milward has observed, the father of Europe was financed by an organisation whose funds almost certainly came from the CIA. That he and the European movement that carried the banner of Euro-federalism made strenuous efforts to keep this secret suggests that they were not unwitting recipients.[63]

Perhaps it would have been wiser—it appears in hindsight—for the Americans to have been more sensitive to British fears. By 1971 they discovered that the Common Market, far from being a genuine free market, did not seem to correspond to anything in the textbooks. It was a 'planned' market economy founded in October 1962 on a programme of action drawn up by Robert Marjolin, the vice president of the European Commission. They soon came to see the European market not as a free trade area in the true sense but as a market managed by its European members acting for once in unison rather than in competition. As one American observer at the time complained, the Common Market's export restrictions were a "merciless retribution administered in a spirit of righteousness" by a Europe that in most other respects had been written off as a force in the world after the Second World War.[64]

One of the new areas of contention was agricultural subsidies, which penalised American farmers who might otherwise have sold their commodities at much more competitive prices. The Americans were also highly critical of the growing number of preferential trade agreements that the European Community (EC) negotiated with the developing world. The preferences given to European exports in manufacturing goods by Third World nations who were party to the Lomé Convention were criticised for discriminating against American manufacturers as well as for violating the GATT principle of most-favoured-nation status. By the late 1970s it was estimated that the Common Market and the European Free Trade Area combined subjected 28 percent of U.S. exports to the Third World and Europe to some form of discrimination.[65]

Somewhat belatedly, the reports to Congress submitted by the Executive every year no longer employed a formula much used in the 1960s, namely that the possible economic price of a unified Europe would be outweighed by the gain in the political viability of the West as a whole. The year 1971 saw the collapse of the dollar and the end of the American balance-of-payments surplus with Europe. At home the misgivings of the Congress were summed up in a report to the Finance Committee of the U.S. Senate, which stated bluntly: "Our other outstanding problems with Europe cannot be viewed in isolation from these economic questions. It is contradictory to argue as some Europeans do that the US must maintain troops in Europe while, at the same time, insisting that Europe must pursue a trade and monetary policy harmful to the United States. These questions are all inter-related, even if specific price tags are not put on specific policies".[66]

It was Britain's long-delayed entry into the EC in 1973 that finally concentrated America's mind on whether the Europeans would continue to subordinate themselves to American leadership indefinitely. Kissinger made his own position clear enough: "For us European unity is what it has always been: not an end in itself but a means to the strengthening of the West. We shall continue to support European unity as a component of a *larger Atlantic partnership*".[67]

Kissinger, however, was the last major American politician to oppose European integration on the grounds that what the United States and the Europeans should be doing was to build "an Atlantic Commonwealth" instead. As secretary of state in the mid-1970s, he believed that the greatest problem the United States faced was not how to regulate competition with its enemies but how to bring its allies to the realisation that there were interests greater than simple self-assertiveness: "The question is whether the nations of the West and Japan are capable of working cooperatively, or whether they are like the Greek city-states in the face of Macedonia and Rome, trying to deal competitively with a situation for which there is no competitive solution".[68]

Of course the reality of the process of European integration was not consistent with the evolution of Atlanticism, as the British had recognised all along. So had de Gaulle, who from the first had correctly seen Britain as a 'front man' for the United States. As a country it was irredeemably Atlanticist. It would have to be excluded from the EC until such time as the Atlantic system had collapsed or European unity had reached a point of no return.

Interestingly, the measures that Kissinger had wanted the Europeans to adopt in 1973 were the same demanded fifteen years later by Bush's secretary of state, James Baker. Both men wanted the EC to abandon the idea of a separate European defence organisation (in return for an American agreement to a specific European identity in NATO). Both wanted the EC to allow a larger role for the United States in its own policymaking process. Both also wanted the Europeans to adopt a free trade declaration to prevent the alliance from fragmenting into two competing economic blocs.

In 1973 Kissinger had talked of revising the Atlantic Treaty. In 1990 Baker demanded a new "European-American outlook", a renewed "European-American dialogue". Both men had to settle for something far short of their demands, in Kissinger's case for the Atlantic Declaration in 1974; in Baker's case for a Transatlantic Declaration that provided simply for biannual U.S.-EC consultations at the presidential and foreign policy levels.

Unconscious, perhaps, of the irony, Kissinger talked in 1992 of the need to transcend mere institutional links and political agendas, the need to reach out for something "more intangible, like the special relationship that has always existed between America and Britain".[69] The more he clung to sentiment, of course, the more he suggested its inadequacy in terms of mitigating conflicts of interest that had been contained. Faced with the Europeans' reluctance to dream on command, to arrest the process of

European integration, the Americans were reduced to the rather despairing measure of hoping that all would be for the best in the best of all possible worlds.

Today Europe appears to be as much a fortress as ever. Protectionism, even in Germany, is real enough. Telecommunications, banking and the chemical industry are all virtual cartels. Without a German partner it is impossible for American companies to enter these markets at all.

Other barriers include restrictive practices and massive government subsidies. In the European Union (EU) at large nineteen bilateral agreements protect European textile producers from competition. Sixty percent of the EU's imports come from countries that have entered into preferential trade agreements with the European Commission. The new rule of thumb, writes Lester Thurow, is that if the rest of the world wishes to be treated equally in Europe, it must change its rules so that they are identical to those that exist in Europe at present.[70]

The irony of course is that Europe is becoming less competitive. It may trade more with itself, but it does so at the expense of its trade with the rest of the world. The United States, for its part, had been moving for some time to secure its own future. It has operated on a number of fronts, negotiating the North American Free Trade Area (NAFTA) and passing laws to protect particular U.S. industries at home.

The politics of trade has not been resolved. Competition is still divisive. If the Americans are a little less inclined to be as critical of Europe as they used to be, it is only because they no longer treat the continent as the centre of economic gravity in the world. It is a measure of the strength of America's trading position at the end of the century that Europe takes two-thirds of its exports. Given such a structural imbalance the Americans have no interest in constructing a North Atlantic Free Trade Area of the kind proposed by the British. It is doubtful whether the European economy would be strong enough to enter it.

Europe Since 1989

I have tried, using a Braudelian schema, to show that the three keys to building the European Community (and the Union that followed it) were opposed to the three themes of the Atlantic idea. The Atlantic Alliance in Britain's case, and the European Community in France's, did not comprise the only context in which the policymakers chose to act. They did provide the context, however, in which they found themselves consciously engaged.

To have attempted to turn the British into good Europeans would have meant, at least in the minds of many politicians, repudiating those distinctive qualities that made them 'British'. Churchill and his successors nevertheless were naive to believe that Britain could, by locking itself into a U.S.-

dominated world, somehow escape finding itself on the margins of history, a distinctly dangerous position for any nation in the twentieth century. The French, by contrast, used Europe to refashion themselves as well. In this they were more successful than the British. As one German commentator sourly complained, "Europe is the continuation of France by other means".[71]

Both countries lived in the past—or at least for a future not so very different from the past. That is why for both of them the events of 1989 were so cathartic. Since 1990, Germany's unification has compelled the French to force the pace of European integration, with far-reaching social and political implications for themselves. The British have found themselves drifting in its wake without a policy or even a known destination. Both countries have been caught up by events not of their own making. The French have been forced to confront the reality of a united Germany, the British the prospect of an absent United States. The influence they once enjoyed in their respective communities is now much diminished. With the end of the Cold War France too has lost its hold over Germany where it hurts most—in the German people's imagination.

During the Cold War France was able to balance Germany's economic weight with its political influence. In the context of a stable European order underwritten by the United States the French were able to play a larger world role than they would have done otherwise—based on a nuclear capability, a seat in the Security Council of the United Nations, and an ambiguous relationship with the Soviet Union that they sometimes played to good effect. All the while Germany was largely impotent politically: a giant emasculated by the memory of its own past, which it tried but failed to exorcise from its own consciousness as well as from that of its closest allies (the United States excepted).

With the end of the Cold War Germany is once more united. With a population of 80 million people it has a newfound freedom of action. There are persistent calls for a German seat in the Security Council. It has reestablished much of the influence in Eastern and especially Central Europe that it had lost in 1945. By a July 1994 constitutional decree German soldiers are once again allowed by law to be deployed outside Germany. All these developments leave the French, in the words of the arch-Gaullist Alexandre Sanguinetti, "at the end of the journey . . . with [their] back to the sea".[72]

France remains what it was in the early postwar years—a regional power, its influence largely confined to the Luxembourg-Saarbrücken-Bonn triangle, the old Europe of the Six. At the end of the century it finds itself walking a tightrope between wanting to play a world role and the acute need to do something to contain Germany. It finds itself trapped between its wish to realise its potential and to assuage an old fear. How will it respond? In the only way possible. As the veteran commentator André Fontaine once remarked, "France has a German policy. She has no other".

The French have invested their entire postwar identity in this one friendship (as the United Kingdom invested most of its historical capital in its association with the United States). Their original reason for opting for Europe with the ECSC in 1952 has been greatly strengthened, not weakened, by the end of the Cold War. It is the one measure that carries with it the promise of a lasting solution to the German problem. It is the one measure that offers it peace of mind. It is the one measure that can save France from Germany and thus, perhaps, Europe from itself.

Unfortunately, further integration, far from transforming the EU into a major world actor, may make it more provincial in its own eyes as well as America's. Europe's politicians seem to be addressing a more conditional future. The Maastricht Treaty revealed that inflated hopes and limited ambitions are not a contradiction in terms. A more united Europe may be a weaker American partner. The cost of pressing ahead with unity may be tied increasingly to the small print of treaties, to the kind of opt-out clauses that the British and the Danes negotiated for themselves at the Maastricht and Edinburgh summits.

A more integrated Europe may have a bias towards framing issues more narrowly, especially when its members are preoccupied with parochial concerns. Risk aversion may be as much a performance standard as problem solving, carrying with it a preference for avoiding open-ended commitments. If this is the path that Europe is about to negotiate, then the prospects of partnership with the United States will become less and less compelling. Out of a position of weakness, not strength (as originally feared), a more united Europe may only hasten the forces already at work that are producing ever greater Western disunity.

Europe already displays some of the hallmarks of a declining power—defensiveness, lack of confidence and mediocrity. Its "grounds of historicity" (as Sartre and Merleau-Ponty would have understood them) are no longer of its own making. History is being made elsewhere. A new generation of leaders seems to find greater reassurance in the nation-state. Bleaker, more muted expectations of the future seem in keeping with a world that seems to be growing greyer and less heroic by the day. All these features have made a nonsense of Chancellor Helmut Kohl's boast that "the 1990s [would be] the decade of the Europeans and not that of the Japanese".[73] Instead Europe is beginning to resemble one of the minor prophets to be found at the end of the Old Testament—an Obadiah or Habakkuk, a Nahum or Haggai, who uttered their testimony while the business of history went on in other hands.

5

The (De)Construction
of Europe

The process of the *evolving* European ... will probably lead to results which
would seem to be least expected by those who naively promote and praise it, the
apostles of 'modern ideas'.

—Nietzsche, *Beyond Good and Evil* (1886)

A culture is not a 'given' any more than is a nation or a society. It is a pattern of relationships within its ranks and between itself and the outside
world. What we identify as a society such as Monnet's Europe is for the
most part an abstraction from a field of complex and competing interrelationships. In identifying different societies we are imposing a unity that by
its very nature is ephemeral. It is bound to change over time. That unity in
turn tends to be more pronounced at the centre than at the periphery,
where the outside world intrudes. That was one of the principal reasons
why the founders of the European Union were mostly 'border men' like
Adenauer and Schuman.

Cultures more than societies are also a series of processes that construct,
deconstruct and reconstruct ways of categorising the world. We constantly
re-perceive the world and our place in it, and more so in the modern age
than in any other. It is this constant flux that Hegel meant by modernity.
We are constantly re-creating ourselves in accordance with our perceptions
of reality. A culture is dialogic, and if at the end of the twentieth century it
is more of a dialogue between societies than groups within them, that is because of the increasing globalisation of history.

In the case of Europe external relationships have become particularly
pronounced. Its periphery is ringed by unrest from Algeria to Bosnia. It also
forms the hinterland of the world's most violent continent: Africa. After the
United States it is the society into which the second largest number of people are pulled rather than pushed. As they enter the twenty-first century

both societies find themselves dangerously placed at the confluence of historical forces, particularly the flow of refugees.

If we look at Europe as a system of relationships that are more or less intense, and more or less cohesive according to events, we can appreciate the force of Marx's dictum that men may make their own history but not under conditions of their own choosing. They do so in the framework of relationships that change frequently as events, not states, determine.

Any attempt to essentialise a culture, as the French have tried to do with Europe and the British with the Atlantic community, is bound to fail, especially when the attempt is at the expense of relations with the outside world, or worse, in spite of them. At the end of the twentieth century we have discovered that interrelationships are essential. They define cultures. The world system, rather than creating massive cultural homogeneity on a grand scale, is replacing one diversity with another, and the new diversity is based relatively more on interrelationships and less on autonomy. This is particularly true for the societies that are members of the West. Both the United States and Europe are interpenetrated more than any other. Both face a similar challenge: whether two multiethnic and increasingly multiracial worlds can transform themselves successfully into functioning and stable multicultural societies.

Multiculturalism takes us back to my discussion of phenomenology in the previous chapter. The phenomenologists set out to explain the opposite phenomenon: how the entire world was 'becoming' European. Phenomenology *was* the European contribution to twentieth-century philosophy, one that since 1945 has spawned a series of imitative or mutinous offshoots.

In the 1920s Edmund Husserl set out to ask what was Europe's 'being', or authentic self. He was insistent that all consciousness pointed beyond itself. It constituted a desire *for* something, or fear *of* something, or curiosity *about* something. Any of our experiences as they appear within our stream of thought necessarily refer to the object of our experience. There is no such thing as thought, fear or remembrance. Every thought is a thought of something, every fear is a fear of something, every remembrance is a memory of the object thought, feared or remembered. The term coined by Husserl to describe this relationship was 'intentionality'. The intentional character of all our thinking necessarily involves a sharp distinction between the act of thinking, fearing and remembering and the object to which these acts refer.[1]

This way of thinking had certain echoes in Eastern philosophy, but for the most part it was definingly European in arguing that only by grasping the object, or in this case the outer world, could the subject formulate its own 'authentic' identity. It was a theme that was particularly pronounced in Western literature, in the realist novels of Flaubert and Zola that depict the artists' desire to incorporate the whole world into their work, or to ensure that their heroes or heroines 'possess' the world of their own experience.

The great novelists of the century, Joyce, Proust and Mann, expropriated the whole world, or tried to. The world was the subject of their novels. Proust embraced a whole section of Parisian society in a single historical moment. In *Ulysses* Joyce tried to capture "the all-including chronicle" of history in a single day. In the most representative novel of all, Mann's *Magic Mountain*, the text begins with the announcement: "Only the exhaustive can be truly interesting." Mann then proceeds to illustrate the history of prewar Europe in one subjective experience, just as Joyce attempted to do in recounting a single day in the life of his protagonist in early twentieth-century Dublin.

The totalising experience was more pronounced in the modern novel than it was in philosophy. Modernism gives us words for the process by which the hero expropriates the object of his reflections, 'an objective correlative' or moment of epiphany. The conception of the objective correlative implies the vision of the connectedness of all things. The notion of epiphany that Joyce took from Aquinas draws from the totalistic vision of existence the idea that truth resides in the object that the subject must retrieve if he is to transcend his own life and thus grasp the reality behind life itself.

It was unfortunate, of course, that what began as an aesthetic and literary idea was appropriated by philosophers and politicians. If the essence of the age was contained in the subjective act whereby it is brought into consciousness, concluded Husserl, what was not 'European' would be swallowed up in the act of recognition. History was the story of man achieving a harmonious unity of becoming that corresponded historically to his transcendental being. Non-Western societies, he added in 1923, had discovered that they could survive only by becoming part of a "European cultural endeavour".[2]

Ironically the nearest Europe came to essentialising itself was when it attempted to eliminate the differences between itself and the world beyond its frontiers. Some philosophers, of course, including Heidegger, were concerned about this process. Man could only attain his true humanity, he wrote in the 1930s, through the fulfilment of historically ordained tasks. He had no doubt that in this struggle Europe held the key, that it was the continent in which "the fate of the earth is being decided". He was concerned nevertheless that "the complete Europeanisation of the earth and of man" might one day end in an ironic dilemma. Europe would have no one left to talk to. When that happened it would cease to exist in its own imagination. Its eventual fate might be to experience the decline of its own *being*.[3]

Adorno later attacked Husserl on the grounds that his reductionism was the last attempt of bourgeois man to construct a world accessible to universal reason. Husserl, however, was the first to admit that the Europeans had tried to establish the meaning of metaphysics out of fear, to ground culture on a metaphysical principle, to locate it in the flow of history by uncovering the meaning of history itself, and thus "to bind together the chain of future generations," to secure their own future by forging the future of humanity as a whole. That is why, like Heidegger, he insisted that by the early twentieth century, history had become "the Europeanisation of all other civilisations".[4]

Even before his death, however, he had begun to question whether there was a single history of mankind cast in Europe's image. Once he accepted that culture, tradition and convention defined the *Lebenswelt* or 'life-world' of a specific community, he had to recognise, however grudgingly, that each community had its own history, and that Europe's could no longer be the world's. "In the social group united with us in the community of life we arrive at secure facts . . . but when we are thrown into an alien social sphere that of the negroes of the Congo, Chinese peasants etc. . . . we discover that their truths, the facts that for them are fixed, generally verified or verifiable are by no means the same as ours".

He went further than that, for his insight that the very idea of a phenomenologically defined world, the life-world, was itself historically conditioned, that it was quintessentially European in tone, could only lead to one conclusion: that the 'Europeanisation' of the world was only a moment in history. As he wrote three years before his death, that moment was rapidly coming to an end through Europe's own actions, its tendency to tear itself apart in war. "The dream is over," he admitted at the very end of his life.

What strikes one most forcefully about contemporary Europe is the extent to which the Europeans have since discovered that their own history, to quote the philosopher Alasdair MacIntyre, is no longer universal but 'autobiographical'. The European project is not a great venturing out into the world but a disengagement from the world, a withdrawal behind the *'limes'* as it attempts to essentialise itself. In the words of a former French president, François Mitterrand, speaking in the early 1980s, Europe is "returning in its history and its geography like one who is returning home".[5]

European Essentialism

There is, however, another philosophical school in contemporary Europe that sees the life-world in larger terms. It is one whose apologists number Paul Ricoeur and Emmanuel Levinas. Both writers have been prominent in criticising the phenomenologists for regarding other people primarily as phenomena to be seen and known. Both reject the idea that issues such as responsibility are secondary to philosophical inquiry. If we are to take ethics as our first obligation, then our main concern must be the quality of our relations to other people, those at present (for example) outside the European Union. Many contemporary philosophers have begun to reject as intensely self-regarding a philosophy whose leading words are consciousness, self, identity and being.

They are much more interested in returning to the Enlightenment idea (which Marx rejected) of understanding the world, not transforming it. They have broken with an ontology that reduces everything to itself. They have shown a much more heightened interest in 'others', not merely their own subjective freedom. Their argument with Heidegger and Husserl is prompted by the latters' tendency to reduce all discourse to one totalising schema of thought. For them the task of philosophy is not to close the circle or to centralise knowledge but to keep open a plurality of discourse, to resist the temptation to make it monolingual.

Levinas, in particular, has promoted a new ethical philosophy that shows how man's relationship to man can transcend the natural search for power and belongingness in search of a Good beyond Being. His phenomenological descriptions of our finite being-in-the-world lead him ultimately beyond the limits of phenomenology to the ethics of transcendence based on the primacy of the other over the same.

Such thinking is in step with the realities of the time. Indeed it reflects them. The relationship, as usual, is a symbiotic one. Europe is in the process of *becoming* a multicultural society, one radically different from the society the United States pledged itself to defend in 1949. With the end of the Cold War a new Europe has been discovered. Two new Central European and Mediterranean worlds are beginning to emerge in the Western consciousness. Neither of them is 'Western' as the term was understood in the days of the European intellectual emigration or in the postwar years when Monnet and Schuman worked closely together. Identities are becoming more fluid and ambiguous. Europe's centre of gravity is changing. The New World and the Old are beginning to debate increasingly with themselves rather than each other. The dialogue at the heart of the Western community is beginning to be conducted in a thinner register, in a much more muted tone.

Camus and the Mediterranean World

Historically the fates of North Africa and Europe have been closely linked through war, trade and the movement of population in both directions. In ancient times we can identify a Mediterranean world, or even a West and an East in the Latin- and Greek-speaking portions, but the West included North Africa as well as Europe. With the spread of Islam North Africa became culturally and economically part of Asia. The Arabs not only created an empire in Spain that survived for 700 years but also settled the area of the present Côte d'Azur in the eighth and ninth centuries—in total for almost the same length of time that the French were later to colonise Algeria.

After the Christian reconquest of Spain the Spanish were drawn into the southern coast of the Ibero-Africa channel, occupying a number of ports in present-day Morocco. Only the conquest of the New World created what

Fernand Braudel called "one of the great missed opportunities of history". Spain, half European and half African, failed to carry out "its historical mission". For the first time in history the Strait of Gibraltar became a political frontier dividing two very different worlds. It was this lost and later repudiated conception of North Africa as a Europe bounded by the Sahara that the French fought to uphold in the 1950s war in Algeria.

Long before then, in 1937, the young Albert Camus gave a lecture in Algiers at the Maison de la Culture in which he insisted on the fundamental difference between the north European and the Mediterranean worlds, between the political doctrines elaborated in the north and the more tolerant attitudes towards life to be found in the south. It was a thesis that already anticipated the essence of the argument of his most influential book, *The Rebel.*

Camus took as his starting point the premise that European unity could only be brought about by an internationalism based no longer on ideology (on spurious political doctrines preaching the brotherhood of man) but on human needs. Its unity would lie not in essentialising the continent but in recognising its different worlds. In company with many of his contemporaries, such as André Gide and Le Corbusier, he set out to ask whether there was a distinctive Mediterranean culture within the grasp of its people. He came up with five answers.

The Mediterranean represented for him a style of life that was different from and stood in contrast to the conventional Protestant world of central and northern Europe through which he had travelled two months earlier. It would be wrong to claim—and Camus did not—that it was in any way 'superior' to that of the north. What he claimed, less reductively, was that it represented a dimension of life itself, that the Mediterranean world was to be found in north European man too, that the European was much diminished in repressing a dimension of himself.

Secondly, Camus also identified a specific 'Latinity' or Latin temperament: a refusal to sacrifice the present for a higher good; a willingness to tolerate ambiguity and difference rather than eliminate them from political life. These were the values that other writers with a close connection with Algeria such as Gide valued most about the Mediterranean as well. In Gide's case it led, despite his earlier uncritical admiration of Soviet Russia, to his later alienation after visiting it a few years before Camus's lecture. Camus contrasted this Mediterranean tolerance with the world in the north—one of order, violence and an unimaginative genius for war that characterised the German people.

Thirdly, the Mediterranean was the only theatre in Europe in which the ideas of the East met those of the West, in which the Islamic and the Christian worlds intersected. The Western Mediterranean world formed what a Spanish foreign minister was later to call "a cultural interface" between two different worlds. What was quintessentially Mediterranean about that world, Camus added, sprang from that historical encounter. The Islamic dimension had been part of European life for hundreds of years, as it had once been part of East European life until the late nineteenth century. It is becoming so again, of course, through migration.

Camus's fourth theme was the existence of what he termed "a Mediterranean collectivism". It was an unfortunate phrase, but all he meant by it was that the Mediterranean world had set a series of problems for its people to meet, a series of challenges for the future. In the late 1930s the civil war in Spain presented Europe with its first external conflict between liberalism and fascism, a dress rehearsal of the larger war that was waiting offstage. Today the Mediterranean poses a greater challenge still. Can a continent that is already both multiethnic and multiracial negotiate its transformation into a multicultural one?

Finally, and most important, the Mediterranean world represented, in Camus's words, a defence against "the lies of history". At the time he was writing, the lies of history were Marxist or fascist fables or myths battling for the soul of man. In contrast, Camus insisted, "politics are made for men and not men for politics". The Mediterranean sensibility seemed to embody that understanding.

Camus's Mediterranean, let me concede, was a European construction. When he spoke of a Mediterranean culture he used the word culture in its French meaning—a culture of language and ideas, a literary culture, a very European conception.[6]

The irony of course is that many of the traditional distinctions between Islamic and European societies, between modernity and premodernity, have been eliminated by modernity itself. French culture is also becoming more regional in its influence, confined largely to the western Mediterranean as German culture extends east once again. Ironically, this makes Camus's idea of a Mediterranean world a far more compelling theme of political life than it was at the time that he wrote.

No one can be certain of what will be the consequences for Europe as the population of the non–European Union countries of the Mediterranean doubles by 2024, making even more pronounced the per capita economic disparities that are already of the order of 10:1 between the northern and southern coasts. These accelerating problems are demographically inevitable. In an attempt to mitigate them the European Union committed itself at the 1995 Barcelona Conference to promote development across the region. But this is unlikely to be sufficient given the scale of the problem. The closeness of North Africa will continue to prompt in its inhabitants a sense of 'right of access' that will have to be addressed.

In short, what we may witness is the emergence of another Europe in which its citizens find themselves meeting up on a ground of history that would have been totally foreign to Monnet and Schuman. In time we may see a fusion of both, a new world. It will of course be one of more limited horizons. It will not be part of that wider Western community as Western Europe has been since the mid-twentieth century. It will present a particularly tough challenge, of course, for a society like France, which has long been accustomed to a high degree of cultural homogeneity and which has made the preservation of its values a dogma of its political faith.

In the end Nietzsche may be proved right. "The process of the evolving European" may lead to results that would seem to be least expected by those who today naively promote and praise it, the "apostles of modern ideas". Those apostles are the "club class" of Europe, the professional politicians and bureaucrats whose horizons tend to be delimited by the Europe of the Six, the original Common Market countries. It is that Europe that is being transformed in ways we are only just beginning to recognise, but not yet comprehend.

If that transformation is resisted, the prospects of a conflict are very high. Updating and relocating Auden's famous lines from his poem 'Spain, 1937', and taking his metaphor of delirium in the body politic, we might observe that "on that square of hot Africa", split from "inventive Europe, our fever's shapes are menacing and alive".

Rediscovering Central Europe

Contemplating the economic and social disparities between Eastern and Western Europe in 1904, the geographer Halford Mackinder pointed out what, for him, the first geopolitician of the English-speaking world, was the most significant. In a lecture that he delivered to the Royal Geographical Society entitled 'The Geopolitical Pivot of History' he noted that while the Europeans had ventured west in the sixteenth century to the New World, Russia had turned east, carrying its power and culture across Siberia. By the early twentieth century both had finally met up on the western rim of the Pacific.[7]

Mackinder himself was not an inward-looking man. Far from it. He was even briefly a politician when he was appointed Allied High Commissioner for south Russia during the Russian civil war. After the Allies pulled out of Russia the following year, of course, they disengaged completely, leaving Eastern Europe at the mercy of Germany and Russia, the two powers with whom the West was later principally engaged. What is so important about Mackinder's vision was that it totally excluded the Eastern European world. This remained the case until the very end of the Cold War. The East Europeans were simply excised from the consciousness of the geopoliticians who followed where Mackinder had led.

It has been Eastern Europe's misfortune to be excluded from that European consciousness for most of its history. It was definitely not part of the 'Western world'—the West—that the Allied powers pledged themselves to defend in 1949 when they signed the Atlantic Treaty. Take, for example, a handbook of Western civilisation that was completed by a Chicago historian in the same year and was typical of the genre. There were small subsections on "the peoples of Western Europe", including unspecified Indo-European tribesmen. But there was none on the peoples of Eastern Europe in any period of history. There were scattered references to the Slavic or Slavonic people but no indication that they represented the largest of Europe's Indo-European groups. And though there were chapters on Western Christendom, there were none on the Eastern Christian world.[8] The book was an excellent example of the extent to which, in the minds of most historians, the East simply did not exist as a significant entity.

The collapse of communism not only freed Eastern and Central Europe from Soviet control; it also made a number of countries eligible for membership in such defining Western institutions as NATO. It is clear why governments in Prague and Warsaw are so keen to join these organisations, from which they are still excluded. They wish to reenter the Western imagination. As Czech President Václav Havel put it with his usual eloquence in 1994: "If we in [the] post-communist countries call for a new order, if we appeal to the West not to close itself off to us . . . this is not because we are concerned about our own security and stability. We are concerned about the destiny of the values and principles that communism denied and in whose name we resisted [it] and ultimately brought it down . . . the traditional values of Western civilisation".[9]

It is quite consistent with history for the East Europeans to ask where they figure in the Western imagination. Europe has always been a construct of its historical consciousness rather than an obvious single cultural, geographical or even economic expression. As the Swiss writer Denis de Rougemont wrote in a seminal work, *The Idea of Europe* (1966), "to search for Europe is to find it".

What makes Europe 'European' is that it is conscious of its own existence. What makes it impossible, by contrast, to speak of Asian values, or even Asia as a single cultural unit, is that Asia does not live in its own imagination. Europe does—and that is what makes it definingly European.

Before the West Europeans referred to Europe at all, of course, they talked of Christendom. As late as the Treaty of Utrecht in 1713, treaties often referred to Europe as a 'Christian republic'. It was of course a Latin, not an Eastern construction. It was the Latin Christian kingdoms that went to war in the Crusades and who expressed no guilt in plundering Constantinople in 1204, even though it was the centre of Eastern Christendom.

When the word Europe first began to replace Christendom in the mid-seventeenth century, it was a reflection of a new consciousness. Europe differed from the barbarians (such as the Turks) in terms of technology. It could defend itself against barbarian incursions as it had not been able to in the past. As Edward Gibbon wrote much later, to conquer Europe the barbarians would need European technology. To develop that technology themselves they would have had to cease to be barbarous. The defeat of the Turks before Vienna in 1683 was the last time a major European city was attacked by a non-European power.

It is significant, however, that the Poles who helped to liberate the city received very little thanks. Poland could not prevent itself from being partitioned three times in the course of the eighteenth century by its three neighbours, including Austria, which remained singularly ungrateful for its own rescue a century earlier.

Hegel unintentionally sanctioned this act by removing the whole of Eastern Europe from the Western imagination. In *The Philosophy of History* he insisted that only a people who were a significant part of 'History' could consider themselves to be historically important. All others were without history. They had nothing to say to the world. Their cultures were particularistic and geographically bound.

Hegel felt able to dismiss the Slavs with some brief comments:

> These people did indeed found kingdoms and sustain spirited conflict with the various nations they came across. Sometimes as an advance guard—an intermediate nationality—they took part in the struggle between Christian Europe and un-Christian Asia. The Poles even liberated Vienna from the Turks; and the Slavs have to some extent been drawn within the sphere of Occidental reason. Yet this entire body of people remain excluded from our consideration because hitherto it has not appeared as an independent element in the series of phases that Reason has assumed in the world.[10]

When Hegel denied that anything that happened in Eastern Europe was part of History he was not denying that interesting things had happened there from time to time. He was only asserting what rapidly became a Western *idée reçue*, that the history of the region was without significance in the grand scheme of things, in that "bloody dialectic" of war and revolution that History had become.

What is significant is that many East European thinkers agreed with Hegel in their moments of deepest gloom and introspection. As Mr. Nagy tells the hero of Zsigmond Moricz's novel *Be Faithful unto Death* (1921), the Hungarians had always been sidelined by history even though on two occasions they had saved the West from Asiatic invasions. It took the Magyar tribes a millennium to leave the depths of Asia and migrate to Europe, where they settled in the Carpathian Valley. As for the second thousand years, the first great calamity was the Mongol invasion of 1241:

> The Mongols didn't get past Hungary. That was always our destiny: we were the ones who had to stop the hordes from the East. Hungary was always the

last battleground. It was the bastion where the Asiatic hordes had to stop. Isn't that amazing, that the Hungarians should have come here from the East to protect the West from the Easterners. ... The alien westerners have remained strangers for a thousand years and have despised us.

What was true of the Mongols was equally true of the Turks, who inflicted a decisive defeat on the Hungarians at the Battle of Mohacs in 1526, leaving the middle third of the country to be ruled by the foreign invaders for the next century and a half. "Isn't it terrible," Nagy remarks, that "we are here in the middle of Europe . . . and that there isn't a single other nation . . . who understands our language. We are condemned to be on our own".[11]

It is ironic that the novel I have just cited with its deeply felt reference to "alien westerners . . . who have always despised us" was serialised in *Nyugat* (or *West*), which was both the title and the political credo of the country's most significant literary magazine between the wars. Moricz was expressing a widely held aspiration to be included in the history of a world that seemed to make its history on its terms, not anyone else's.

It was the misfortune of Moricz's generation, of course, to be condemned to live in the shadow of the invaders from the East after the Second World War, the third wave of 'barbarians' battering at the gates. "Asia begins on the Elbe", Konrad Adenauer concluded in the late 1940s. Even the Americans, those "gentle barbarians", as Thomas Mann called them when living among his neighbours in Pacific Palisades, were considered definingly un-European even if they were Western. The humiliation of Europe's division led to the creation of the European Common Market, a "civilising process" that was intended to render Europe at peace with itself for the first time.

It was of course a process that merely highlighted the incivility that existed behind the Iron Curtain. The Hungarian critic István Bibó was quite right, writing in 1946, to suspect that the West Europeans were inclined to dismiss their Eastern neighbours as a people defined by "an innate barbarism", a people who were as much a danger to Western Europe as they were to themselves.

The Second World War threatened the Central European identity that had established itself briefly in the Western imagination. Not only did it divide the continent politically into two opposing ideological blocs, but also it destroyed the cultural bridge that had existed in the early years of the century. When Thomas Mann, for example, visited Budapest in 1937 he was welcomed by the Hungarian poet Attila Jozsef not only as a German but also as a European, an important consolation for a man who could no longer be proud of his own country.[12] When Husserl had given his lecture series 'Crisis of European Humanity' two years earlier he had voiced his defence of the German idea of *Lebenswelt* (of a life beyond the horizon) to the two audiences to which he felt closest—to those who were part of a German-speaking world, to the intellectual circles of Prague and Vienna. How could he have done otherwise when it was a world that had produced Kafka, Musil, Broch, Gombrowicz and Freud, men who more than anyone else in the West had stamped their own authority on the early twentieth century.

That was the world that was sundered from the West after 1945. The geopolitical division of Europe separated even Vienna from Western Europe and made the great cities of Budapest and Prague closer to Moscow than to Paris. The disappearance of the Jewish communities, which had given the region so much of its cosmopolitanism and literature in the interwar years, also contributed to its intellectual sterility.

The division of Europe produced three responses. The first was a tendency to emphasise what made Eastern Europe different from the West. When Béla Bartók used the expression 'Eastern Europe' he was staking out a claim that Hungarian music, which is pentatonic and Asian in origin, was a distinct and autonomous entity, that it had more in common with the Slav folk legacy of the Danubian tribes than with the musical heritage of Western Europe. It was not a response of course that recommended itself to the majority of his countrymen, especially after the Soviet invasion of 1956.

A second response was to deny that there was any division between East and West, that culturally Eastern Europe was still part of the Western cultural tradition, notwithstanding its political divisions. It was consistent with the earlier reaction against Vienna among Croatian intellectuals like Miroslav Krleza who had always looked to Paris not Vienna, and regarded Freud and Kafka as provincial writers. It was a questionable strategy, of course, because it denied what made Central Europe interesting—its own unique contribution to European culture, one that was different from that of the West but no less authentically European all the same.[13]

The third response that gained ground in the 1970s was the rediscovery of what made East European culture European and not Soviet. The reaction of writers such as György Konrád in Hungary and Václav Havel in Czechoslovakia was a natural response to decades of Soviet social realism and antidecadentism in the arts. It took a very pro-European form, for it stressed the power of a culture that could not be silenced even when writers lived in exile, like Kundera, or were marginalised, like Konrád, or briefly imprisoned, like Havel.

Denied a chance to settle in Paris or Vienna or Berlin, isolated from the cultural hinterland of Western Europe, writers such as the Hungarian György Mihály Vajda championed Hungarian literature as a striking affirmation of his country's European credentials. It was a 'virtual Europe', of course, as it had to be because the reality of political oppression cut off Hungary from any other links except economic.

In the words of the Serbian writer Danilo Kis, writing in 1986, Eastern Europe had been caught between two kinds of reductionism: ideological after 1945 and nationalistic before it. Though tempted by both in the course of the twentieth century, Central Europe's intellectuals had realised very late that the ideal of being part of Europe lay in neither. They found their legitimacy instead in a language and culture, "that strange, mysterious consolation" spoken of by Kafka.[14] Small nations tend to emphasise their cultural identity. If they are more intense in expressing it than, say, the Germans or the French, that is because at one time or another they have had to live with the reality of their disappearance or extinction. Larger cultures, for the most part, have not.

The awareness of belonging to a culture known as Central Europe was ultimately an act of dissent. The writers who stressed their country's close association with the West, once they were exiled or imprisoned, were left with nothing but their language. It was the mark of their exile. Language was destiny, added Kis. It was inevitable that once the Berlin Wall fell it would be Central Europe's destiny to rejoin Europe as a world with its own unique heritage.

The East Europeans, or those in the first wave of NATO expansion, will begin rejoining Europe in 1999. Their admission has given the alliance a normative as well as a pragmatic purpose. The reasons for including Poland, the Czech Republic and Hungary are not that different from the decision to forge NATO in 1949. Fifty years ago the U.S. Senate Foreign Relations Committee recommended ratifying the Atlantic Treaty as the best way of rescuing the West Europeans from "a haunting sense of insecurity". Membership in NATO, it added, would enable them to plan "with confidence in the future."

The same process is under way in Eastern Europe. The changes since 1989 are not irreversible. In the late 1940s the French and the Italian voters were tempted to endorse communist parties in general elections. The possibility of the same threat in the East today is not that remote, even if the new communism is likely to be more populist than ideological. Membership in NATO is a way of anchoring the new democracies in the Western world, at the same time as giving the West itself a historical role.

What seems to be in the offing, however, is not the expansion of the Western Alliance as it was conceived in 1949. What seems to be in the air is the creation of a European security community to which Russia itself may one day be admitted, a much looser alignment of European states, something that may absorb or replace sometime in the future the Organisation for Security and Co-operation in Europe (OSCE).

The Berlin communiqué of June 1996 has increased the pace towards establishing a European security identity inside NATO. It has given credence to the concept of Combined Joint Task Forces (CJTFs). France's intention to rejoin the integrated military command will force the pace still further. NATO's intervention in Bosnia also saw its willingness to work together with other, non-alliance members—including, significantly, Russia. The evolution of a pan-European security community would significantly transform the security environment.

Two different but complementary entities are beginning to emerge. In the West, the European Union appears to be evolving into a 'hard core' of countries linked by an indissoluble monetary union, with Britain and other peripheral countries outside. In the East, the Commonwealth of Independent States (CIS) is similar; it has its own 'hard core'—Russia and Belarus—with the other former Soviet republics on its periphery but within its sphere.

Many of the countries in between are likely to find themselves in Western institutions, but as part of a new security relationship between Germany and Russia based on a common desire to exclude the United States from Europe. It is not at all clear in the long run whether this would be unwelcome to the Americans themselves. Germany, after all, is a country with which the United States can work perfectly well (as it could not in 1914 or 1939). If little has come of the security partnerships offered by both Presidents Clinton and Bush in 1989 and 1994, this is due, in part, to German reluctance to get involved in military operations. Since 1991, however, there has been a serious drive on the part of the German government to achieve the same military status as its allies. A true partnership with the United States would require Germany to play a more active role still, to overcome its historical reticence. In the debate on whether Germany should send forces to enforce the Dayton accords Chancellor Kohl spoke of the national honour. A nation can only speak with a decisive voice if it has a distinctive identity and the self-confidence to assert it. In the past both have been lacking. There are signs, however, that this is about to change. Once again Germany holds the key to the future of Europe.

The German Problem Revisited

The population looks on greedily through the windows. Culture is advancing again . . . the defeated are well provided for. A transatlantic bishop arrives and murmurs: my brethren. A humanist appears and chants: the West.
—Gottfried Benn (1947)

After Germany's defeat in 1918, Max Weber wrote that the German people needed "an educator" to teach them to make something out of their experience.[15] They did not get one. Instead they challenged the West for a second time and almost destroyed themselves in the attempt. Forty years later that consciousness appears to have been transformed.

Countries do, of course, still regard themselves in a certain light as hardworking, or militarily proficient, or technologically advanced. But a histor-

ical character can change over time, as was shown by one of the most com-
prehensive surveys of public opinion ever conducted. By the 1980s the
German people had begun to judge their virtues by a different set of categories from those they had employed in the past. Military proficiency was
rarely mentioned despite the fact that when the poll was conducted the
Cold War was still far from over and Germany itself was still in the front
line. Instead they valued cultural and technological inventiveness as their
most important national attribute. Technologically they considered themselves to be far superior to the Soviet Union. In terms of culture, however,
they rated their principal ally, the United States, far inferior to themselves.
Most significant of all, they considered the Russians to be their cultural
equal, a far cry from their view in the 1930s, when they had been encouraged to see all Slavs as no better than semi-Asiatic savages.[16]

If Heidegger once called Germany "the most metaphysical of nations",
the German people now seem disinclined to reconstitute themselves as a
community with an existential mission. They seem unwilling to repossess
the past and thus secure the future by asserting themselves historically.
Economic success has become its own reward. They seem to have little interest in realising their 'moment' or 'destiny'. They are no longer disposed
to see history in apocalyptic terms.

In short, Germany has experienced the same transformation of historical
consciousness as every other European country. If Max Weber thought that
the West had become "religiously unmusical", that it no longer had an ear
attuned to God, it has become historically unmusical since. It is no longer
attuned to the great historical ideas or political texts that haemorrhaged
into Europe's consciousness in the course of the twentieth century and in
the process plunged it into war.

In Germany's case, of course, this change of heart was self-conscious. It
was largely a strategy of survival. Germany needed to be accepted into the
community of states that made up the West. The only opportunity left to
the Germans after the war, writes the historian Michael Sturmer, was to
play the West's game, to be the most European of the European powers,
and to become one of the most Atlanticist at the same time.[17]

In the immediate postwar years the philosopher Karl Jaspers insisted that
there could be no turning back, that the new German state would have to
forswear some of its traditional ways of thinking if it was ever to recover its
soul. In an interview with *Der Spiegel* in 1965, Jaspers reiterated the central
theme of his book *The Question of German Guilt* (1947), namely, the need
"for every German to transform his approach to the world". For Jaspers
the way to do this was to become part of a Western consensus, or what
Hannah Arendt, who arranged for the book to be translated into English,
described at the time as "the harmony that can be felt to exist from
America to all the European countries".[18]

Europe was the other club. Of the two, it was far more important in the eyes of the politicians and even the public at large. As a people the Germans are likely to remain far more committed to the European project than they are to the Western. The European orientation of its elites, the commercialisation of its culture and what Jürgen Habermas calls its "constitutional republicanism", in short, its *bourgeoisification,* will not easily be reversed. But then again Germany can afford to remain European if only because it is well on the way to effectively institutionalising its power. Most of the proposals currently mooted for a federal Europe are modelled on German institutions. The European Court of Justice is a version of Germany's Constitutional Court. A future European Bank will be modelled on the Bundesbank. To these institutions one could add the principle of 'subsidiarity', which was included in the Maastricht Treaty as a copy of the German *Länder* system.

In economic terms the German economy accounts for more than a quarter of Europe's gross national product as well as a quarter of its intracommunity trade. Faced with that scale of influence all the Europeans can do is to persuade the Germans themselves to give up the deutsche mark, not so much in an attempt to control German decisionmaking as to dilute it into a European decisionmaking process.

It is more difficult, however, to be equally sanguine about Germany's continued membership in the *Western* community. Even before unification there were writers who saw the Federal Republic not as a country but as an atonement for the past, a society with responsibilities but not interests, a community that had been co-opted into the West, of which it was not really part. It was a price that some writers considered too high. The Federal Republic, complained Heidegger, was a country that existed to teach the German people how not to be German. As a state it was expected to stand forever in the shadow of the Third Reich. It was denied the right to 'become' something other than what the Allies had made it in 1949. It was a strange state of "being", he concluded, when a country was denied the right to "become" something else.

Heidegger died in 1976. As long as the Cold War persisted his complaint failed to strike a popular chord. Since reunification his dissatisfaction has found an echo across the political spectrum. As the respected British commentator Timothy Garton Ash noted in 1994, just because Germany has shifted westwards geographically it does not necessarily follow that it will move in that direction culturally as well.[19] Indeed, only now, adds Zbigniew Brzezinski, "has the great test come for Germany's ties to the West since the East no longer exists in the political sense but only as a collective hardship case. . . . Now we will see whether the oft-extolled Western Community of states will collapse, whether . . . the West's cohesion was simply a useful idea, or whether it is a reality in which the Germans can also feel at home in the future".[20]

Some of the most prominent writers on German foreign policy have contrasting views about which destiny the new Germany will choose. Let me mention three of them.

Germany, writes Timothy Garton Ash, will probably choose not to choose. True to its foreign policy tradition, the government in Bonn will choose to look in every direction at once.[21] A similar prediction has been made by Josef Joffe, the leading foreign affairs correspondent for the *Süddeutsche Zeitung*:

> Like many other countries [Germany] is battling a paradigm change that seems to indicate that the classical goals of foreign policy are no longer pertinent. Territory used to be of prime importance. Today, additional land more often means more over-production in the agrarian sector, more subventions, more taxes etc., a decrease in welfare. Welfare not warfare is the name of the game. In such circumstances there can be no clear foreign policy. . . . In the postmodern world . . . Germany will try to increase options and reduce commitments.[22]

A very different prediction has been made by Hans Peter Schwarz, a professor of political science and contemporary history who believes that in the future, Germany will find itself compelled on objective grounds to make its foreign policy more self-centred in the service of a national interest, more narrowly defined.[23]

There is something to be said for all three predictions. What should also be taken into account is that in periods of anxiety or uncertainty such as that through which the Germans are passing as the twentieth century draws to a close, nations often seek to reaffirm their sense of community. The challenge the German people face is no longer what it was in 1949: to reinvent themselves (as Alfred Weber put it), to make themselves as Western as possible. The challenge today is to defend themselves against the threat of 'Easternisation' as they grapple with the horrendously high social costs of integrating East Germany (now running at DM2,300 per second) as well as the fallout from the eventual integration of Central Europe into the European Union. Will this entail Germany's progressive de-Westernisation—a return to the cultural first principles of the past?

Unfortunately, reunification has not made the Germans feel either happier or more secure. It has made them all too aware of the deep social divisions that still obtain between the East and the West Germans. By 1996 unification had cost the taxpayer DM1,000 billion in net transfers to the east, a staggering sum that has created neither the promised era of prosperity in the east nor achieved the political objective of giving the German people the sense that they live in a united community. It has also added 17 million more poor people to the national population, refugees from a bankrupt, inefficient industrial sector and a ruined housing stock.

Unification has created a severe social malaise. Westerners are upset at having to finance a 'solidarity' tax for the reconstruction of the eastern economy; East Germans have become disillusioned at the social costs of freedom, the most important of which is structural unemployment, which may last well into the next century. In short, the German people have become disenchanted and concerned about their future. A wall of mutual resentment has replaced the old Berlin Wall.

In fact even before the end of the Cold War many of the old themes that distinguished German history in the early twentieth century had begun to reemerge. The Germany struggling to be born in the postwar era was heir to impulses that it only half understood. It is naive to think that forty-five years of economic competence alone could be spiritually rewarding. Old tendencies are transmitted at the deepest level of a culture. That is where we should look for them. What could be identified in the closing years of the Cold War was an undertow of redemptive yearning, a wish to be exceptional of necessity, not choice—once again to be 'German'.

On the Right a number of politicians declared that the country's Western integration was an ideological façade that had outlived its usefulness. On the Left many writers as early as the 1950s 'rediscovered' a much older debate when intellectuals such as Alfred Anders had supported a humanistic socialism and Jacob Kaiser a fusion of Christian-Socialist elements in both East and West. Both writers had located Germany in between two worlds, no less forcefully than earlier writers such as Max Weber who had located German culture between the two very different worlds of Anglo-American materialism and Russian authoritarianism.

Let me tease out three themes that coloured the debate in the 1980s. The first was a suspicion of the United States, which also took the form of a criticism of modernity, specifically in its American version. Upon returning from East Berlin, where he had been West Germany's permanent representative, Günter Grass complained that the Federal Republic had paid a high price for becoming politically, culturally and economically part of a Western world with which it had never really identified before 1949. It had lost something of its "essential substance" in the process, a sense of community as a nation.[24]

Another theme resonant of Germany's past was the idea of a political community based on a national mission. In 1983 the radical writer Rudolf Bahro insisted on seeing the peace movement as a way of integrating nationalist emotions into an entirely new vision of society, as a way of "fusing together" the ideas of direct democracy and the community, and thus rescuing the country from the "unpatriotic capitalism" demanded of it by its membership in the West.[25]

Even on the Right similar voices were to be heard. In his book *The German Nation* Bernard Willms explored the possibility of developing "a new nationalism" based on German idealism and its rejection of Western liberalism. Willms was an interesting writer who openly appealed to Carl Schmitt's philosophy of self assertion—the idea of 'self' based on the differences rather than similarities between political communities. Like others on the Right, he wanted to build a new national ideal that would transcend the liberal constitutionalism at the heart of Germany's postwar political system.[26]

This longing for the politics of the general interest, this search for a suprapolitical communal idea in which interest parties would play no part, was an important attitudinal seed of the Green movement, satisfying as it did the need for a cause that seemed to stand above the bourgeois, materialist political world that had made the Federal Republic in the eyes of many of its leading intellectuals a mere *Ersatzvaterland*.

A third theme that reemerged was Heidegger's complaint that the Federal Republic was not a proper state. As the French philosopher Philippe Lacoue-Labarthe observed at the time, Germany existed in the Cold War only in the act of not existing in the German people's imagination.[27] "The denationalization of our country has almost reached the limits of the absurd", complained one conservative writer. Another observed that Germany had been denied a suitable peace settlement after the war. It had thus been robbed of the most fundamental right of self-determination.[28]

What all of these disparate themes shared in common was a growing preoccupation with what made Germany quintessentially 'German'. Today that debate has been joined by writers who remained largely silent in the Cold War years. For the German playwright Botho Strauss, a nation is only as strong as its sense of community or 'togetherness'. Strauss is no longer what he was in the 1970s, a child of the Frankfurt school. He is a born-again nationalist who believes that the modern German state is inauthentic, that it actually produces disenchantment because it is what the Allies made it in 1949—the construction of rational thought. A true community for him is a historically rooted one, a society that lives by myths. History "does not call for a disgusting and ridiculous masquerade of dog-like imitation, nor does it call for a slide into the second-hand shop of the history of mischief. It requires a different act of rebellion: one against the total domination of the present which weeds out and deprives the individual of any *presence* of unenlightened past, of historical coming-into-being, of mystical time".[29]

Strauss cannot be easily translated into English. And an English reader will find his sentiments no less foreign than the language in which they are expressed. Nevertheless they have roots in the thought of early-twentieth-century writers such as Tönnies. They also echo the empirical conservative English school of Burke and Oakeshott, despite a romantic gloss that insists that a nation must find a sense of 'enchantment' against a hostile market and the constant threat of technological change that threatens to dispossess a people of its historical birthright.

Traces of such thinking are to be found in the works of other writers who have abandoned the Left such as Hans Magnus Enzensberger, or the historian Walter Grossheim, who argues that his country's Western orientation "is not necessarily the result of rational decisions but rather a dogmatism founded and perpetuated by both liberal and conservative intellectuals".[30] They are important because they represent a typical German response to modernity that never really disappeared, even in the days when the Federal Republic was most self-confident, in the 1960s. It is still possible that the German response to history will be different from that of France, that in the end some of the old German cultural assumptions will be reasserted, albeit in a very different historical context.

Let me return to the circumstances that made Germany 'Western' and 'European' at the same time, those higher identities in which the Germans were instructed to believe as a passport to their readmission to the international community. Circumstances have changed, as Nietzsche would have been the first to recognise. When he spoke of a nation's genealogy he insisted that nations do not evolve into a predetermined or retrospectively determined community. A people's destiny cannot be mapped out in advance.

Early in the next century continued membership in the Western Alliance may offer Germany an *a*historical perspective. It may confront it with a history whose function is to compose and finally reduce the diversity of time into a totality fully closed upon itself, a historical foreclosure. It may be more sensible to admit that history is a process of social and political evolution that gives rise to conflicts of ideas that in turn generate different historical movements.

As David Calleo warned back in the 1970s, just as we cannot understand the present without a knowledge of the past, so we cannot really understand the past without anticipating the future. As we contemplate that future it cannot be taken for granted that the present condition of Europe or of Germany will be fixed indefinitely. Even if the integration of Europe does go ahead German thinking may be more influential than it was in the past. Europe may become a German rather than a French cultural entity. The upshot for the Anglo-American world would be profound, for this would effectively mark the end of the Western project. As Calleo warned, the German Problem might one day be transformed into the European Problem, "an appropriately Hegelian revenge upon the Anglo-Saxon victors".[31]

Conclusion

In retrospect we can see that the French hoped by essentialising Europe to construct a two-pillar alliance, with the United States and Europe as equal partners. It was to have been a community based on a respect for each other's cultures rather than a mute accommodation with the prevailing norms of the Anglo-American world. The French now find themselves overtaken by events. The world is changing fast. In the Islamic hinterland of Europe and the borderlands of Germany the Europeans are beginning to confront a new demand of history, that they reinvent themselves.

Camus anticipated a world in which Europe would be 'other' than it was in the 1930s, in which the austere nationalism of the Protestant north would play much less of a part. The reconciliation between France and Germany after 1950 was indeed an attempt to refashion Europe along different lines. But Germany is changing as much as France. If France is being asked to reinvent itself, Germany is being challenged to rediscover aspects of its own past that have been forgotten in its obsessive pursuit of a Western identity. Neither of these demands will transform either society into something radically different from what they are now. But they may change the accent of their policies; they may force both countries to revalue themselves in ways that are not consistent with the roles they have sought to play during the past forty years.

France and Germany are not being asked to abandon their internationalist agendas, but they are being asked to define them less reductively. They are being asked to show greater imaginative empathy with their neighbours who have been on the outside looking in for so long. The problem is that both France and Germany have embraced their old missions with such enthusiasm that they are in danger of neglecting what those missions were supposed to accomplish. Central Europe cannot be left outside the Atlantic Alliance without betraying what the West said it was trying to accomplish: the freedom of the satellite European states. The attempt to construct a European superstate must also inevitably discriminate against the 'second-class' Europeans seeking a way in.

The new Europe awaits its moment of awakening. If it is delayed the United States is unlikely to remain the European power we know today, for it too is experiencing many of the same pressures, though in a rather different form, as we shall see in the next chapter.

6

The (Re)Construction of the United States

Each man prefaced his commination service with "I am an American by birth ... an American from way back". It must be an awful thing to live in a country where you have to explain that you really belong there.

— Rudyard Kipling, *American Notes* (1891)

Papini's way of loving America was to thrash it into consciousness.

— German Arciniegas, *America in Europe:
A History of the New World in Reverse* (1986)

In 1869 the writer Mark Twain set out to search for the archetypes and differences between Americans and Europeans in the hope of discovering an authentic American identity and thus determining what made his countrymen different from the Europeans. He concluded his account of his travels on a note of resignation. America was everything Europe was too. All that Americans such as himself could do was to return to Europe, chipping away at the fragments of their past, at a culture to which they clearly belonged.

His journey ended in Egypt with him standing before the Sphinx (memory and retrospect wrought in a tangible form). He stood in silence until he saw on its jaw "an excrescence of some kind". Further perusal revealed it to be a fellow tourist, an American, who was clambering over the monument in search of a souvenir. "We heard the familiar clink of a hammer and understood at once—he was chipping away at America".[1]

These were the days when 90 percent or more of immigrants to the United States came from Europe. Today 90 percent of immigrants, nearly a million a year, come to its shores from Latin America and the Pacific. The upshot is the growth of a multicultural society that may swiftly lose contact with its European roots. By the year 2050 today's ethnic minorities will be in the majority.[2]

A nation of course is constantly renewing itself. It is not a single personality. As Jules Michelet wrote of France, a country is a multitude of personalities that are in constant flux.[3] The problem for the United States is that, as the most modern society in history, it is witnessing changes faster than ever before. Many Americans have begun to complain that as their country becomes increasingly multicultural it may also become increasingly 'un-Western'.

Their first fear is that multiculturalism will prove to be politically divisive. The new Americans will have little interest in what happens in Europe. The United States will remain European for a long time by virtue of its culture. Nevertheless, in determining its own identity 'the West' will no longer be its principal frame of reference as it has been since 1941. The point of reference is likely to be Asia or Latin America.

The second fear is that today's patterns of immigration may divide the nation socially and economically, compromising in the process its ability to defend the Western world. Unless present trends are reversed, warns one writer, the United States will become a Third World country. Leaving aside the homeless, the number of working poor is increasingly dramatically. In the inner cities the infant mortality rate is rising and life expectancy decreasing. Ten percent of the population now owns 90 percent of the nation's wealth. These are not the conditions, he writes, that are normally associated with the developing world.[4]

These days Americans tend to be more upbeat about their future. They no longer fear the 'Third Worldisation' of the United States, but some do fear the growth of a Third World in the inner cities, a predicament that may make the nation much more introspective and isolationist than it is at present.

A third fear not always stated, but nonetheless often entertained, is that the United States will no longer represent everything that has made the West 'Western'—the defence of a particular version of civilisation and civil life. As America changes, its citizens are unlikely to be inspired by the claim made by President Bush that the United States is a contract with history, "a promise to the world implicit in the words of its Declaration of Independence". Nor are they likely to be reassured that America will continue to be based on what Bush's secretary of state once termed America's 'Enlightenment spirit', the spirit of the eighteenth-century philosophes whose own writings were so essential to the vision of what the founding fathers wanted their creation to become.[5]

One traveller to the United States, G. K. Chesterton, predicted when he returned to England in 1922 that this would happen. He could not conclude his account, he told his readers, without testifying to his belief that America's ultimate test would come at the end of the century, "when eighteenth century ideas formulated in an eighteenth century language [had] no longer in themselves the power to hold all those pagan passions back".[6] Of the eighteenth-century ideas that Chesterton may have had in mind, three ideas the United States had of itself were instrumental in confirming Americans in their 'Western' identity. Let me discuss each of these themes in turn.

America and Its Atlantic Identity

The idea that without a purpose or role in history the Americans would have nothing to say to the world was particularly disturbing to the generation that emerged into the Cold War. Throughout their history Americans have had a great deal to say about their association with Europe. The United States often saw itself as a pilot project of the Enlightenment whose fate was to become more European than it was already. The New World, complained the poet William Carlos Williams, was "the inspired invention of European thought", and looked as though it would remain so indefinitely.

In the early years of the Cold War that sense of identity became central to America's self-understanding. We have seen already how the German-Americans differed from their compatriots in their objection to Anglo-American universalism, or what the radical writer Randolph Bourne called the colonisation of American foreign policy, its 'Magyarisation'. In the 1920s even the Italian immigrants were suspect because of their ideological affiliations (more supposed, to be sure, than real): their alleged association with anarchism, socialism and radicalism, which came to a head with the Sacco-Vanzetti affair.

It is deeply ironical, therefore, that the Americans were brought into the Atlantic world in part through the immigration of thousands of German thinkers in the 1930s, the refugees from Hitler's New Order. Never before in its history had America attracted an intellectual elite to its shores. The result was portentous. Even on its own, predicted Thorstein Veblen in 1918: "The outlook would seem to be that the Americans are to be brought into a central place in the republic of learning". The arrival of Central European émigrés speeded up the process dramatically. Almost twenty-five years later, in June 1941, Veblen's forecast appeared on the cover of the annual report of the Emergency Committee in Aid of Displaced Foreign Scholars, an organisation that assisted thousands of refugees to establish themselves in American institutions of higher learning.[7]

The United States did indeed move to the centre of European thinking through this unique emigration. It found itself the home of some of the great centres of European intellectual life—the Vienna Circle, which had influenced thought on mathematics, linguistics and philosophy; the Institute of Mathematics at Göttingen; many members of the Frankfurt school; and almost the entire staff of the Berlin School of Politics. Even the leaders of Gestalt psychology joined the migration.

The Europeans themselves looked upon the emigration with a faint sense of foreboding. Two German writers recognised from the first that something momentously important was happening. "Strangely sterile those Semitic intellectuals are, but think themselves very superior and global", complained the German poet Gottfried Benn in 1939, on the eve of the war. But a few years earlier when the first refugees began to leave for the New World, he had seen them in a very different light as "an aristocratic milieu" that was "superior and un-Nordic".[8]

The playwright Bertolt Brecht also recognised the significance of the exodus. "Emigration is the best school of dialectics. Refugees are the keenest dialecticians", he claimed in his *Refugee Dialogues:* "They are refugees as a result of change, and their sole object of study is change".[9] Brecht believed that they had involved their adopted country in a historic dialectic with the Old World from which they had fled. They had made their own unique contribution to the dialectics of the West, that unique colloquy among its members.

First, the refugees brought to America a quality totally consistent with the American character, a willingness to see the world in terms of change. With the exception of the Gestalt psychologists, who were unable to find a permanent position in the graduate departments of psychology and therefore unable to keep alive their own tradition, most of them succeeded in placing themselves at the heart of American intellectual life. In the words of Edward Shils, they "brought the awareness of the possibility of decay of the social order, and the possibility of disruption of what once seemed stable". They were among the first to warn the Americans of the danger of events in the outside world that were beginning to force themselves into their consciousness.[10]

They were among the first to find themselves involved in one of the most profound changes in history: a change of consciousness in how America began to see itself and the world. In the 1950s American writers were challenged by the émigrés in their midst to take the 'idea' of America much further—into the realm of *Western* history rather than, as in the nineteenth century, to create a non-Western history for themselves. As another émigré, Theodor Adorno, later wrote, their presence in the United States forced Americans of all political faiths to "search for fresh concepts not yet encompassed by the general pattern".[11] One of those concepts (to which Adorno himself was opposed) was the creation of a Western community.

Secondly, the émigrés were members of a specific generation that they themselves did much to fashion. Karl Mannheim, one of many who settled in England rather than the New World, was fascinated all his life by the his-

torical and sociological conditions by which individual members of a generation become conscious of their common situation and what makes this
consciousness the basis of their group solidarity.

The generation that escaped from Germany and Central Europe in the
1930s was conscious of its own importance in the conflict that was about
to unfold. It achieved so much because it was so self-confident. Its members
had the confidence of the survivor. As Alfred Kazin describes: "It was the
best of times for Jewish intellectuals who, as Rob Lowell said with as much
truth as spite 'were unloading their European baggage'. Yes, we Jews were
older; we embodied 'the school of experience'; we had been centre stage at
all the great intellectual dramas and political traumas of the century".[12]

In that respect the exiles challenged the Americans to be more conscious
of themselves as well as of what they were meant to accomplish in history.
If Brecht can speak for the refugees as men interested in change, Mannheim
can speak of them in terms of a communication between the different members of the Western community. The role of the exile, Mannheim wrote,
was "to serve as a living interpreter between different cultures and to create
communications between different worlds which have so far been kept
apart".[13] Of no two societies was this probably more true than America
and Europe. In no country was this 'communication' more important than
in the United States, a country that during the exodus from Germany had
retreated into isolationism.

The refugees added a third dimension to American life. Many, like
Hannah Arendt, moved from philosophy to political theory, from a life of
contemplation to that of action, and to the recognition that the 'political' in
the twentieth century had an urgency that could no longer be denied. The
ideas of the émigrés were fundamentally shaped, after all, by their experience of political repression.

Their personal encounter with totalitarianism demanded commitment
and engagement, and ultimately the mobilisation of the democratic West. It
was an antidote to what they saw as the naive liberalism, the dangerous
moral relativism and the facile historical optimism that had characterised
the American political science tradition in the period that followed the First
World War.

Their commitment also took the form of coining the ideological currency
of these years. At Chicago Hans Morgenthau and Leo Strauss did much to
invent the language of American realpolitik, or realism. Hannah Arendt
was the first to coin the term 'totalitarianism' to express the new adversary
with which her adopted country would soon find itself engaged.

Once the Cold War began in earnest, of course, it became essential to
produce an ideological consensus that would unite an ethnically diverse nation. In 1950 Samuel Eliot Morison, the president of the American
Historical Association, complained that the isolationist school of histori-

ans, of which Charles Beard had been the leading luminary, had left the younger generation on the eve of the Second World War "spiritually unprepared for the war they had to fight". Beard's writing, in retrospect, seemed doubly dangerous because he had demanded an ultimate act of faith—renouncing "the diplomacy of the dollar, the navy and the marines". The Historical Association's president the year before had denounced Beard's views as "unorthodox" and therefore dangerous. In the Cold War, he had added, historians were under as much obligation as nuclear physicists to serve the community as best they could. As one undersecretary for education argued at the time, "History textbooks should not read as if they were written by neutrals in the struggle between freedom and slavery".[14]

What American historians in this period chose to present their readers was a highly selective view of the past that highlighted what appeared to be true of the moment, and useful for the ideology of the hour. Their selective reading of the past was a conscious attempt to inspire their readers, to call them to arms. For twenty-five years American historians answered the call, and no one more devotedly than Arthur M. Schlesinger Jr. Of the many presidents he had known in his lifetime he was closest to John F. Kennedy, a man who believed America had been "commissioned by history" to redeem the world from communism just as in 1776 it had contracted to strike a blow for liberty against the principles of dynastic rule. Years later Schlesinger took Jimmy Carter to task for not communing with the nation in the language of the past, for spending too much time addressing questions of policy. Instead of communicating a sense of purpose he had left the American people "spiritually adrift", just at the point when the Cold War reached a new level of intensity.[15]

What the historians of this period were mandated to write was an Atlanticist version of the past. In that endeavour the Western civilisation courses that became popular in American schools and universities in the 1950s played a vital role. They were designed to inculcate in the students shared values that would make it possible for the United States to enjoy an enlightened political consensus in the Cold War. That consensus depended on a unity of curriculum and knowledge. As the historian William McNeil could be found insisting in the closing years of the conflict, the whole purpose of education was to create an active citizen, one who was not only aware of his public duties but who was also willing to perform them.[16]

Even more important, of course, was the attempt of American historians to rewrite their country's history in terms consistent with its nineteenth-century understanding of itself. It may not have been an altogether successful exercise, but it was certainly an important one. American historians understood the Cold War to be a conflict between two contending ideas of political action and accordingly tended to treat the country's story from the very beginning as a historical parable.

What was America's membership in NATO, asked one historian, but the 'reification' of American history?[17] Between the wars most American historians had stressed the distinctiveness of American society. After the Second World War they tended to see the 'Atlantic Community' as the only appropriate framework in which to anchor their own history. "To those who are interested in the survival of democracy", wrote Richard Hofstadter in the 1950s, "it is probably more important to see American democracy as part of Western European democracy than it is to stress its uniqueness".[18]

In the 1950s many sociologists began to assert that the Cold War had reaffirmed America's ideology as the basis of its national identity. *The American Way, The American Creed,* and *The American Idea* were the titles of three particularly influential works in the postwar period, all of which argued that the United States was the embodiment of the idea of equality, an ideology that was both universalistic and practical in its appeal.

Becoming an American was still an act of will. It was open to all who were prepared to subscribe to the American idea, irrespective of their cultural or racial origins. What seems clear is that whatever the elite's idea of national consensus meant, its thinking was in step with the popular response to assimilation during the same period. Indeed, the southern Europeans who had begun arriving after 1910, only to be discriminated against as 'nonwhites', were the first to benefit from the transformation of the American idea into the force of equality. This ideology became in turn a mainstay of the government's own effort at mobilisation. It facilitated its own attempt to unite the nation behind the rhetoric of the Cold War. For one historian it marked the historic moment when the ghetto whites, the Slovaks, Poles and Ruthenians from Eastern Europe, "felt fully accepted as Americans".[19]

In that sense, the Old World would be conjoined with the New. The Atlantic Alliance was lauded precisely for this reason. It offered, wrote the historian Hans Kohn at the time, a vehicle through which "the nations on the two shores of the Atlantic" had started to realise their communality for the first time. Although they had not shared a common past, they would at least share a common destiny. A fellow historian looked forward to a time when the 'nationalistic' view of American history would be replaced by "an international view treating America as part of a great historical civilisation with the Atlantic at its centre". One of the most respected of all, Garrett Mattingly, went so far as to insist that American history *was* Western history. The United States and Europe were "moved by the same rhythm, stirred by the same impulses, and inescapably involved in the same crises".[20]

Long before the end of the Cold War, however, the historians had jumped ship. They were no longer willing to be co-opted or conscripted. Revisionists even challenged the official interpretation of the origins of the Cold War. As the much-respected historian Daniel Boorstin wrote in the early 1960s, "What ails us most is not what we have done with America

but what we have substituted for America. . . . We are haunted not by reality but by those images we have put in place of reality".[21]

In addition, history gradually ceased to resonate in the popular consciousness as it once had. What began to chip away at America's Western
identity was not the rewriting of history so much as its disappearance from
the syllabus. At the end of the Cold War what impressed critics most was
how little history the American people knew. In the mid-1980s a report by
the National Endowment for the Humanities found that 68 percent of high
school children did not know in which century their own Civil War had
been fought. Forty percent had no idea when the Declaration of Independence had been drawn up. What the Americans wanted, claimed Barbara
Tuchman, "is not history but news", or "history by the ounce". To borrow
a metaphor from Susan Sontag, the force of historical argument had become the force of collage.[22]

There was a much more profound force at work—the rise of a multicultural consciousness, a phenomenon that in turn was part of what
Chesterton had foreseen in 1922: the deconstruction of the United States as
an eighteenth-century society. History does not have a method, but it does
have a critique and a topic, the French historian Paul Veyne has noted. The
term "topic" he borrowed (via Vico) from the Aristotelian theory of *topoi*
or "commonplaces", which were at the heart of the Greek tradition of
rhetoric.[23] These commonplaces constituted a stock of appropriate questions that an orator had to possess in order to speak effectively before the
assembly. The purpose of history's topic is to expand the questionnaire.
History is the art of asking questions about oneself, one's past and one's
destiny. It allows historians to conceptualise events differently than the contemporaries who took part in them. It enables them to rationalise history,
to give it meaning.

Today the American people and their politicians tend to ask fewer questions of the past. The questions they do ask, moreover, are not part of that
useable past, that nineteenth-century series of myths we are discussing, but
of the histories of minorities and marginal groups who are only now discovering their history for the first time.

Not only are Western civilisation courses now challenged on American
campuses, but also interest in other cultures has become increasingly pronounced. Often the process is questionable, especially when students are
encouraged to see Western culture as an irredeemable record of imperialism, persecution and slavery. But is this not to miss the point? The point is
not that historians are no longer conscripted to the fight. The point is that
American history is being reinterpreted as society changes, as it begins to
demand a rereading of events in the light of present social needs.

Historians looking at the American Southwest, for example, are beginning to acknowledge that Mexican influence is about as abiding a charac-

teristic of the region as its desert topography. The native Spanish speakers or Chicanos have continued to speak Spanish in Texas for at least 150 years. The majority have also learned English and adopted some English customs without losing touch with their Hispanic heritage. Many believe that the Anglo-American era of their history, which dates from their forcible incorporation in 1846, is about to end. In the process they see a redrawing of the ethnic map, a fusion of English and Spanish speakers—the growth of a distinctly Anglo-Spanish political culture.

For their part, many Chicanos, instead of calling themselves Mexican-Americans as they did in the 1960s, have begun to recognise that the English language is as much a medium of that fusion as Spanish; that General Scott, who entered Mexico City in 1846, in a war that dispossessed the Chicanos not only of their land and their rights but also of their history, is as much a Mexican figure as an American one, for he was the catalyst by which the fusion took place. What we may be witnessing is a new community of consciousness in the making. "If we want to predict changes in the American continent, we should look at the Chicano", says one writer. "We must look at ourselves, for we reflect the Western hemisphere in a state of cultural and social change".24

What makes all Americans 'American' is their ethnic past as well as the national past they share in common. Ethnic histories are their past; American culture is their present. The present, however, is only real in the context of the past. The two cannot be separated any more than individual ethnic identities can be suppressed, if only because the kind of past we see ourselves sharing is bound to influence our present view of ourselves.25

Self-consciousness is the key. It is not that the United States is in any sense 'un-Western' with respect to the traditions, values and conventions it still shares with Western Europe. No longer, however, can it see itself as a 'European' nation, a product of Enlightenment thought. It is finding it increasingly difficult to apply those eighteenth-century ideas of itself that seventy years ago Chesterton recognised would one day lose their hold on the American imagination.

At the same time, we can see a deconstructionist process of a different kind, this time involving Europe. If the presence of European intellectuals in the United States helped to mould the West in the early years of the Cold War, in the long term their escape from Europe radically altered the balance of intellectual power between the Old World and the New, with results that may well have been permanent. In the 1940s the Paris school in arts was virtually dead. The Bauhaus was not reestablished in Berlin. Vienna lost its philosophical dominance altogether. One must not exaggerate, but I think it true to suggest that Europe never quite made up the intellectual deficit.

European philosophers no longer seem to have time for 'grand narratives', only for 'particles', 'fragments', the heterogeneous elements of language games. So much of Europe's political discourse since the 1960s has been a deconstruction of those 'metanarratives' that Europe, having constructed, tried to export to a large part of the world.

Instead of producing new ideas the Europeans seem much happier deconstructing old ones. It is not purely coincidental that deconstructionism, in the words of the American critic Harold Bloom, is "thoroughly European". For Europe it marked "the completion of its reconstruction". Indeed, the reconstruction of a 'new' Europe demanded a "temporal disjunction" with the past. Could the European community have come into existence at all, Bloom asks, without the deconstruction of those historical narratives and missions that had distinguished its history from the early nineteenth century onwards, those metahistorical texts that had led to the great European wars?[26]

As one of its critics concedes, deconstruction is, after existentialism, *the* European cultural export of the age. What is deconstructionism, after all, but what Bloom calls "a school of resentment" on the part of a culture that once saw itself in universal terms? Whereas once the Europeans were renowned for addressing the great questions in an attempt to solve them, they are now *dissolving* them. They are proud of showing how terms such as 'truth', 'spirit' and 'meaning' are in reality flawed. A minimalist account of the truth is all that is required. In the end deconstructionism appears to be definingly European in origin if not in style. In a sense it is symbolic of the loss of confidence that has been the defining mark of so much of European politics since 1950, a loss of confidence in the grand ideas that it was once so eager to communicate to the world at large.

Deconstructionism, after all, represents not so much a belief that everything has been said as a belief that nothing more can be said. It represents a recognition that nothing can be the same again. The very word, writes Michael Wood, has "an austere sound to it which makes it some sort of sign of our timid and disabused times".[27] In the future the intellectual gap between Europe and America is likely to grow, driving them even further apart in that ultimate act of deconstruction—the passing of the Atlantic Age.

America as a European Country

In 1976, the bicentennial year of the founding of the United States, the journalist-historian Theodore H. White returned to the Jewish ghetto in Boston where he had lived as a child. He did not like what he found—a landscape of blank places, burned-out hulks of cars and boarded windows. All pointed to a society that had lost its spirit of place. The school in which he had been taught his first lessons in American history had also burned down. The street in which he had played as a child he found flanked by empty lots and tumbledown ruins. In place of a once vibrant community he found a fearful society at war with itself.

It appeared that this suburb of Boston had become a microcosm of America writ large. After a lifetime's reporting he found the United States slipping away in his imagination. It no longer offered a great dream. The America he was now reporting seemed to be swelling with strange forms that his understanding could no longer shape into clear stories. America had become a society that he could no longer understand. In short, it was clear that the old English political culture had lost control over the 'other' people who had filled America's vast spaces and crowded cities. The polyglot people of America no longer shared a common heritage. At issue, wrote White, was whether "America could be transformed simply into a Place—a gathering of discretely defined and entitled groups, interests and heritages, or . . . could it continue to be a nation where all heritages joined under the same roof".[28]

What was the idea that he himself had learned so early in his youth? It was the idea that America was the promise to which all mankind, including his own immigrant grandfather and father, had been marching. It was a promise that had inspired White all his life. It had taken him from the ghetto, transforming him in the process into a successful journalist and historian, inspired to even greater effort. Now he knew that as an idea it made nonsense of the current story.

Sixteen years earlier White had 'discovered' something else that made him highly critical of suburban life. Just as the census of 1890 had announced the closing of the frontier, so the census of 1960 had announced "the passing of the city". The great crucible in which America had been forged, the frontier and the cities, had given way to a more suburban, parochial setting for the future: the suburban life of ethnic minorities who had crowded into the ghettos, shutting themselves off from the American Dream.

It was in fact a familiar complaint. A hundred years earlier James Russell Lowell, while also strolling through Boston, had been disturbed to find two Irish immigrants at a loss as to what to make of an equestrian statue of George Washington. Like White, Lowell recorded how he had been brought up "among the still living traditions of Lexington, Concord, Bunker Hill. . . ." To these Irish-Americans America was not a country but a place—not, of course, as it was in the 1960s, a place of entitlements and welfare payments, but "a place to earn their living".[29]

What White found most disturbing was much more than the alienation of an ethnic group or series of groups from mainstream American life. He also feared the alienation of the mainstream itself. As he had written twenty years earlier, a society without a common identity, or fixed points of reference, or a mainstream political tradition, could never constitute a genuine society. When one is a stranger to oneself, one is often estranged from others too.[30]

Today an increasing number of Americans are beginning to share White's fear that their country may be transformed into a multicultural society that may have much less respect than in the past for the values that inspired two generations of Americans to see themselves as members of a society that had been "commissioned by history" to defend Western civilisation at a critical moment in its life.

It is important not to exaggerate this fear, but it is also important not to underestimate it. It is useful to remind ourselves, in fact, how strong the historical memory of the nation seemed to be even in the confusion and chaos of the debate on the Vietnam War. Indeed, one of the phenomena that most astonished the radical writer Sacvan Bercovitch in 1968 was the strength of that remembrance:

> Nothing in my Canadian background had prepared me for that spectacle. . . . It gave me something of an anthropologist's sense of wonder at the symbol of the tribe. . . . To a Canadian sceptic, a gentile in God's country . . . [here was] a pluralistic, pragmatic people . . . bound together by an ideological consensus.
>
> Let me repeat that mundane phrase: ideological consensus. For it wasn't the idea of exceptionalism that I discovered in '68. . . . It was a hundred sects and factions, each apparently different from the others, yet all celebrating the same mission.[31]

What Bercovitch found most surprising was the spectacle of the Jewish anarchist, Paul Goodman, berating the establishment for turning its back on the promise of the American Dream. He was even more astonished to find the descendant of an African slave, Martin Luther King, denouncing the injustices of American society as a violation of 'the American way'. In fact Bercovitch found the black community's response particularly revealing, for in keeping with its evangelical tradition, King had called upon America "to be born again".

In short, Bercovitch found hundreds of different factions, each radically different from each other, yet all celebrating the same messianic American purpose, "a vast *Pequod*'s crew, engaged in a ritual which kept society together". It was precisely that process that White believed had broken down. As unrest in the inner cities became the norm, he thought it inevitable that history would begin to tap into that restlessness, drawing from it an energy that might, for the first time, give the alienated poor a voice.

What makes White's own voice important was that he was one of the first observers to see multiculturalism as a threat to America's Western identity. The number of Third World immigrants of course is now much higher than it was in White's day. It is higher, in fact, than at any period in American history, including the years 1900–1910. Numbers alone, however, are a misleading basis for analysis. The population is larger now than it was at the turn of the century, but the rate of immigration in fact is much lower. Though the proportion of persons living in the United States who are foreign born is high by recent standards—about 8 percent according to the 1990 census—it is still lower than it was for every decade between 1850 and 1950.[32]

It is the racial origins of the new immigrants, of course, that are considered to pose the most immediate challenge. For those who believe that nationality must be defined in explicitly racial and ethnic terms the current high rates of nonwhite immigration threaten to increase the 'extended American family', that ethnocultural society that is becoming more ethnic over time. In 1960 the U.S. population was 88.6 percent white; today that proportion is 75 percent—a drop of 13 percent in thirty years. The demographer Leon Bouvier has projected that by 2020 the proportion of whites could fall to 60 percent or less.

During this period the proportion of Hispanics is expected to rise by 25 percent, and that of Asians by 8 percent. Both will overtake in importance the African-American community, which is expected to rise in number by less than 2 percent. The true importance of the figures is highlighted by the age distribution. By 2030 the white population may constitute less than one-half of those under the age of eighteen, but three-quarters of those aged sixty-five or over. California could have a Hispanic majority by then, ensuring, as is so often the case, that it remains ahead of the field.[33]

The challenge of immigration is one of the most compelling of all because it strikes at another of Chesterton's eighteenth-century ideas found in America's constitutional dispensation. In a recent book, *Heteropolis* (1993), Charles Jencks provides a fascinating anatomy of Los Angeles, a city that has become a confederacy of thirteen major ethnic groups, occupying eighteen definable urban cores. Some are de facto city-states speaking Spanish or Chinese or Vietnamese; some are fortified towns guarded by private armies. As Jencks points out, Los Angeles is the paradigm migrant city in the sense that every citizen can claim to be a member of a minority group.

In examining the cultural uniformity of each of these city cultures, from the Barrio, Koreatown and Little Saigon to Beverley Hills and Malibu, Jencks reveals that their inhabitants have little in common other than a superficial understanding of a collective American culture. In particular, they are out of sympathy with the essence of the eighteenth-century constitutional settlement, "the atomisation of society into individuals and the suppression of minority cultures". For Jencks "modern liberalism has been challenged by the politics of cultural difference". There will be no reversion, he argues, to the old universal ideas that inspired generations of earlier American immigrants. The Third World has arrived in the First with a vengeance.[34] It is a change that may well signify the end of the Anglo-American state.

Before the Americans despair of their future, however, they might recall that there have been many American writers who have questioned the attraction of assimilation as the Anglo-American elite understood it. What the writer Horace Kallen sensed as early as 1918 was that America was a society constantly *renewing* itself. "A living culture is a changing culture. "Majorities are minorities in combination; minorities are majorities in division. Majorities are orchestrations of the difference; minorities are dissociations of the difference. The 'American way' is the order of these constant combinations and dissociations in all the enterprises of living".[35]

Kallen recognised earlier than most of his contemporaries that first-generation Americans had often found 'assimilation' to be a myth. Confronted with a hostile society on arrival, they had been forced to promote their own ethnic identity. What distinguished America from Europe in the nineteenth century was not the power of assimilation but the right of immigrants to preserve their separate identities, the acknowledgment of group rights, in all but name. No laws prevented immigrant taxpayers from repatriating their wealth. No legislation forbade them from establishing their own churches, hospitals or social services. Private schools were even eligible for state funds. Ethnic communities were allowed to educate their children as they wished. In 1920, in a celebrated ruling, the Supreme Court refused the right to the State of Washington to make public education a state monopoly. Unlike immigrants in Western Europe, those who came to the New World were never forcibly assimilated. America was defined not by the inclusion of its ethnic cultures but by their self-creation.

As another dissenting sociologist, Marcus Hansen, argued thirty years later, the history of immigration was a history of alienation. Wrenched from their historic roots by the passage across the Atlantic, they had reestablished themselves in the New World. As a group they were no longer identified by their relationship with the land but with the ethnic group to which they now belonged. They read ethnic papers or joined mutual aid associations. Such actions, in the end, were steps towards their eventual Americanisation because ethnicity worked only within larger societies like America. At the same time, the very experience of displacement introduced to them what was essential about the situation of most Americans, displacement itself (in some degree the experience of modern men). As the most modern of societies America experienced that displacement more vividly than any other.[36]

In other words, in terms of their memories and customs, most immigrant cultures were really the creation of the New World, not the Old. Immigrants who wished to be assimilated, and found they could not, chose to celebrate a past different from the past they had escaped, or fled from. They did not import their ethnicity with them in a suitcase. Confronted with a society that was so unwelcoming, they created an ethnic class culture. It was of course an ethnicity very different from that they had known at home, if only because they had to manufacture past memories in a totally new setting.

Seventy years ago the distinguished anthropologist Randolph Bourne saw no threat at all in the "small narratives" (i.e., the alternative visions of the future) associated with the nonwhite groups in America's cities. The best test of democracy, he believed, was the intercultural cooperation of all groups on loose, functionalist lines. Bourne championed the idea of the "unintegrated self" (the alienated immigrant). He argued passionately that the immigrant is more than the man he was back at home. He carried his "nation within him" to the country that he had come to, his nation of choice. In the process immigrants reinvented themselves and became agents of mediation, fully capable of taking part in the life of the community. In reversing the conventional depiction of immigrants as marginalised political figures, Bourne transvalued the meaning of marginality itself.[37]

Marginality was an anchor that kept the immigrants from being sucked into the big cities as an amorphous mass. It saved them from being scattered into atomised isolation by the forces of eighteenth-century liberalism. Without this "spiritual internationalism", Bourne maintained, "America ran the real danger of becoming a queer conglomeration of the prejudices of past generations, miraculously preserved here, after they had mercifully perished at home. [Those who] fondly imagine that they are keeping the faith ... have not really kept the faith. The faith is a certain way of facing the world, of accepting experience. It is a spirit and not any particular form".

Assimilation, by contrast, had divested immigrants of their traditions and cast them out on the fringes of American life. In the last years of his life Bourne railed against an increasingly anglophile culture that, because it had denied the new immigrants a chance to create an authentic tradition, had also "unconsciously belittled" a "distinctively American spirit".[38]

What was common to all three writers was that they were writing about the response to the *white* outsider, to the new white immigrants who flooded into the United States at the turn of the century. Large-scale immigration is not a new phenomenon. By the end of 1910 one in three Americans was an immigrant or had at least one foreign-born parent. The fact that the new immigrants came principally from Central and Eastern Europe made this particularly problematic. Not only did they outnumber immigrants from Western Europe by six to one, but also they spoke little or no English and brought little wealth with them. So threatened did many Americans feel that twenty states were persuaded to introduce compulsory English language courses into public schools to promote "the language of America", and to inculcate "American values".

The early years of the century, in fact, saw the appearance of numerous Jeremiahs arguing that the new Americans would share little in common with second-generation Americans, not even a common language. The United States, they predicted, would soon become a country divided between a predominantly white political elite and a predominantly 'nonwhite' population. As H. G. Wells warned during a visit to America in 1908, contemporary immigration had "produced a marked degradation of political life".[39]

It is doubtful, in fact, whether today's poorer immigrants are discriminated against any more than were the poor southern Europeans, the Croats complained about in Owen Wister's *The Virginian* (1902), that "darker haired, darker eyed, uneducated proletariat", a group that Wells described as "a coloured invasion".[40] It is doubtful whether today's poor Hispanics working in underpaid areas of the retail trade are any worse off than the Ruthenians who arrived at the turn of the century and were able to find work only in the most depressed and depressing sectors of the economy. "My people do not live in America", complained a Ruthenian priest, "they live underneath America". Many were impressed into mining or disappeared into the sweatshops of New York. America, he added, "goes over their heads".[41]

The difference between today's immigrants and those of the past has nothing to do with the values of Western civilisation. It has everything to do, however, with the fact that the new immigrants come from the non-European world. Only 5 percent of all immigrants in the 1980s were Europeans. What is at threat in the new America is not the ideals that were once extolled so vigorously in the Western civilisation courses of American universities. What is at threat is the umbilical link between the United States and Europe that is still considered by many to be the bedrock of America's Western identity.[42]

It is true that this new generation of Americans may no longer suffer from "that superstitious valuation of Europe" about which Henry James complained a century ago. It is probable too that we will no longer see any more of those literary transatlantic pilgrimages that once dominated the Anglo-American literary discourse. It is most unlikely, however, that the United States will lose touch with European values. Far from it. In successfully promoting them it will ensure that they no longer seem Western, but universal.

The history of the next hundred years will turn on the answer to two questions: Will 1.6 billion Chinese living predominantly in cities for the first time and enjoying a reasonable per capita income for the first time be able to function as a politically stable society without repression? Secondly, will 350 million Americans be able to live together in a multicultural society as a microcosm of a world in which the West is no longer in the ascendant? As usual China crouches behind its Great Wall, looking inwards. As always, the United States looks outwards posing a problem of importance to the entire world.

America as an Enlightenment Project

What many Americans find most threatening about the demographic changes that are changing the face of the United States is that they are undermining America's Western identity. At the Republican Party Convention in 1992 the most important protectionist politician, Pat Buchanan, declared that the United States was threatened with an invasion across the Rio Grande, an infusion of Mexicans that would dilute the racial stock and challenge the work ethic.

He did not appear to understand that the city in which the convention was held, Houston, had been Spanish speaking for 150 years. By framing the issue in apocalyptic terms he virtually ensured the acrimony of the debate on America's future. Competing analysts of a possible event can reach agreement about its basic meaning; rival interpreters of a catastrophe cannot.

Buchanan's jeremiad was a very old one, however, couched as it was in the hypertrophic rhetoric of invasion. Nearly a century ago Henry James was shocked to discover on a visit to Ellis Island that he had to "share the sanctity of his American consciousness" with "Italian immigrants coming from Sicily and Calabria"; 300,000 arrived in 1914 alone. Later in an electric car he found himself confronting the face of the alien: "The car-ful again is an alien car-ful, a row of faces up and down testifying without exception to alienism, unmistakable alienism, alienism undisguised and unashamed". He was so disturbed by the sight that he was moved to ask where "does one put a finger on the dividing line, or for that matter . . . on the particular phase of the conversion, of any one of its successive movements?".[43]

James in fact was intelligent enough to recognise that immigrants became American simply by helping to construct it. For Frederick Jackson Turner the process was the colonisation and settlement of the West that transformed weak, protein-deficient Europeans into Americans. For the writer William Barrett, writing in the 1950s, the process was "an existential adventure", for the immigrants committed themselves to becoming free men.[44]

Every generation, in short, produces a different process of transmutation. As James recognised, neither the concept of the 'American' nor that of the 'ethnic' could be defined separately. Put simply, there is no 'American Scene' (the title of his 1904 study). There is only an interpretation of it. That is why we must be careful not to design 'case studies' from which to draw universal laws. We must be careful not to dehistoricise economic data. We must be especially careful not to remove it from its place in time or to divorce it from its cultural context.

Non-Western immigrants may bring with them non-Western values, working habits and performance levels, but in a non–Third World context those factors may operate quite differently. This is particularly true of the Hispanics, who are in fact a creation of Anglo-American culture, a group that unites the disparate elements that make up the Spanish-speaking population, the immigrants or children of immigrants from societies as different as those of Uruguay, Cuba or Argentina. Only Hispanics have that identity because they work and live in the United States.

Of no other group is this more true than the Chicanos, who make up 60 percent of the Hispanic population. If they had not already dispersed to cities as far away as Chicago, Kansas City and Detroit, the American Southwest would already be predominantly Spanish speaking. Spanish speakers will certainly be in the majority in California by 2020.

Most Hispanics only began rediscovering their identity in the 1960s, when a distinctive Chicano culture arose, with its own poets and writers, prominent among them Rudolfo Anaya, Rosae Arias and Arturo Islas. For such ethnic writers, writing is not an activity within life but a way of experiencing life, of communicating the truth of their own experience. The rise of this particular culture was prompted in turn by urbanisation in the 1950s, which produced a radical political consciousness for the first time.

Long before then, however, the probable future of the community had been glimpsed by the now forgotten writer Waldo Frank. In the 1920s he was one of America's most celebrated authors, one of its bright young men who helped the United States come of age. He was editor of *The Seven Arts* magazine and an experimental novelist whose works were translated into French and German. For a time he was even a European figure. Only after the Second World War did his reputation decline. His message in the 1950s, an era in which Americans were at their most self-confident, was not one that most wanted to hear.

Frank believed that America's consciousness was incomplete. He hoped that the Spanish-speaking and English-speaking Americans would rediscover each other for the first time since they had gone their separate ways in the 1820s. America was only an experiment that was half realised, he claimed, "a conception to be created . . . a step in consciousness", a bridge between a Western and a semi-Western world.[45]

Frank believed that the Hispanic-American encounter would mark a potentially decisive stage in the evolution of American society. One day the memory of their respective histories would displace the memories of Europe within each other, "those de-natured elements of a transplanted world", of a European world that had been built by Europeans. This is why Einstein told him that America was only a two-dimensional world. What it lacked was its third dimension, an authentic American consciousness, one forged from a fusion of the true "American nation", a combination of the English and the Spanish traditions.

It was this Latin American world that Frank wrote about so eloquently in the 1920s. He claimed to find in the common history of the two Americas, in their respective myths and traditions, a vision of a shared destiny: "Across the frontier of the Rio Grande two cultures face each other. Both are incomplete, awaiting some crucial element of wholeness; both in varying degrees long for completion".[46] If the South Americans lacked what northerners had made for themselves, a stable government and economic growth as well as a working political order, the North Americans lacked a 'creative' life, with confidence in their own values. The two were mirror images of each other in a distorted looking-glass that reflected back not the image of their 'being' but the image of what they might become.

Even today Mexican children are encouraged to see the United States as 'the other'—both inseparable and yet radically different. In the north of the country the expression "the other side" is used to mean the United States. The other side can be geographical (the border), cultural (another civilisation), linguistic (another language) or historical (another time). The United States is running to keep pace with the future; Mexico appears still to be tied to the past. "The other is above all metaphorical", writes Paz, "it is an image of everything we are not". Mexico is 'American' nonetheless.[47]

Can there be a more imaginative creative dialogue between the two societies? Paz believes that the initiative will have to come from the United States, not only by virtue of its power but also because of the presence of 'the other' in its midst, its own Hispanic population. By the mid-twenty-first century it is possible that 40 percent of Americans will be either Spanish speaking, or of Spanish-speaking descent.

For the United States turning inward is not an answer to the current debate. Indeed, the construction of a North American Free Trade Area (NAFTA) makes this probably impossible as well as undesirable. The Americans are being asked to be more imaginative still, to dig deeper into their inner consciousness. They are being asked to become existential adventurers, to question again the purpose of America as an Enlightenment project, and in questioning it to reformulate an answer.

As Paz insists, a national identity is not essentialist. It is always in flux. It is a constant exercise in reflection and revision.

> What is called the "genius of the people" [national identity] is only a set of reactions to a given stimulus. The answers differ in different situations, and the national character, which was thought to be immutable, changes with them. Despite the often illusory nature of essays on the psychology of a nation, it seems to me there is something revealing in the insistence with which a people will question itself during certain periods of its growth. To become aware of our history is to become aware of our singularity. It is a moment of reflective repose before we devote ourselves to action again.[48]

It is worth quoting Paz at length, as I have throughout this book, because of all contemporary Latin American writers he comes equipped with the best stock of terms. He embodies twentieth-century man's anguished quest for meaning. If 'time', 'the fall', 'innocence', and 'redemption' are his concerns, they also happen to be America's. Paz's observation is so acute because how he reads America is how an increasing number of Americans are beginning to read themselves.

Reinventing America

The world has changed enormously since 1989. In the long course of history the United States has no alternative but to march on, to become something other than what it is. It was with that prospect in mind that President Clinton referred in his inaugural address to a new mood in the world's oldest democracy. It would test whether America would have the courage to 'reinvent' itself.

Clinton was probably unaware that this was one of the central messages of the country's greatest philosopher, John Dewey. Dewey found much to fault in the America of his day. What he opposed most was the burden of the past (not history) in whose name so many young Americans of his day were conscripted to fight. Dewey was not against historical myths or what another American writer, Van Wyck Brooks, was the first to call a "useable past". He was only against a manufactured national history when it failed to inspire those who had inherited it, when it was more life denying than life affirming.

If a myth gives rise to spirited actions and useful initiatives it is socially useful. He also believed it to be true, for its truth lay in its intrinsic value as a spur to action. Truth was not a cause of success. It was an effect of holding to a belief. Dewey judged the rightness of all beliefs by their effects, not their causes. The power of a people to remake itself is what he called "instrumentalism".

Waldo Frank once compared Dewey with Emerson. Emerson was a very old European; Dewey was a very young American in asserting that the United States was always being reborn.[49]

Dewey's ideas had an immense impact outside the United States, particularly in Japan and the Soviet Union. In the early 1920s the education department of Columbia University, whose faculty was very much influenced by Dewey's thinking, was commissioned by another of Dewey's admirers, Lenin, to put together the first Soviet school curriculum.

Dewey himself was intrigued from the first by the new Soviet state. "Freed from the load of subjugation to the past it seems charged with the ardour of creating a new world". Equally impressed was Woodrow Wilson, who saw the Russian Revolution as the second greatest event in history after America's own revolution in 1776. Both men were to be disappointed, of course, not least because the new Soviet state inherited so much that was bad about the old.

Japan too imported much from the United States, including Dewey's ideas. Dewey in fact was so widely read in the first Asian country that had set out on the road to industrialisation that he was invited to lecture at the University of Tokyo in 1919. In the lectures he gave there (which were published in 1920 as *Reconstruction in Philosophy*) he told his Japanese hosts that they would have to revalue many of their own traditions if they wished to keep in step with the modern world. They would have to redefine their culture if they wished to succeed. Upon their success in reinventing themselves would depend their chances of rising to the challenge of modernisation.[50]

As in the Soviet Union, it was a challenge to which the Japanese did not rise until much later in the century, but rise they did, not least because they were prepared to revalue their values—because, in Dewey's words, they were prepared to "substitute faith in the active tendencies of the day for dread and dislike of them".[51]

That challenge faces all modern societies, including the United States. As I shall discuss in the next chapter, it will determine whether the non-Western world will be threatening enough to justify maintaining the Western Alliance in another form, and for another mission. All the evidence, it must be said, suggests that it will not.

The Future Is History

Even if there is no master text that binds Europe and the United States together, there is a common challenge they face together. If they cannot meet it successfully then they may go their separate ways. Immigration is now a phenomenon that threatens to divide the Western community rather than unite it as it did in the 1930s.

The challenge that both societies face is a product of geography as much as history. Europe may no longer be in its own eyes what it was for philosophers in the 1930s, "an idea imminent in its own history". It may no longer see itself as the future of other worlds. But the rest of the world is most certainly intent on becoming part of the history of the West. The United States and Western Europe are the only points of destination for those who seek safety overseas. If the capital-intensive world will not invest in the future of its neighbours, the labour-intensive world will move in search of jobs. Both the United States and Europe are already multiethnic as well as multiracial societies. The early twenty-first century will determine whether they will accept cultural diversity as the basis, not the negation, of their own identity.

The United States is likely to rise to the challenge; Europe may not. Nothing in its history encourages us to be optimistic on this score. In the political violence that already disfigures the political landscape of Germany, Italy and France we can catch a glimpse of a past that is struggling to be reborn.

If things go badly, an increasing number of American politicians may become critical of Europe. Already some are employing the language of the 1920s, the language of a country that asked itself in the aftermath of the First World War whether it should have entered the conflict at all, whether it would not have been better to have left the Europeans to their own devices. To be sure, both the circumstances and the themes of the debate are different. Nevertheless, there is one stark similarity: Many Americans are inclined to ask more frequently than they did in the recent past whether the Europeans are capable of defending themselves from within, or whether the old forces of barbarism are still there, waiting to break out.

Once again Europe seems to be troubled by a past that it has failed to exorcise. Let me quote a passage from a book published in 1989, the year the Berlin Wall was breached, the year the European project seemed finally to have come into its own:

> Europe is dangerous. If the United States goes wrong we have, we think, a fairly clear idea of how we expect it to do so—apocalyptically, as befits the scale of the country and no doubt democratically, carrying the national logic to the bitter end. The European possibilities are more subtle and European history suggests they would be more original. Americans should worry about Europe and consider what the American relationship with Europe may become as the existing alliance weakens.[52]

William Pfaff, the journalist whom I have just quoted, may not be entirely representative of his age or even his countrymen, but he has been writing for a predominantly European audience for many years. He writes of a Europe that is inherently different from America. He also writes of a continent that is in conflict with itself. The realities that inspired the European project in the first place still seem to prevent the Europeans from coming to terms with their own history.

One of those realities is fascism. Only now are the Americans beginning to recognise that it was not defeated in 1945. It held on tenaciously throughout the Cold War years. By the early 1980s neofascist parties could draw as much as 10 percent of the vote in local elections. Today they are strongly entrenched in France in Le Pen's National Front, in Austria in Jörg Haider's Freedom Party, in Belgium in the Flemish Vlaams Blok and the Walloon National Front, and in Germany in neo-Nazi movements such as the Deutsche Volksunion and the Republican Party.

Many European countries are beset by a confused identity. Nationalism has returned even in the rhetoric and programmes of conventional politicians. It is tempting, writes Tony Judt, to see in their programmes and agenda a return to the fascism of the 1930s, but it is not the same. The historical context has changed. The nationalist ideologies of Le Pen, Haider, and Italy's Gianfranco Fini are not totalitarian but populist. They represent a new fascist generation, all the more worrying for that, for they represent "the ghost of Europes yet to come".[53]

There is a phrase of Italo Calvino's that seems especially apt: "The more enlightened our houses are, the more their walls ooze ghosts". The Western community will not long survive the suspicion that the Europeans are really permanent recidivists who may once again be reverting to their old ways and old habits; that the great ideas and endeavours that dominated the Western imagination for much of the century and that led to the great conflicts between nations did not, in fact, achieve any permanent change in the long-term unfolding of European history.

There is a verse by the Russian poet Anna Akhmatova that captures this suspicion:

> *The past is rotting in the*
> *Future*
> *A terrible carnival of dead*
> *Leaves.*

What is so interesting about the present debate is that its echoes of the 1920s are quite uncanny. It has a resonance with a decade in which the United States turned its back on Europe and withdrew into isolationism.

America's visceral distrust of Europe in the 1920s was represented in American literature that told the story of the encounter between a new generation of Americans and a new and more troubled Europe. The Berlin stories of Robert McAlmon, Glenway Wescott's *Good-bye, Wisconsin*, William Carlos Williams's *A Voyage to Pagany* and the writing of Louis Bromfield and Henry Miller all dealt with this theme. As Malcolm Bradbury writes: "These were no longer tales of Jamesian encounters between American innocence and European experience. Arriving Americans were no longer naive spirits from a safe simple world but critical bearers of the message of change. Likewise the Europeans here depicted no longer carry the weight of . . . moral complexity but the flavour of crisis and defeat or corruption . . . they were not the manipulators of history but its victims".[54]

In 1923 William Carlos Williams urged the United States to break with a continent in which the dead had risen in 1914 to claim the living, in which men still lived for the past or in its shadow and in so doing had repudiated their own future. America, he warned, should separate itself from a civilisation of "fatigued spirits".[55] In the 1920s the past, though dead, was still dangerous enough to require defence against it.

In such criticism there is of course a uniquely American idea that as members of a polyglot and still largely European culture they are more capable of understanding Europe's past than the Europeans. We find something of this in T. S. Eliot's commentary on Henry James: "It is the final consummation of an American to become, not an Englishman, but a European, something no born European, no person of European national identity, can become". We find it also in Auden's comment in his preface to James's book *The American Scene*: "It is from American critics like James and Eliot that we Europeans have learned to understand our social and literary traditions in a way that we could never have learned by ourselves, for they with natural ease look at our past as it is extremely difficult for us to look with contemporary eyes".[56]

Today's criticism, however, runs deeper. Europe, writes Pfaff, has once again shown that it is one of the most unpredictable places in the world. For Americans this is particularly disconcerting, for what appears to be happening is not the rebirth of the past so much as the denial of the future. What we are witnessing is not "the end of history", but an equally momentous structural change. What has ended for the moment is not history but the most elementary dialectic by which it used to be articulated, that of 'before' and 'after'.

It used to be true of Europe that you could measure the periods that began with defining events and ended in victories or defeats, leaving history to begin anew. Those events were the defining moments of the twentieth century, the years from the First World War to the Second, from the Russian Revolution to the fall of the Berlin Wall. However destructive they may have been, they were also self-defining. Europe may have been a disaster area in 1945, but it was also a tabula rasa on which the United States could prevail upon the Europeans to build a better future. Now, writes Gilbert Adair, the Americans find themselves in a world that has relapsed, where nationalism has once again reappeared, where the present is unending, where nothing seems to be drawing to a genuine conclusion.[57]

Europe will certainly forfeit American support should the United States find itself having to treat the future too as a *historical* concept. What would a fundamentally transformed America have in common with a community that failed to *revalue* itself? It is to the question of cultural revaluation that we must now turn.

7

The Challenge of the Future and the Revaluation of Values

One cannot but confront the probability of a general European state. As for the occasion that will suddenly bring the process to a close, it might be almost anything; a Chinaman's pigtail appearing behind the Urals or a shock from the great Islamic *magma*.

—José Ortega y Gasset, *History as a System* (1940)

Modernity is an open-ended process. Hegel was right in arguing that the modern age was the last. Our own age will not be seen as the beginning or end of an era even though we are encouraged by our imminent exit from the millennium to use the prefix 'post'. The prefix suggests that our existing world is in some sense beyond what has happened in the past and thus beyond further change. Whether we are addressing the postmodern era (Etzioni), the post-Bourgeois (Kahn), the post-civilised (Boulding) or the post-industrial (Bell), the changes in each have been dramatic. The industrial, economic, bourgeois and modern have all renewed themselves and will continue to do so long into the future. Much though we are given to speaking of the postmodern or post-industrial, what we mean by these terms is not a 'going beyond' in terms of self-transcendence but a 'taking further' of what the modern age began. History has become the permanent revision or reinterpretation of what we have achieved.

In that sense, of course, every one of our achievements is conditional. Every one is historically contingent. There are no final solutions or final answers, no ends of the road stretching ahead of us. That is the problem of modernity for those who are impatient for history to come to an end. It is also what devalues it in the eyes of its critics, for it makes every answer provisional.

What we have come to understand at the end of the twentieth century is that dissatisfaction is the engine of change. It is what drives us on. The modern era does not allow a politics of loss and retrieval. Kant stands permanently at the door preventing us from going back.[1]

Hegel too stands at the door as the first philosopher of modernity. Contrary to his popular image forty years ago, he did not as a philosopher try to transform the world into a concept, a programme or an agenda to be enacted and realised through action. That was the work of Marx. Instead he attempted to do justice to the process whereby the world not only must be conceived by us as intelligible but also must be *reconceived* by other generations. They, after all, will have to make sense of it for themselves.

The Western world spent a century or more trying to impose its own voice on history. It made the egregious mistake of thinking that it represented an historical epoch as well as a culture: that it was, in Husserl's words, "a philosophical idea imminent in its own history"; that it represented, in short, the future of others.[2]

Contemporary philosophy has departed from such a narrow understanding of history. It has decontextualised rather than deconstructed it. Let me quote one of the most influential French writers, Paul Ricoeur:

> An essential characteristic of a literary work is that it transcends its own psychosociological conditions of production and thereby opens itself to an unlimited series of readings, themselves situated in different socio-cultural conditions. In short, the text must be able from the sociological as well as psychological point of view to 'decontextualise' itself in such a way that it can be recontextualised in a new situation—as accomplished precisely by the act of reading.[3]

A textualised dialogue reveals that a language is never entirely our own. We can appropriate it for ourselves but not for our children. Similarly, the value we place on our social practises cannot be limited in time. Modern societies, compared with those in the past, tend to reinterpret values in the light of their own experience.

We have discovered that a dialectic is open-ended. This is the precondition, in fact, of every civilisation that is genuinely 'civil'. Winning the right to live by this discovery was the main prize the West secured by its victory in the Cold War. If the peace is also to be won we will have to accept that the non-Western world must be allowed to revalue itself. Whether the dialectic between our civilisation and others will be conducted in positive and peaceful terms will depend on two critical factors: whether the process of revaluation is successfully accomplished, and whether their own systematisers or 'fundamentalists' are defeated as they were within the Western world.

The Challenge of East Asia

Long before the West prevailed in its long civil war (1914–1989) some writers had a presentiment of another conflict, this time between the West and the outside world. Even before the end of the nineteenth century many

Europeans had begun to ask whether the next war would signal the end of Western domination, whether a revived China and Japan would challenge Europe's own ascendancy in the East.

From the first, Westernisation was seen as an ambiguous process. By 1900 the Japanese were capturing markets in Europe by outperforming European companies. They were said to work harder, to be better educated, to be more efficient in their working habits. European companies began relocating their plants from Europe to Japan, where labour was cheaper and government policy noninterventionist.

The emergence of an industrialised Japan occasioned a debate that was even more fundamental in its implications. If the Japanese were successful not only in acquiring but also in improving upon Western technology, could the Europeans continue to see themselves as the most inventive race? Could they, in turn, think of their own industrialisation as a uniquely Western process rather than one that, beginning in the West, was destined to extend beyond their own world?

Intelligent writers were concerned, from the first, with the threat that an industrialised Asia might divide the European powers against one another as each state struggled to preserve its market share. Many were in favour of a new Conference of Berlin, this time not to partition Africa but to ensure that the Japanese and Chinese came into the world economy on the West's terms. Their fear of China was much greater because of the size of its market. If its workers were introduced to new machinery and techniques, what chance was there for the increasingly lazy, strike-bound workforce of Western Europe?

No one doubted that the West would remain the source of new technology, but some began to wonder whether its role would be that of a 'noble race' capable of inventing machines that only the Asians would successfully exploit. Even after Germany's defeat in the First World War the statesman Gustav Stresemann was so concerned about this threat that he warned his countrymen not to rejoice at the decline of England's position in East Asia. "The liquidation of the East Asian branch of the British economy" and its transfer to Japan, he claimed, would "mark a significant defeat for the entire white race".[4]

What worried the Europeans even more, especially after the First World War, was that they had lost their moral ascendancy in the eyes of the Asians. The war had exploded the idea of progress, the working faith of the West, as a sham. It had exposed Western superiority as a mere superstition. The French writer Romain Rolland had already predicted that in the event of another war between France and Germany, Europe would be "its own inescapable victim".[5] By the 1920s glimpses of mortality were becoming more pronounced. As the poet Gottfried Benn despaired, the Europeans looked as though they were living through the last cycle of their civilisation.

He predicted that Europe would soon fall to the Slavs and the Mongols, "the last strenuous, self-assertion of an ancient race".[6]

What is interesting about the debate was that the United States looked to East Asia with a confidence the Europeans did not share. It was symbolically important, perhaps, that after revolting against French rule the Vietnamese nationalist Ho Chi Minh based the draft of his own declaration of independence on that of the United States rather than the French Declaration of the Rights of Man. In short, the Americans began to steal into the Asian consciousness just as the Europeans found themselves becoming eclipsed.

Let me propose three reasons for this. First, the Pacific states emerged into America's consciousness in the twentieth century, not the nineteenth. The settlement of California was one of the major demographic events of the twentieth century. In the period between the wars its population doubled and then doubled again. With the growth of population economic development followed. D. H. Lawrence may have been a keen observer of American life, but he was wrong when visiting Los Angeles to complain that California had "turned its back on the world" by deciding "to look into the void Pacific".[7] The Pacific was not a void, it was a vacuum that the United States expected to fill. It was not Lawrence, the novelist, poet and dreamer, who proved to be the greater prophet, but the Californian rail magnate Henry Huntington, who only a few years earlier had pronounced that the Pacific Ocean would be that of the future, the Atlantic that of the past.

All geopolitical musings, of course, are intensely subjective. Every generation explains the past according to expository themes that often extend well beyond what the evidence suggests. Demographic changes explain very little unless a nation already has a view of historical demography, as the United States did in terms of its own 'manifest destiny'. It was that myth that enabled the Americans to draw different conclusions about their future than the Europeans did about their own. It defined the possibilities rather than the limits of their power. To that extent, manifest destiny was a peculiarly powerful myth created by historians for an American audience. It was one of the most compelling myths of the twentieth century.

A second point of difference between the United States and Europe was the Americans' confidence. At the turn of the century the geopolitician Brooks Adams had predicted that by the 1940s the United States would find itself in conflict with Japan, in a battle that would determine whether or not it would hold the Pacific as "an island sea". Adams was only one of many writers of the time to believe that history was marching westwards, a view apparently confirmed by a series of defining events, including the construction of the Panama Canal, the laying of the first telegraph cable across the Pacific and the retention of the Philippines after the Spanish-American War.[8] Even at the time, these were seen by many as the opening moves in a coming conflict between the United States and Japan. In other words, long before 1941 the Americans were preparing for the great challenge of the twentieth century, in the theatre in which they felt their own future would be determined, not the Atlantic but the Pacific.

The third reason for America's optimism was its sheer ambition. Objectively there was little that gave the Pacific region coherence. It had no common adversary, no common frontier and no common culture. But there did exist one common reference point—the promise of the region's Americanisation. No country figured more prominently in America's imagination than China, which contained a vast consumer market and was also, according to a Rockefeller Foundation report in the 1930s, "plastic in its democratic possibilities". The Pacific seemed to fit America's energy, to offer scope for its ambition. In its own eyes, at least, it was the chief protagonist in the Pacific story.

Indeed, towards the end of his life Henry Luce believed that his country's capacity to continue to shape world history would be determined by whether the Pacific Ocean would become the theatre of its future energies. The Americans had rescued Europe from itself and in the process become "leaders of the West". The second half of the twentieth century, he told an audience in San Francisco two years before his death, would see a greater test of American leadership, perhaps the most demanding of all: "whether we can do our part in bringing East and West together".[9]

Luce was typical of his generation in his belief that the East had little to say to the West. He was atypical, however, in challenging the idea that the future of humanity would be fashioned by the West alone. It would be fashioned, he insisted, by the response the East made to the West. It would be determined by its receptivity to Western ideas. From that he concluded that "the responsibility of the West is to know what it has to say and to say it well".

More recently the Americans have been confirmed in their confidence in the future by a naive interest in something called the Pacific Century. Compared with an increasingly provincial Europe, an ageing uncompetitive society in a young, highly competitive world, the Pacific appears to present a greater promise as well as a greater challenge. It is not altogether surprising, of course, that the American imagination should be increasingly engaged with its own prospects. Many of the issues that have penetrated the American consciousness recently come from the Pacific—the emergence of China as an economic power, one, moreover, that is experiencing the fastest growth of any society in history, the continuing challenge of Japan, and the emergence of newly industrialised countries, or the "Asian Tigers". By almost any measure, the Asia-Pacific region is now the most economically vibrant in the world. The Pacific Rim accounts for almost half of the world's gross national product as well as 50 percent more trade than the United

States conducts with Western Europe. There is in Washington a tenacious belief that a changing of the guard is already at hand.

Yet, despite all the hype, we are more likely witnessing the dawn of a Pacific moment, not a century; it is certainly not on the scale of the American Century, as understood by the Americans themselves. History has moved on. Centuries are no longer appropriated by societies speaking in their own name. The vision of a Pacific Century is a nineteenth-century concept that was coined for the first time by Theodore Roosevelt in 1898. It is a political fiction, not a reality, the description of a moment in history, not an era. It is a picture promoted by special lobby groups. It is precisely such interest groups that have given shape and meaning to the term.

Even now, of course, many Americans are acutely anxious to second-guess history. Some are still sensitive to theories of great historical movements, those neat caesuras into which their own history is still divided. The notion that America has a Pacific destiny is a potent myth, to be sure, since it is much older then the century. What is more compelling than to see the movement of population to the West Coast and rising immigration from East Asia, not as a historical footnote but as part of the master text of history? These factors, however, are the stuff of a previous era, the political clichés of a former age. The Pacific Century already looks set to become the greatest cliché of all.

Ultimately the Pacific Century is a product of optimism about the future. For the more pessimistic, the future holds out only the prospect of conflict in Asia, which the United States may find itself meeting alone. Faced with the challenge of China, some political scientists envisage a very different challenge, a clash not of countries but of cultures, a conflict that will be all the more dangerous if the West fails to remain united.

As Samuel Huntington argues, optimism about the future is based on a dubious assumption that commercial interchange is invariably a force for peace. However, he contends, Asia's economic development and growing self-confidence are already disrupting international politics. Economic development has enabled the Asian states to expand their military capabilities and at the same time to bring to the fore issues and rivalries that were suppressed during the Cold War. It has also increased the intensity of conflicts between Asian societies and the United States. Finally, the growth of Chinese influence in the region may well force its neighbours to find some security either in appeasement or in a regional balance with the United States at the head.[10]

Huntington's thesis is an attempt to formulate a new paradigm for international relations. It also offers the West a chance to redefine itself and thus to survive into the next century as a viable political force. It offers a master narrative of history. As such it may remind the reader of one of the most contentious arguments of Spengler's *Decline of the West,* one that he argued with particular passion. Spengler's book, which appeared in 1918, was the first of the great blockbusters with which we are now familiar. It brought the author instant fame, rapidly selling 100,000 copies despite its formidable oracular style, apparent lack of organisation and exhausting prolixity. It was a book that supplied his German readers with the terms in which to interpret their experience of defeat in the war. What made it sell worldwide was that it also fitted the anxious mood of the twentieth century. It resonated in the minds of those who feared that the West was in decline even when they disagreed with Spengler's analysis. Since its publication it has never been out of print.

One of his arguments that has never proved very popular with his readers, however, was his insistence that different cultures are doomed to a dialogue of the deaf. They can never communicate with one another. Spengler took this theory to its logical conclusion. Even the Europeans, he argued, could not understand cultural changes in their own past, those that were "out of phase" with the contemporary age. Even the painting of Rembrandt and the music of Mozart, he predicted, would one day cease to resonate in the Western imagination. Such thinking, of course, led him into a deep impasse: if we can understand neither what is "out of phase" or "out of style" with us, then apparently we can only understand ourselves.[11]

It was an argument with which even his admirers took issue. André Malraux agreed with Spengler up to a point. As the hero of one of his novels, *The Royal Way*, pronounces: "In the last analysis, of course, no civilisation is ever understood by another". It was a theme on which all of Malraux's subsequent writings were but variations. Nevertheless, he took issue with Spengler in his claim that different cultures could borrow one another's styles. If Hegel peopled the past with the 'spirits' of nations, Malraux peopled the history of art with what he called "those imaginary super artists we call styles". Throughout his life he had an uncritical conviction that the visual arts provided the shortest root to understanding the mentality of other civilisations as well as that of another age.

In reaching this conclusion Malraux specifically referred to Nietzsche's "revaluation of values". So did many other art historians of the period. The rediscovery of El Greco in the 1920s, argued Max Dvorak, was to be explained by a change of consciousness, an abrupt reconceptualisation of the Western perception of the world, which he mistakenly attributed to a shift of emphasis from matter to spirit. "If we have recognised in Greco a great artist and a prophetic soul we owe it to this momentous change". Some years later Hans Tietze went further in arguing that cultures can revalue themselves in communion with other cultures. As an example he took the 'invention' of primitivism, the introduction of an Eastern and an African aesthetic into European art, one that he ascribed directly to Nietzsche's principle of "the transvaluation of values".[12]

Interestingly, Spengler grounded his belief that there could be no intercultural exchanges, or dialogues with the past, on a specific refutation of Nietzsche's theory. He accepted that the process of revaluation could take place, but he saw it in negative rather than positive terms. It was interpretative, not creative. When a society tried to reinvent itself it merely confirmed that it was in decline. Revaluation did not transform the soul of a culture, only its style.

The West, he argued, had tried to revalue itself at the end of the nineteenth century but had failed. A nonmetaphysical religion had replaced one based on dogma; natural law had replaced historical law. Artists had begun to experiment with different styles. The West, he concluded, had exhausted its zest for life. It had begun to draw on its capital reserves. It was living off its intellectual annuities. In its belief in socialism he saw the nadir of what had made it great: its will to power. The political experiments of his own day, such as the October Revolution, merely disguised the fact that all the West's ideas were nineteenth-century in origin. The twentieth century merely provided the technical means to realise them.

Though Spengler has been proved wrong in his criticism of Nietzsche, I am of course using Nietzsche's concept as a metaphor, not in the way he intended or in the way it has been interpreted by others at different times. His thesis at least lends itself to the view that history is a permanent dialogue between the past and the present as well as the anticipated future. Cultures can learn from each other, for they too comprise a dialogue between their own internal and external worlds. It could be argued of course that the process is dangerous: that it may drown out debate, or discourage it, or make it more difficult than it might otherwise be. In this respect, there are two arguments that must be treated seriously. The first is that in the case of the Western world's relationship with East Asia, the Asians themselves may arrive at Spengler's conclusion that the West is indeed in decline in large part because it has *devalued* those values on which its previous success was built. This is the idea that there is such a thing as 'Asian values' that are either superior to those of the West or that were once those of the West's (Victorian) past.

It was on this understanding that the Japanese, after all, went to war against the United States in 1941. As a senior Japanese official told reporters in November 1942, the key to victory lay not in the material fighting strength of a nation but in its superior spirit. General Hideki Tojo frequently told audiences that guns only served as the means of fighting. The Japanese could fight without them. At the end of the conflict the head of the Japanese Air Command told his American captors: "We believed our spiritual confidence in victory would balance any scientific disadvantages". In the run-up to the Pacific War the Japanese quite self-consciously challenged what Sir Kenneth Clark once dubbed the Western world's belief in "heroic materialism".[13]

The language may differ today, but the thrust of recent criticisms of the United States sometimes echoes themes that have not been heard for fifty years. In the mid-1990s the Malaysian prime minister, Mahathir bin Mohamad, published a book with a Japanese politician, Shintaro Ishihara, entitled *The Voice of Asia*. In a specific reference to Spengler the authors accused the West of hedonism:

> Materialism, sensual gratification and selfishness are rife. The community has given way to the individual and his desires. The inevitable consequence has been the breakdown of established institutions and diminished respect for marriage, family values, elders and important customs, conventions and traditions. These have been replaced by a new set of values based largely on the rejection of all that relates to spiritual faith and communal life.[14]

Spengler had written of a world in decline and saw revaluation as evidence of it. Ishihara and Mahathir speak of a world that is decadent because it lacks an idea of social value. The only source of value in the West, they contend, is a market that has lost touch with the religious values that Max Weber identified in the 1920s when explaining why capitalism had taken off in Europe rather than Asia.

In this reading of history Asia has nothing to learn from the West except what *not* to do. What it should learn most urgently is that unrestricted economic growth may fatally undermine even its own social structures. As Singapore's first president, Lee Kwan Yu, warned in a speech in Munich in June 1996, there is even a risk that one day Asia's traditional values will be undermined by unimpeded economic growth.[15]

The idea of Western decadence is not easy to sustain. As a civilisation it is still far from having mined all its ideas or exhausted its possibilities, and on the existing evidence, it probably never will. We must also acknowledge that there is a deep difference between the political speeches of politicians from Southeast Asia and those from South Korea and Taiwan. What the former often identify as decadent may well be the features of a mature economy, as more developed societies such as Japan have begun to recognise. A belief that social values should not change over time may be symptomatic of a society that cannot face the demands of the modern era. It is a dangerous form of essentialism from which Western Europe suffered so egregiously in the past.

A second danger would arise if any self-conscious attempt at revaluation were to encourage Asian societies to stress the differences rather than the similarities between themselves and the rest of the world. If those differences are presumed to be profound, then there would be little hope of an intercultural exchange. As Spengler predicted, history would render the major powers deaf mutes to one another.

This is certainly what happened in Japan in the run-up to the Second World War. The interwar period stimulated a search for a philosophical response to the challenge of Western imperialism. An early example is Watsuji Tetsuro's *Studies in the History of the Japanese Spirit* (1926), which explicitly denied the possibility of universal values by polarising Asian spirituality and Western materialism. Whereas Heidegger had grounded the authenticity of a culture's 'being' in a Western understanding of time, Japanese philosophers tried to ground it in terms of space. They tended to stress a spirit of place: a belief in the household or family rather than the self-determining individual who was at the centre of the Western philosophical discourse. In the eyes of Kitaro Nishida, the most important Japanese thinker of the century, a sense of *topos* (or *basho*)—place—was essential to identity, for it was timeless, or independent of history.[16]

It is clear why the Japanese should have put forward these claims. It was a defence against being drawn into history on the West's terms. Heidegger had asserted that once metaphysics had been recognised as the destiny of the West, through their own Westernisation outsiders could authenticate their inauthentic (that is, historyless) existence for the first time. Such thinking persisted well into the Cold War era. As Sartre wrote as late as the 1950s: "The plurality of the *meanings* of History can be discovered and posited for itself only upon the ground of a future totalization. . . . Our historical task, at the heart of the polyvalent world, is to bring closer the moment when History will have *only one meaning,* when it will tend to be dissolved in the concrete men who make it in common".[17]

In the interwar years many Japanese writers chose to assert their autonomy as a people with a history in terms of a 'being' that was timeless, rather than the individual as "a being in time". We find in the writing of linguists such as Tokieda Motoki, or the folklorist Yanagita, or the romantic writer Yasuda Yojuro, who was particularly anti-Western, a belief that Western temporality was ultimately dangerous because it denied permanent historical meaning. The West was always trying to impose a meaning on history in the present. It was bound to fail since individuals disappear from time.[18]

Such musings might not have mattered much, perhaps, but for the Japanese challenge to modernity. At the Bungakutan seminar in the autumn of 1943 on the theme 'Overcoming the Modern', one speaker complained that modernity had alienated the Japanese people from their own traditions. In another paper, however, the critic Nakamura Mituso was one of the first to appreciate the paradox of the exercise. If the intention of the conference was to 'seal' the decline of the West and encourage self-consciousness in Japan, then the modern could indeed be overcome. But if its intention was to go beyond the modern, then the modern would prevail. Japan would have to borrow even more in order to survive. Had not the sacrifices that the Japanese had made in order to challenge the United States in 1941 been too great? To have survived Western encroachment, had the country not Westernised itself too much? Had changes in social life not robbed the Japanese people of confidence in their own identity? "How have the requirements of . . . the ruthless age in which we live by adapting ourselves to necessity distorted our identity"?[19] Some of the other participants at the conference also recognised the irony of the exercise. Though some expressed the hope that a Japanese victory might help the country to "overcome modernity" by prompting its move to a higher stage of intellectual development, they were unable to agree on what higher development would mean without further modernisation. One seemed to presuppose the other while at the same time contradicting it.[20]

In the end the war compelled all but the most implacable traditionalists to accept that they would have to come to terms with the promise of modern life as well as its challenge. Indeed, some time before the end of the war, the philosophers associated with the University of Kyoto began to see their country's impending defeat as a unique opportunity not to repudiate traditional beliefs but to revalue them rather differently than they had after the Meiji Restoration.

Two years after the Bungakutan seminar, in March 1944, Watsuji Tetsuro convened a seminar in Kyoto to study "the reevaluation of the modern age". It was attended chiefly by members of the Faculty of Ethics at Tokyo University, where he was at the same time senior professor of moral philosophy. Watsuji was very much at ease with the Western tradition. He had translated Byron and Shaw and was one of the first philosophers to introduce existentialist thinking to Japan. He even studied for a time with Heidegger. Indeed, much of his criticism of the West was cast in a Western idiom, in "chic, scholarly methods" that Marxists such as Tosaka Jun in the 1930s found challenging precisely because the critique made the defence of Japanese tradition so compelling.[21]

What made his critique particularly important was that he saw the battle between East and West as one not between two cultures but *within* two traditions in Japan.[22] It was continued after the war by three of the more prominent members of his school, Tanabe Hajime, Nishitani Keiji and, above all, Nishida. Nishida too was strongly influenced by Western thinkers, in particular Fichte, Schelling and Hegel, and sought to extend their philosophical writing by undertaking what he believed the West could not. As one of his pupils later wrote, he wanted to lay "new foundations . . . for the Western philosophical tradition that could not be laid in the West" by uniting three different strands that were mutually exclusive in contemporary Western thought: speculation, experience and existentialism. Only by reconciling these three schools could Western metaphysics progress. In synthesising them the Japanese could transform them into something non-Western, something universal as well as new.[23]

In the past the international community had lacked a common language in which to express its common concerns. In the future international peace would depend on whether it found a collective voice. The importance of Nishida's synthesis turned on his recognition that Western philosophy could only be universal if it spoke to the whole world. It was, he claimed, still the product of a particular historical experience, or what he called "the self-formation of historical life", and therefore not free from what Hegel would have called the "particularity" of Western culture. In Nishida's opinion Western metaphysics had transcended the empirical realm in order to find a universal principle. In doing so, however, it had moved away from experience. As for the Japanese, they needed to engage in "trans-descendence" to a more direct experience of themselves.[24]

Looking back at the debate today, we can see how much has changed since the 1930s. What has resulted is a threefold change of consciousness in which Asia and the West see their common future. The first is a response to the alienation that is at the heart of our experience of modernity. We have both come to recognise that there is no such thing as an 'authentic' person, if by authenticity we mean an attempt to eliminate the conflict at the heart of modern life—in short, to escape alienation.

Hegel had hoped that the French Revolution would abolish alienation and reconcile nineteenth-century man to his own age. Marx dreamed of challenging the class principle of history and thus eradicating the anomie at the heart of the industrial system. Locating an authentic Japanese identity in a timeless principle or *topos* was merely another attempt to deal with alienation in time. Whereas the Germans identified a specific historical moment when they could realise their destiny, the Japanese searched for a *timeless* principle that would help them to escape from the acute anxiety they had experienced in a world dominated by others.

Both cultures now recognise that alienation is at the heart of modernity, that humanity is not to be found in time or redeemed from it. Humanity *is* time. Alienation can be mitigated but never resolved. We are condemned to live in the shadow of a past we have not forged and in anticipation of a future we will never experience directly. The present, that "narrow ledge of history", as Milan Kundera calls it, is the only ground of history we have.

There has been a second change in the metaphysical debate that also takes us back to Japanese thinking in the 1930s, in particular to its concern that it lacked a scientific way of thinking. As Tetsuro recognised, a country needed more than to import science or to copy foreign technology. It needed to master it. This is a theme that can be found in his book *The Closed Country*, which was based on a series of lectures he delivered in April 1947.

Today the challenge of globalisation is an experience that East and West are experiencing together.

It has begun to encourage a synthesis of Eastern and Western philosophical thought, an attempt that may encourage both societies to see the world through what Nietzsche called a "trans-Asiatic and trans-European eye".[25]

Indeed, Nietzsche was the first writer of note to put forward this claim to an unusually synoptic and global perspective. It is interesting that he moved to endorsing a synthesis of Western and Eastern thinking at the time when he first began to indict the nationalism of his own era, in response to which he endeavoured to become "a good European".

Among Asian thinkers Nietzsche himself (rather than Hegel or Heidegger) is now a much read author, a man who believed that one of the problems of modernity was its failure to embark on long-term intellectual initiatives. Perhaps an intimation of his early death made him wary of going far down that path. He nevertheless went further than any other Western philosopher.

Looking back at the end of the twentieth century, however, it is clear that globalism has begun to generate renewed interest in Asian thought in the West. Also new developments in quantum physics have fostered an interest in Eastern mysticism.[26]

One of Nietzsche's greatest fears of course was that a scientific world-view would lack sacramental value and thus be deeply alienating. In objectifying everything it would encourage a mechanistic and materialistic mode of thought. His own writing stressed that science conferred no value as such, that it could not produce a faith, an ideal or a goal. It is a complaint, adds the author Okochi Ryogi, that can be found in the work of his own country's philosophers, particularly that of Nishitani Keiji.

As the critic Charles Newman has noted, it is even more a part of the postmodern condition than the modern: "Post-modern means the first culture in history totally under the control of twentieth century technology, and the first in 500 years in which information is codified in ways which do not depend on literacy. All we have discovered, thanks largely to mass communication, is that 'reality' is often more hollow than is verbal configuration, and that meanings date even faster than styles".[27]

In contrast with the literate cultures of the past that stored knowledge in writing and learned to automate it so that it could become information, our information age seems to demand the reverse. Given the constant stream of information, we must be sceptical of any structures of meaning that narrow its flow. For us, no single overarching order can set up proper channels for incoming information. We have no centre around which to organise it. We live in an age that is eroding the gravity of experience, the patient, painstaking ear and eye for meaning.

For the Japanese this challenge is especially important. Their first attempt at revaluing their culture in the light of modern experience placed great emphasis on the sacramental as well as the scientific. Instead of being used as a means to an end, in this case modernisation, religion set the end— which is to say, wrote Robert Bellah, that when religion maintains its "commitment to the source of ultimate value", it remains religion.[28] In the

Meiji era growth became a strategy for survival. In that respect it was very
much an existential experience, a struggle to compete with the West on
equal terms, an experience that no Western power in the encounter with the
non-Western world has had to confront. The survival of Japan's culture did
indeed appear to be conditional for much of the twentieth century. It followed that its modernisation had to be a moral exercise if it were ever to
become a strategy for survival.

Today economic growth has brought its own problems. The poison gas
attack in 1996 on the Tokyo subway by a religious sect revealed how religious terrorism could thrive in a society that for fifty years had been intensely trained on a goal of material success alone. Japan is in a state of
painful transition. But then so is much of the industrialised world. For the
first time, the world faces that challenge together.

What also distinguishes the philosophical debate from that of the past is
that the discourse is no longer principally with German metaphysicians but
with American writers like Richard Rorty and John Rawls. It is a debate
not only about cultural identity but also about democratic values. This was
not a debate that was much encouraged by the West in the first half of the
twentieth century. Despite their protestations to the contrary, the Western
powers made little effort to promote democracy. They found themselves
compromised as colonial administrators. Even countries like Britain were
not convinced of the necessity of promoting democracy nearer home.
During the Second World War the Foreign Office was notably doubtful
about the wisdom of restoring democratic regimes in Latin countries, even
in Italy, with which it was at war.[29]

Democracy was imposed on Japan by the United States, as it was also
imposed on Germany. Both countries were forced to choose whether to retain their cultural independence at the cost of political impotence or join a
community that was about to enter into a prolonged war with Soviet communism. In Germany the Allied occupation consolidated democratic forces
that had been weak but identifiable for a long time. In Japan the outcome
was different again.

It is still American folklore, of course, that Japan owes its democratic
system as well as its economic resurgence to the five years of American occupation. General Douglas MacArthur propagated this view by referring to
the Japanese as an adolescent nation, a country still in its teens, one
younger than more adult powers such as Germany. The Japanese, he remarked in 1948, were "thirsty" for democracy. In his memoirs he recorded
how under his own trusteeship they had experienced a "spiritual revolution" that overnight had transformed a collectivist society into one in
which individual liberties were held in high esteem.

In retrospect we can see that there is still a long way to go. Japan has still
to demonstrate its ability to deliver "quality-based growth" rather than

growth based on adding even larger quantities of capital and labour. To do so it will have not only to become more innovative but also to combine further development with economic freedom on a much greater scale than it has thus far.

What is prompting this debate is the slowdown of the Japanese economy. Japan has been there before, of course, particularly after the oil crisis of the 1970s, when leading firms shed jobs and asset prices plunged, and growing crime rates added to the gloom. But then it managed to pull out of the recession. This time the economy has been languishing since 1990 and is still showing little real sign of improvement as it begins a second descent into another downward cycle.

These trends are of much longer duration than often supposed. Output per unit of work, which gave an annual raise of 6–8 percent for much of the century, began to slow in the early 1970s. This does not shock economists who believe in the 'convergence hypothesis', the idea that productivity rates tend to even out among industrialised countries. What *is* surprising is that Japanese growth seems to be stalled prematurely at the point where output per worker is well below American levels. Even more surprising is the fact that Japanese productivity rates have slowed in spite of a sustained investment effort that has exceeded the U.S. rate of capital accumulation. This would suggest that the average return on new investment in Japan is well below the return in the United States. Unless Japan manages to increase its rate of productive growth, living standards will undoubtedly decline.

What the Japanese economy lacks is what the United States economy still has: a freewheeling culture that allows rapid change and encourages innovation. Japan will simply have to become more innovative. A culture that relies so heavily on the group, glorifies consensus and concentrates financial decisionmaking in the hands of a few large institutions is going to have a very tough time producing its own Silicon Valleys in the future. The revaluation of values that followed the war hardly touched the workforce. It largely affected an elite that encompassed the country's corporate managers, academics and political leaders. If Japan is to continue to develop as a modern society its people will have to be revalued too.

That is the message of Patrick Smith's excellent book *Japan: A Reinterpretation* (1996). His conclusions are in many respects not dissimilar from mine. Japan, he writes, is in the habit of reinventing itself and is in the process of doing so once again. It has an urgent need to because its economic overdevelopment conceals the social and psychological underdevelopment of its people. In setting out his argument Smith talks of "a retrieval of history or part of it"; the Japanese must revisit the past in order to march into the future. If they are successful, this will have a significance quite beyond Japan itself—for it will confirm that the world can move beyond the old assumption that the 'modern' is by definition 'Western' as well.[30]

In the near future, of course, it is not Japan but China that clearly poses the greatest challenge. From being Public Enemy No. 1 in the last years of the Cold War, Japan has been demoted in the popular demonology. From being a silent partner in the Cold War China has become the society with which many Americans believe they may find themselves at war in the early years of the twenty-first century.[31]

It is much too early to say whether China will continue to flounder between state control and the market, as some Chinese become very rich and others very poor, or whether its civil consciousness will disintegrate altogether. Or whether, engulfed in what Nicholas Kristof calls "Market-Leninism", it will succumb to the peaceful evolution that the present Chinese leadership most fears, its own nonviolent disappearance.[32]

China may emerge as a fully modern state or dissolve into a vast Third World country dominated by a rapacious elite with the cities arrayed against the countryside and wealth against pervasive poverty, a society in which technological advance will conceal desperate social ills. The country still appears to be on a collision course with its future in areas such as Shanghai and the coastal enterprise zones that have sprouted since the 1980s. It is still left with countless unresolved conflicts from the past that threaten to *devalue* life for the majority of its people.

In the 1930s the China on the hinterland of the Western spheres of influence in cities such as Shanghai seemed to exist in a perpetual state of confrontation with the countryside. The situation today is not very different. The urban Chinese still tend to regard the peasants as a source of cheap labour, or the source of crime and instability, or all three. Fifty million or more migrants have moved to the cities. Two hundred million more are permanently unemployed. If the inland areas are allowed to continue with their backwardness while the coastal areas take off, there will be little stability nationwide. Already the clocks are running backwards, with a disillusioned peasant population rejecting the modernised reforms that have left them even more impoverished. Many have revived the cult of Mao. Others are rekindling old faiths such as Taoism. It is a potent and unstable mix of chaotic economic change and deadening political immobility that can only increase the risk of a social explosion.

There are also ominous echoes of the intellectual debate that engaged the Japanese in the 1930s. Already a group of young intellectuals, Marxist fundamentalists in all but name, clustered around the Ministry of Propaganda and associated with journals such as *Seeking Truth,* are convinced that China is on course for a "historic clash" with the West. Another faction—a new wave of nationalists writing books like *China Can Say No* and *Viewing China Through a Fourth Eye*—is of the same opinion, though the premises on which it arrives at its conclusions are different again. Both groups are fighting for the 'soul' of the nation much as the Japanese intellectuals did in their own country in the run-up to the Pacific War.

But much has changed in the interim. If China does find itself at war with the United States the causes are likely to be more mundane. It is unlikely to be historically conditioned. Instead a political leadership fighting for its life may play the nationalist card in an attempt to cling to power. It is by no means obvious that it would succeed. Despite the party's longevity, it is already running against the grain of history, not with it.

On the other hand, China may revalue itself successfully. The Communist Party may change—or have to. It is beginning to become clear, even in Asia, that the next phase of economic growth will depend on a nation's ability to innovate and to develop American-style management skills. And for that to happen it will have to mobilise and educate its population in order to improve what Asia still markedly lacks—factor productivity. It would seem that this type of progress can only be achieved in more pluralistic societies. If East Asia is to continue to compete successfully with the West it may have to resemble it a little more in its commitment to some form of popular democracy.

The confidence of the Western world should be enhanced by this development. It looks very much as though other cultures are not intrinsically different from its own. Modern societies tend to be democratic, though perhaps of *economic* necessity rather than choice. Those who used to claim that Asians were only interested in making money, in economic freedom not human rights, have been confounded by the rise of the democratic movements in prosperous societies such as South Korea and Taiwan. These societies, of course, are still in the early stages of deciding what the proper balance between collective and individual interests should be. It is the process of modernisation, nevertheless, that has prompted that debate.

Modern societies seem to produce democratic pressures. Wealth creation seems to lead to a greater emphasis on human dignity. If this really is the case, then we should expect to see the growth of many more pluralist democratic systems in the future. If it is also true that democratic societies do not go to war against each other, this should make for a less dangerous world.

The Challenge of Islamic Revivalism

If, as Simon Schama has written, the French Revolution was "the crucible of modernity", we should expect it to have an impact on the non-Western world. It did. The French Revolution too intruded itself into the Islamic consciousness as it did that of Hegel and Goethe, whose debate between themselves anticipated that "general crisis" in which the West emerged the victor.

Napoleon's invasion in 1798 may not have been recorded by the Arab chroniclers of the time, except as a side event that interrupted the pilgrimage to Mecca that year. But there were people who saw it for what it really marked: the return of the West after its defeat in the Crusades, and this time so powerful that it would not be easily defeated. The Egyptian chronicler Abdul al-Rahman al-Jabarti saw the emergence of a new order. The fact that he participated in the General Council that Napoleon set up to administer Egypt after the defeat of the Mamluks did not reconcile him to the "new era" of catastrophe that he predicted was about to descend on the Islamic world.[33]

What distressed him most was the French belief that they had nothing to learn from the East, but the East had a great deal to learn from them. "Soldiers, you are undertaking a conquest with incalculable consequences for civilisation", Napoleon told his troops as they set off for Egypt. France considered the process of civilisation to be complete at home. It had become the standard-bearer of civilisation in foreign lands. It was on that understanding that the West dismissed the Islamic world for the next hundred and fifty years. As T. E. Lawrence wrote, the Arabs had centuries of history but no experience. Or as one British scholar opined in the 1930s, the Islamic world represented nothing more than a "historic fossil". Even today French schoolchildren learn from a popular text—written in the 1950s—that the Algerian people had only emerged into history when they were brought by force into the French empire.[34]

So calamitous was Napoleon's invasion that Sayyid Qutb, one of the founders of Islamic radicalism in the 1920s, saw it as the "greatest rupture" of all in Islamic history, for it had prevented the Islamic world from living out the divine message. It was only after this foreign incursion that "God's attributes of exclusive sovereignty and lordship were appropriated by human beings".[35]

The Islamic world faced a threat from outside—Westernisation—just as Europe faced a threat from within—nihilism. Both were nihilistic in the sense that Westernisation denied the Arabs self-respect. In much of the Islamic world a foreign culture intruded in everyday life with devastating effect. The secularisation of knowledge devalued Islamic creativity.[36] The Western division of knowledge into disciplines shaped by other people's perceptions, ideologies and concepts of the world made the Islamic worldview subordinate to that of Western civilisation.[37]

The second aspect of the general crisis in the Islamic world took the form of an Islamic *trahison des clercs*. In the 1920s a number of European writers regretted the willingness of the intellectuals of the day to allow their thoughts to be used by politicians, often in ways that conflicted with the spirit of their ideas. "The best answer to the betrayal of life by intellect", wrote Ernst Jünger, "would be the betrayal of intellect by intellect and one of the great joys of this age is to participate in this work of destruction". Many Islamic writers, looking back on a disastrous twentieth century, find a depressing betrayal of another kind, by socialists, neo-Marxists and even liberals who sought to revalue life on the basis of ideas that, though critical of colonialism, nonetheless devalued the Arab experience.

Both crises were reinforced by something absent from Western history in this period: a fatalism or refusal to protest, which derived from the low priority traditionally accorded to political action in Islamic thinking. Since the Koran enjoins believers to obey those who exercise authority unless they depart from Koranic teachings, Islamic theologians have tended to be quietists. Since the Koran tells its readers that all human power tends to be unjust, it matters little who is in power or how power has been acquired, only whether or not the rulers obey the injunctions of the *shari'a*. The upshot was what sociologists call a "culture of dependency", a term first used in the United States to describe a people who believed poverty to be external to themselves and as a result felt that they could do little about it.[38]

In these circumstances it is hardly surprising that Islamic fundamentalism has grown. Nor is it surprising that so too has a much more significant movement, Islamic revivalism, which is of a very different nature. What *is* surprising is that the latter should be ignored in the interest of the former, that fundamentalism should be seen by so many observers in the West, including the former NATO secretary-general Willy Claes, as the next historical challenge. It is a perspective that locates Islam and the West in a quasi-Hegelian view of history, one that posits not a clash of peoples but one of ideas.

What the West was confronting, wrote one conservative observer at the end of the 1980s, were "deep historical currents" that might, if not negotiated successfully, pull it along the slipstream of history.[39] More dispassionate scholars such as Bernard Lewis who have been studying the Islamic world for years appeared to be cognisant of a new moment in history: "It should now be clear that we are facing a *mood* and a movement far transcending the level of issues and policies in the governments that pursue them. This is no less than a clash of civilisations—that of perhaps a rational but surely historic reaction of an ancient rival against our Judeo-Christian heritage, our secular present and our worldwide expansion of both".[40]

In the mullahs' fierce attacks on Western civilisation American observers tended to be confirmed in their conviction that the worlds of secularism and Islam were as fundamentally incompatible as those of capitalism and communism. Of the two protagonists, indeed, the Islamic world appeared to be the more intractable. It was seen by many as a force similar in its intent to fascism and Marxism: not a break with history, but a continuation of a historic trend—the revolt against modernity.

As we move from the twentieth century into the twenty-first, however, a different reading of history seems to be in order. In most of the Islamic world a quite different historical force is at work: that of Islamic *revivalism*. This is a modern ideology that allows its followers to rediscover the original meaning of the Islamic message and so to translate it into action. It is a modern, acculturalist ideology shaped by the forces of the modern world to which it has responded while developing its own distinct idiom. In particular, it is fully consistent with three major aspects of modernity that helped the West to prevail in its long struggle against totalitarianism.

The first is the modern scientific tradition. Before the beginning of this century science was considered to embody an absolute truth with an independent existence. In political life societies were encouraged to perceive absolute truth directly and to construct theories like Marxism around it. In the course of the century, however, science changed significantly. It became self-referential. Scientists now acknowledge that it does not matter what, for example, quantum mechanics is about. The important thing is that it works in all possible experiential situations. Modern science has done away with the idea of a one-to-one correspondence between reality and theory. The mind cannot grasp reality, only ideas about reality. Whether something is true depends not on how closely it corresponds to absolute truth but whether it is consistent with our own experience. Most Western scientists would agree with Niels Bohr's contention that there is no point in seeking a model of a reality that can be conceived independently of our experience of it. Nor is there much point in trying to rationalise these experiences (as Marx tried to) in order to formulate a single principle (the class principle of history).

What proved to be the undoing of the Soviet version of modernity was that in the three spheres of culture, politics and the economy each were made to obey a logic that was absolutist rather than relativist, and thus deeply unscientific. They often worked at the expense of each other and in the process unbalanced the relationship among all three. In the political sphere, the needs of the party took precedence over all other aspects of political life. The need for political control also made the Soviet economy increasingly autarkic. In the cultural world the claims of Marxism-Leninism to represent a scientific worldview led to the invention of a series of pseudosciences; in the case of genetics, the result was disastrous for Soviet agriculture in the 1950s.

Ironically, what makes Islamic fundamentalism so dangerous in the eyes of many Western observers is the appeal of science and technology in the modern Islamic imagination. Indeed, one of its most interesting features is that, compared with the sustained iconophobia of the nineteenth century, there has been little if any Ludditism in Muslim societies. There has been no smashing of machines, no repudiation of the Western sciences.

This should not be surprising. Islamic fundamentalists are likely to be the children of *urban* immigrants rather than rural peasants, as was not the case a hundred years ago. Unlike their parents, many of them have had an education. A large number of Iranians are qualified in the applied sciences. Many of the followers of Ayatollah Khomeini were computer programmers and electrical engineers. Only few were students in disciplines that explore the ambiguities of meaning or analyse the grand narratives that govern life in terms of myth. Many, in other words, have been trained in the applied, not the pure, sciences. An applied scientist who espouses fundamentalism need feel no sense of contradiction, any more than an air force pilot or even a nuclear physicist.

Islamic revivalism is different again. The majority of economic and scientific techniques in the Islamic world are fully consistent with the modern scientific tradition. If the modern mode of production requires order, cost-effectiveness, thrift, a division of labour and a free market; if it requires those who operate the market to be sensitive in turn to notions of obligation and fulfilment of contract; if, above all, it requires us to experience what we preach, then one can hardly argue that Islam is unmodern. If that is indeed what a modern society demands—or more to the point what the construction of such an society may require—then revivalist Islam, in the words of Ernest Gellner, seems to be "custom made".

The second aspect of modernity that was crucial to the West's struggle against totalitarianism is that it is also based on the proposition that knowledge is not culture-specific but universal, even if the values derived from it are shaped by cultural norms. It was the failure to recognise this that undid the Soviet experiment after 1950. Many of the scientific theories that the Soviets espoused after the Second World War were not linked to the modern scientific spirit. Einstein, Bohr and Heisenberg all questioned the existence of rigid scientific laws. Lysenko's bogus work on genetics totally ignored the work of de Vries at the turn of the century, the man who introduced the concept of chance into biology. The Soviet regime entrusted Lysenko with the task, in Camus's vivid phrase, of "disciplining the chromosomes" and thus demonstrating once again the truth of determinism.[41]

The Soviet Union suffered to the very end, even after Lysenko had been disgraced. The problem ran much deeper than the deterministic ideology on which the socialist experiment was based. In a protest letter sent to Leonid Brezhnev in the mid-1970s by Andrey Sakharov (the founder of Soviet nuclear physics) and several other distinguished colleagues, the case was made for democratising public life. What made the task urgent was "the close link between problems of technical-economic progress, scientific methods of management and questions of information, publicity and competition". The world was moving into a second industrial revolution that was going to require a wide exchange of information and ideas. Such a change could not occur in Russia, they warned, as long as the "anti-democratic traditions and norms" of Soviet socialism persisted.[42]

Islam too can be interpreted as a deterministic faith, with its own philosophy of history and thus its own privileged access to the truth. Since the late 1970s a number of Islamic scholars have launched a quest for the Islamicisation of knowledge on the grounds that the Islamic world will never solve its problems until it abandons categories and concepts that are inimical to the ethical spirit of Islam itself. Only when modern knowledge has been 'Islamicised', only when it has been imbibed with the ethical spirit of the faith, will it become an instrument in the modernisation of Islamic life.

There have already been several attempts to teach an Islamic science, including in the social sciences sociology and anthropology. The most sustained attempt has been in the field of economics, a discipline with its own categories and analytic tools. It has even engendered its own institutions such as banks operating on the basis of zero interest. The failure of such attempts so far suggests that most Muslim politicians recognise that knowledge cannot be Islamicised, that it is the heritage of every society prepared to utilise it for its own ends.

Finally, modernity is also the name we give for increasing the effectiveness of means. It does not constitute an end. The end is not the devaluation but the preservation of traditional cultural values, including spiritual ones, for the modernisation of any society must be a moral undertaking if it is to succeed at all.

Nazism claimed to be precisely that. From the very outset of his political career Hitler defined his movement as a "political article of faith". The redemptive character given to the regime was transfigured into the flow of secularist politics, constructed on the faith of a people in a better future, or what Hitler himself called "a mystical hope". Even in the early days of the party he defined its structure in sacral-religious terms. National socialism demanded that faith precede understanding. In the Third Reich religious concepts were not invalidated. They were retained as a part of a racial theory. The Nazis merely deprived them of their original theological content and converted them into a critique of Western humanism. In so doing, of course, they ultimately subverted Germany's moral code. They replaced it with an amoral religious philosophy.[43]

One of the reasons for the apparent success of the Soviet Union in the early years of its life was that it was committed to a spiritual principle, the creation of a new society, even a new kind of man. Communism owed a large debt to Hegel, who had secularised the Christian doctrine of providence into the "cunning of reason" and converted the belief in salvation into a secular theodicy, or what the philosopher Karl Löwith preferred to call "a metaphysical historicism", a substitute religion that became the faith of those whose scepticism was not vigorous enough to dispense altogether with belief in the redemption of man.

Marxism in fact was definingly Christian in its themes—in its opposition between free will (liberty) and determinism or predestination (history). Not even God was absent from the text. History assumed his functions if not his face, with one critical difference. Unlike the Christian God it did not assume a human form, nor was it an accomplice in the destiny of Marxist societies. Human beings were history's accomplices and it fulfilled its destiny in them.

Communism, however, lost its religious fervour long before the end. From the moment the Soviet Union chose to engage the West in the marketplace, ideology became far less important in Soviet life. The result was a society that was deeply cynical, intellectually sterile and materially minded.

In the early days of the Cold War, there were also a number of Western writers who were critical of how little emphasis the West too had put on the values that it was in the business of defending. Broadcasting to a defeated German nation in 1945, T. S. Eliot expounded the view that Western civilisation stood in mortal peril because nationalism had displaced morality in the European consciousness. Later ideology had replaced religion as the basis of Western humanism. He described what had happened as a closing of "mental frontiers" that had accompanied the closing of political frontiers in the East.

Eliot did not ask the West to rediscover its faith in God. He did plead, however, for it to rediscover its commitment to Christian humanism. At the end of the bloodiest and most barbaric war in its history it needed to remind itself that only a Christian culture could have produced what many considered to be its greatest accomplishment: its body of philosophical thought from Voltaire to Nietzsche.[44]

It was a plea that went unanswered. At a conference on the meaning of history convened by the Ecumenical Institute in Geneva the following year, the participants found themselves at a loss to say what Christianity meant in the modern world. One of them, Arnold Toynbee, preferred to use the term "post-Christian" to describe the West's religious foundations. He was concerned that the gospels had become so associated with the West that Christianity was in danger of becoming culture-specific. The Westernisation of Christianity, he hoped, was merely a historical phase, an episode in a longer history. Writing much later, in 1957, he urged the Christian church to purge itself of "its western accessories".[45]

Toynbee changed his position several times during the course of his career, but at the end of his life he believed in the need—in a world in which the Western powers had engaged the Soviet bloc in a nuclear standoff—for the West to rededicate itself to its own values, to agree to what he called "the reconsecration" of the idea of liberty. It was not a goal that demanded a return to orthodox Christianity, but it would require the West to remain true to the Christian faith.

Long before his death, however, the cause that he had hoped to see 're-consecrated' had given way to modernity itself, to the material enhancement of life rather than man's spiritual enlightenment. It is only at the end of the century that Toynbee is finally being vindicated. Indeed, social theory is now beginning to accept the 'normalisation' of religion in political and social life as modernity is 'demythologised' from the excessive assumptions about human nature, science and progress that have dominated the Western imagination since the Enlightenment. This will be a very different trend from the demythologising of religion that was undertaken by modernist writers at the turn of the century.

Max Weber would lead us to expect a congruence between a modern economy and its associated beliefs. In the Islamic world the role of religion is not anachronistic; it is a vital part of the modern experience. The evidence so far would suggest that the world of Islam is no less favourable to modernity than is the world of the West. "A puritan and scripturalist world religion," wrote Gellner, "does not seem necessarily doomed to erosion to modern conditions. It may, on the contrary, be favoured by them".[46]

Russia and the West's Historical Testament

A civilisation, Octavio Paz tells us, is a translation of common ideas and practises. It does not require one interpretation. There are many ways of saying the same thing, and many things can be said in the same way. There must exist, of course, a common medium. Since the Enlightenment, philosophy has determined the language of politics in the West. It has provided the terms of reference in which its members have engaged one another. In the case of Germany ideas may have been at the root of its claims against the West, but as a society it was rooted in the European tradition. There were neo-Hegelians in England up to the early twentieth century, just as there was a strong liberal tradition in Germany throughout the nineteenth century.

What has always made Russia different from the West was the absence not so much of a liberal as of a philosophical tradition, as Bruno Bauer was among the first to point out when calling for a Western alliance in the 1850s. One can find interesting philosophical works such as Chaadayev's denunciation of the Russian past, present and future in his *First Philosophical Letter.* But these texts are not read by non-Russians. In principle, notes Ernst Neizvestnyi, one of Russia's foremost philosophers of art, literature not philosophy has been at the centre of the Russian tradition. This is in part because there has never been a distinction between philosophy and art in Russian thinking.

What is impressive about Russian literature is its criticism of all things Russian (as even the Marquis de Custine, one of its severest critics, was the first to concede). The self-understanding of the Russian mission is to be found not in philosophy but in the picture of provincial life presented in Nikolay Gogol's *Dead Souls*, in Mikhail Saltykov's picture of officialdom, in Maksim Gorky's diatribes against the peasants and in the satirical sketches of Russian life in the 1920s by Evgenii Zamiatin.[47]

The problem is that Russia is intensely self-regarding in one crucial respect: it is not a universalistic but a contextual society. Russian thought has not expressed as much interest in the nature of the human condition as in the study of Russia. In part this is reflected in its language. If we take the simple word *pravda,* we find that it cannot be translated, and therefore it has no universal appeal. It is a word that is rooted in the Russian tradition, combining as it does two quite different concepts—truth (*istina*) and justice (*spravedlivost*). In West European thought, truth and justice are separate concepts. For positivists justice is a moral imperative, whereas truth is purely objective. Truth can exist without justice. The notion of truth equalling justice, of course, is the principal source of Russian philosophical maximalism. As Neizvestnyi writes, "It is this which accounts for the Russian infatuation with extremism, revolution and counter-revolution, dissidence and repression".[48]

What is also significant about Russia in the Western imagination is that it was the first society in history to embark on a self-conscious exercise in revaluation. It tried to 'Westernise' itself in the eighteenth century. It was the best example, wrote Spengler, of a phenomenon he himself called "pseudo-morphosis" (or what anthropologists now call deceptive cultural formation). It is a concept that throws light on the tenuous relationship between a satellite society and that into whose field it has been drawn.

In essence Spengler's idea is simple to grasp. Whenever two civilisations interact with each other, one is bound to be more powerful, the other more creative. In this situation the more creative will be forced to conform outwardly to the more powerful civilisation's cultural configuration, although the latter's ideas will never really take root.

"Don't believe this Nevsky Prospect ... everything is a dream, everything is deception, everything is not what it seems", wrote Gogol in the spring of 1835. A half Westernised Russia was never at ease with itself, even in the nineteenth century. It was its Western visitors who gave it the benefit of the doubt. They continued to take St. Petersburg, the symbol of its Westernisation, at face value, seeing the city as a modern community in the monotony of its grand façades and the lack of animation in its streets. Dostoyevsky's 'underground man' had its true measure when he famously called it "the most abstract and contrived city in the world".[49]

Whether Russia will once again constitute a challenge to the West will be determined by whether the society it is in the process of becoming is not as abstract and contrived as it was in the past. It will fail in its attempt to become a modern society if it devalues itself in an attempt to become what the West would like it to become. It is a unique culture. Modernisation must work to maintain that uniqueness, not stifle it.

Russia will never be co-opted into the Western political community, nor for that matter into the Western world. To understand why, we need look no further than its émigrés, the writers who fled to the West but, on settling there, discovered how different they were from the people among whom they had settled. One of the most forceful rejections of Westernisation ever penned is to be found in an open letter by the first émigré of all, Aleksandr Herzen, who left Russia in 1847. Herzen lived a large part of his life, twenty years in all, in exile in Paris. He was a cultured man, well versed in the ideas of philosophers such as Ludwig Feuerbach and well read in the French philosophical writings of the late eighteenth century. Towards the end of his life, however, he found himself increasingly thrown back on Russia as a source of inspiration.

In an open letter he wrote in response to the criticisms of his own country made by Jules Michelet, he insisted that the West could make no demands on Russia's affection or expect the Russian people ever to pay it the moral tribute of becoming part of the Western world. "Would you condemn a foundling for having no respect for his parents?" he asked. "The history of the West provides us with certain lessons, but no more. . . . We do not consider ourselves to be the legal executors of your historical testament".[50]

Michelet, as we have seen, was one of the first writers to call for a Western alliance against a common threat—Russian imperialism. He was also one of the first to find most threatening its 'communist' spirit. Michelet found Russia threatening because it was a society based on a communal vision, on the village commune. Herzen, for his part, saw the system as the salvation of the Russian peasant. Indeed, in the last years of his life he wrote eloquent pages about peasant life. What he valued most was its spontaneous Russian character, uncontaminated by the corrosive doubts and moral values of a Western world that appeared to be in decline.

Herzen persuaded himself that the Russian peasantry, with its "natural socialist outlook", would be able, in a way the West had not, to marry the claims of individual liberty with the demands of industrialisation. In short, it would offer the world the chance to preserve a model by which personal life could be maintained in an industrial society, a model of a world that was not alienated from its history.

Looking back at Herzen's arguments we can see that the debate has not changed much over the century. Russia is still fundamentally un-Western and is likely to remain so well into the twenty-first century. It is still struggling with what Herzen called "the greatest problem of the age". In maintaining its self-respect, it is still unwilling to look to the United States as an example, not because America fears it so much, but because it respects it so little.

In this spirit, what the most recent émigrés have to say about themselves and their country's future is as interesting as the conclusions Herzen reached a hundred years ago. No one was more forceful in this respect than the Nobel Prize winner Joseph Brodsky in the last years of his life. Like Herzen, Brodsky knew the Western world at first hand. He lived in the United States for the last twenty years of his life. He felt comfortable living in New York and giving commencement addresses at some of America's famous universities. He wrote exquisite English verse. Yet he felt increasingly

critical of the West's attempts to transform the Russia he loved into something other than it was.

Much of what has happened in Russia in the twentieth century, he insisted, could be traced back to the American belief that it could provide an
example for other countries to follow, that America's own values were indeed universal in their appeal. Surely what the West should have recognised
at the end of the twentieth century was that although values are indeed universal, every society must find them in its own traditions.

Indeed, Brodsky concluded that American exemplarism was as much a
danger to Russia as Marxism had been in the past. Perhaps, he cautioned,
the language of American policy with its call for Americanisation was not
much better at its core than the language peddled by Marx. The United
States still tended to treat the Russians as little better than its own Indians,
as he suggested in an open letter to Václav Havel in 1994:

> Isn't this the juncture at which we find ourselves? . . . Should "Indians" em-
> bark on imitating "cowboys", or should they consult the spirits about other
> options? May it be that the magnitude of the tragedy that befell them is, in it-
> self, a guarantee that it won't happen again? May their grief and their memory
> of what happened in their past create a greater egalitarian bond than free en-
> terprise and a bicameral legislature? And if they should draft a constitution
> anyway, maybe they should start by recognizing themselves and their history
> for the better part of this century as a reminder of Original Sin.[51]

Like Herzen, Brodsky rejected the idea that the Western historical testament was universal in its appeal. He argued not for the approach of the
cowboys, who "believe in the law, and reduce democracy to people's equality before it: i.e., to the well-policed prairie", but for "equality before culture".[52] In that sense the debate in Washington as to whether Russia has
been lost or is about to be lost is meaningless: there was never anything for
the West to win.

At the end of the century the revaluation of Russian culture remains as
central to Western security as ever. It is not in the West's interests for the
Russians to repudiate what makes their culture so distinctive in a naive belief in the virtues of overenthusiastic modernisation. Arrested modernity of
course would also be dangerous. In both cases the self-conscious rejection
of the task of 'remaking' Russian man is surely the central lesson that
should have been learned from seventy years of communism.

It is not surprising of course that so many Americans should think in
terms of 'winning' Russia as if it were a strategic prize to be secured by ju-
dicious diplomacy. For is Russia not another defeated country, one that
though not occupied like Germany and Japan in 1945 could still be anchored into the Western world? In the closing years of his life Richard
Nixon persistently criticised his government for failing "to seize the mo-

ment, to shape the history of the next half century" by bringing Russia into the Western world. Another critic condemned the Bush administration for failing to exploit a unique opportunity to make the twenty-first century happier than the twentieth, for failing to 'win' Russia to the Western cause.[53]

In the case of Russia, of course, there is a specific security aspect that is not to be found in the West's relationship with many other societies. As James Baker hoped, it might be possible to seize "a historic opportunity" to "anchor Russia ... into the Euro-Atlantic community".[54] Such an objective, however, would be desirable neither for the West nor for Russia.

This is not necessarily a pessimistic conclusion to draw. If it is true that the Western world is beginning to recognise that neither essentialism nor universalism is desirable in itself, then perhaps the estrangement of the two societies will be less critical than in the past.

As Nietzsche tells us, we are our own value esteemers. What we value most is the respect of others. But respect has to be won. Russia has never really won the world's respect except (ironically) for a brief moment, the worst in its history, when Western intellectuals visited Moscow to see the future that worked, or admired it for its resolve during the Second World War. To some extent it still lives off of those memories. What the Russian people face is a unique challenge—to become for the first time a nation that respects itself, one that is also less intent on winning the respect of others. Instead of building itself up as another Great Power, it could choose instead to construct a Great Society that will earn the esteem of others.

The prospect that this will happen, it must be admitted, is not good. At worst, however, it is unlikely that Russia will ever again constitute the 'Cossack menace' it did in the Western consciousness after 1870. The frontiers of the Western world are being pushed eastwards. The Slavophile ideology has largely vanished. As the 'Third Rome' Russia exists only in the fevered imagination of a few writers and politicians. Russia is likely to remain a lesser power, and one that, of necessity, will have to turn inwards to its own salvation rather than to seek the redemption of others.

Doubtless Russia will continue to worry its neighbours for some time to come. It is adrift, unanchored in the Western world, undermined in its own. The difference is that this time it will not be seen as a threat to Western values as it was after 1870, for there will be no West for it to threaten. It will be seen as the Germans saw it before 1870: as a great power that may be suborned or deterred, co-opted or appeased, as events may dictate.

Conclusion

In the course of the second half of the century modernity rather than capitalism became the West's main line of engagement with the future. It still is.

The Western world prevailed in its conflict with totalitarianism because it was more modern, and hence more functional.

Nazi Germany was an example of *retarded* modernity. It talked the language of modernity but was frightened of the conflicts and ambiguities it produced. It was not a modern state like mid–twentieth century-Britain or France. It was based on an irrational ideology that, although it used the language of reason, was deeply antagonistic to the values of the Enlightenment. It was an excellent example of arrested development.

The Soviet Union, by contrast, always considered itself to be a more modern society. It claimed, after all, to be the first 'scientific socialist' state. By the 1940s the Soviet state was built on the discovery and application of historical laws whose logical outcome was meant to be the construction of a scientific worldview. Unfortunately, if its scientific status was meant to be the embodiment of the functional principles of a modern society, its actual practice was extremely dysfunctional.

It remained a construct of an alien ideology rather than that of a people struggling to reach the future as soon as they could. Ill at ease with its best traditions, while remaining true to its worst, it never became a genuinely modern state. By the late 1980s even the Soviet leadership had begun to recognise that its economic failure was largely the fault of an ideology whose chief ethos was antiscientific as well as antihumanitarian. When the whole system finally collapsed it did so not because it was illiberal but because it was 'unmodern'.

Most Western Sovietologists (there were a few notable exceptions) placed so little emphasis on the concept of modernity that they were caught off guard by the speed of the Soviet Union's collapse. Most scholars preferred to conduct rather arid discussions about the size of the country's defence budgets or the success of its five-year plans. They were right, of course, to put less emphasis on ideological motivation and more on the utility of the Soviet system. They were wrong, however, to place so little emphasis on the value of modernity itself.

It was a lesson that did not become fully apparent until the last years of the Cold War, in the wake of the nuclear disaster of Chernobyl in 1986. As V. A. Legasov, the nuclear physicist appointed to head the enquiry into the disaster, later reported, the tragedy had been caused not by a failure of physics or technology but by a chronic failure of the men in charge. The subordination of its scientists to the ideological imperatives of the state was proof that, as scientists, they could no longer be trusted. In a socialist society they had grown up with only a utilitarian ethos. In other words, the responsibility of the men who caused the disaster at Chernobyl was not a cause but a consequence of a lack of ethical content in their work.

Without a modern scientific ethic knowledge could indeed be rendered harmful. Was not the prime condition of scientific success, Legasov contended, the adoption of a set of distinctly 'modern values' that necessarily had to include truth, trust, integrity and dissent? In a society in which such values were not respected, did not the scientist have to create them first, to make the practice of science possible?[55]

The Cold War offers the world a lesson for the future. The revaluation of values is not an individual strategy for survival. It is one that modernity demands. It is no longer the mark of the Western world. It is an international phenomenon. It is one that a civil society must undertake if its citizens are not to be totally alienated by modern (or postmodern) life.

One of the few visionaries who recognised what this might lead to was—rather surprisingly perhaps—Raymond Aron, an old Cold Warrior, a man who broke with Sartre and became a voluble critic of a communist world that despite losing its prophetic powers still retained its arms. Long before the Cold War had run its course Aron claimed that the concept of civilisation as the West had defined it since the eighteenth century had lost much of its force. It was becoming devalued. There was an urgent need to transcend it. That is the task that faces the world if civilisation itself is to be defended from fundamentalist forces, such as fear, alienation and superstition. "The phase of civilisation is coming to an end," wrote Aron, "and for good or ill humanity is embarking on a new phase", that of forging a single civilisation which for the first time in history, may become truly universal in its appeal.[56]

8

The Axioms of Twilight

When writing this book I was often reminded of Spengler's *Decline of the West,* his graphic description of Western civilisation in 1918.[1] Like Hegel, Spengler believed that every culture has a destiny or a predetermined life. Like the arteries in the human body, its creativity was bound to harden. Spengler dealt with the 'decline' of the West as the exhaustion of a world that was ageing rapidly. Throughout his book there are constant references to "the metaphysically exhausted soul of the West". "We are a late culture," he wrote, "we have to reckon with the hard, cold facts of a late life".[2]

Spengler saw cultural ageing as the exhaustion of a society's expressive possibilities. Being old is not just a matter of chronology; it is a matter of acting as well. What distinguished the West, Spengler concluded, was a "weariness of spirit". Certain possibilities were no longer open to it at this late juncture in its history.

Spengler was writing, of course, at a critical time: the end of the First World War. He also expressed a general angst that continued long into the twentieth century. As Erich Heller was moved to observe in the 1950s, "The history of the West since 1917 looks like the work of children clumsily filling in with lurid colours a design drawn in outline by Oswald Spengler".[3]

Although I do not subscribe to Spengler's analysis of Western civilisation it does seem to me that, as a metaphor, 'cultural ageing' can be applied to the Western Alliance. This, after all, was very much Henry Kissinger's thinking—Spengler's influence ran deep in his thinking from an early age. He was a man, wrote one of his colleagues at Harvard, who has always walked with Spengler close to his side.[4]

Interestingly, one of Kissinger's most strongly held convictions was that:

> In the life of societies and international systems there comes a time when the question arises whether all the possibilities of innovation inherent in a given structure have been exhausted. At this point immediate problems absorb the attention that should be devoted to determining their significance. Events are not shaped by a concept of the future. The present becomes all intrusive. However impressive such a structure may still appear to outsiders it has passed its zenith. It will grow more rigid and in time more irrelevant.[5]

Kissinger shared Spengler's belief that once its creative life is exhausted a society may linger on but only as "the scrap material of history". To change the metaphor, it may survive but only like "a worn-out giant of the primeval forest thrusting its decaying branches to the sky." The point is that once a society is relegated to such a state it is unlikely ever again to achieve anything of significance.

Another major figure in the Atlantic world who believed that such a process was already at work in the mid-1970s was Raymond Aron. Writing just after Kissinger had left government service, he acknowledged that for the first time in history the West existed as a *political community*. Cultural differences in family structure and traditions might persist, to be sure, but their social institutions were essentially the same, even if they had been moulded by different traditions.

What depressed him was the fear that as a community the West seemed to have reached the end of its creative life. Compared with the 1950s, it had begun to lose "a capacity for collective action". The Europeans were unwilling to translate their economic success into power, preferring to rely on American protection instead. Their historic fate appeared to be integration into an imperial zone dominated by the United States (that 'American commission' that Paul Valéry had predicted before the war might be called into being to administer a Europe divided against itself). Europe, Aron regretted, was "no longer capable of recovering the status of a subject acting in history".[6] When he looked to the New World, however, he also saw little ground for optimism. The Vietnam War had undermined the self-confidence of the American political elite. The result seemed to be an unwillingness to confront the future.

Aron's pessimism was shared by many of his contemporaries, especially in France, the country that was, ironically, most anti-American in temperament. *The Totalitarian Temptation* was the title of another pessimistic analysis, by Jean-François Revel, who had no confidence that the Western democracies would not succumb to communism simply to avoid the effort of resisting it. Around the same time, the Swiss writer Peter Durenmatt was equally doubtful whether the West would hold the line long enough, until the Soviet system collapsed.[7]

Looking back on this period, of course, we can recognise how overdrawn were these fears. Heinrich Heine once said that societies should imprison their prophets of doom until such time as their prophecies came true. In our more enlightened times such measures are unnecessary even if the Cassandras have doubled in number. As it was, the Alliance held to the end. The world was saved from communism. Yet many of the themes of Aron's argument have resurfaced in recent years. Many of the tensions and strains that he identified in the 1970s have been reinforced since the end of the Cold War. The Western Alliance *is* in trouble. Drifting without a purpose, it is frequently unable to coordinate its policies even when it can agree on common principles.

Disputes on free trade and differences of perception about the international order continue to drive the allies apart. Events in the Balkans revealed an alliance whose members were often in fundamental disagreement about its purpose. Like the six characters of Pirandello's play *Six Characters in Search of an Author*, they often appear to be dreaming different dreams of the future. The West, I would suggest, does seem to have exhausted its creative life. It seems to be living off its intellectual annuities. As an ideological construct it would seem to be metaphysically exhausted. To use one of Spengler's terms, it appears to have entered the "winter" of its life.

The Axioms of Twilight

So you will understand why I have always been concerned with the West. This concern seems to you absurd or gratuitous. "The West—you aren't even a part of it," you pointed out. Is it my fault that my greed for misery has not found another object? Where else will I find so persistent a will to fail? ... If I open some history of France, England, Spain or Germany the contrast between what they were and what they are gives me ... the pride of having discovered, at last, the axioms of twilight.

—E. M. Cioran, *The Temptation to Exist* (1954)

Cioran's observation seems to me to be well taken, forty years after he made it. The West as an alliance can no longer be taken at face value. It has long lost that certainty that once made it definingly itself. As it descends into ever more competitive confusion it tends to mask its statements under an ironic guise. Whether it likes it or not, it confronts what Cioran calls "the axioms of twilight".

Let me conclude this book by referring to three axioms of my own that reflect the hallmark of a declining society—irony, the characteristic mode of postmodern thought. What better way to appreciate the West's fate than to see the extent to which it subscribes to an ironic spirit, one that mocks all established styles and challenges the claim of established authority?

1. *An alliance cannot survive long if there is a contradiction between what it says and what it intends its statements to mean.* Whenever the West intervenes in the world, from Bosnia to Somalia, it does so in the name of the international community. "The international community will not tolerate the behaviour of the parties in Bosnia", trumpeted the British defence secretary at the time in reference to yet another atrocity that had come to light in the region.[8] The Western powers leap to life whenever trouble is more than 3,000 miles away. The more distant the walls of Jericho, the more certain the sound of their trumpets.

Of course when they refer to the 'international community' they mean nothing of the kind. They are entirely preoccupied with the much greater fear of what would happen if they lose their own cohesion or belief in themselves. As a famous British historian reminds us, "Victory in a war tends to last only as long as the coalition that produced it remains intact".[9] A.J.P. Taylor was describing what happened after the Crimean War, in which France and Britain, for the first time standing together, found themselves in conflict with Russia. Fifteen years after their victory they found themselves so divided that the Russians were able to reverse the verdict of history, to tear up most of the provisions of the treaty that had ended the war.

In the Western mind, at present, there is a prevailing mood of pessimism, the sense that victory in the Cold War would not long survive their own disunity. Since that victory was won not only for themselves but also for what the Americans euphemistically used to call the "Free World", they must continue to underwrite it. It is a dangerous illusion. The West does not speak for the rest of the world. It needs to speak to it more often, and that will require it to be a little less insistent in seeing itself as the world's conscience or court of last appeal.

2. *The Alliance will not long survive the irony created between appearance and reality.* The West claims to be united, but it is not. It is riven with divisions and differences of opinion. Even its much-vaunted support for free trade is questionable despite the importance attached to it by the Clinton administration, which has chosen it as the principal Western interest in the post–Cold War world. There is much on which the Western powers agree, of course, but there is much on which they do not. At times the very concept of the West seems to have outlived its usefulness, or certainly its usefulness to the United States, the country in default of whose leadership it would have no collective identity. At times it looks less than a coherent political community than a political no-man's-land in which the allies find themselves engaged in continual skirmishing. If the West is indeed a product of the historical circumstances that gave it birth, it is unlikely that it will hold together in the years ahead. It is more likely, in fact, to dissolve into alignments and alliances less than the sum of its parts.

What keeps the West alive in its own imagination seems to be fear of itself. As Cioran once noted, the West has been preoccupied since the nineteenth century with "the art of surviving itself".[10] It still is. The real challenges the West faces are still to be found within its own ranks—declining competitiveness, a reflective distrust of the outside world, a cardinal loss of faith in some of its own first principles. Europe and America still seem to be more fearful of their own disunity than they are of outside threats. Ironically, that is the reason why the concept of the West exercises such hypnotic power over its members, who still crave reassurance. It offers them not so much peace, but peace of mind. This may certainly be important as a litmus test of its longevity, but it may also be the wrong test for the time.

3. *An alliance cannot long survive the difference between what it says in its communiqués and what it does in the world at large.* Irony here is deeply corrosive, for the Alliance no longer believes in its own statements. Disbelief is part of its postmodern condition and is not something it can easily escape. The Alliance no longer speaks for history. It has no ground of action on which to stand.

Let me illustrate these themes by returning to where I began this book, with reference to Hegel. He was seen in the Second World War as an enemy of the open society, particularly by the refugee philosopher Karl Popper. Whether this reading was accurate or not, Hegel was certainly a man who set the terms of our modern engagement with history, just as Goethe established the line on which the Western powers eventually decided to fight.

Let me quote three observers, all modern voices, to illustrate what has happened. On the eve of the Cold War Hegel's chief twentieth-century interpreter, Alexandre Kojeve, could still write that every interpretation of Hegel was only "a programme for struggle and work". A work of Hegelian interpretation had the significance of a work of political propaganda. It was possible, he added, "that the future of the world and therefore the meaning and direction of the present and the significance of the past depend in the final analysis on the way in which we interpret Hegel".[11]

Thirty years later Paul Ricoeur was speaking for an entirely different generation. Hegel's interpretation of history, he wrote, had lost its credibility. This was no less than a major "event in thinking", a change of consciousness of the kind that we experience rarely more than once in our lifetime. It was an event so recent that its outcome was ambiguous. "We do not know if it is indicative of a catastrophe that is still crippling us or a deliverance whose glory we dare not celebrate".[12]

Writing only a few years ago the French philosopher Jean-Luc Nancy could acknowledge Hegel as a man who had set the terms on which history was engaged for a large part of the twentieth century. But history itself had moved on. The West now reads Hegel "as history", as a voice that once resonated in its own imagination but does so no longer.[13]

All versions of history, idealist and empirical, are produced in specific historical situations and serve particular needs. None of them deserves a central canonical status. We should not regret the passing of the Hegelian age. The trouble is that we have not replaced it with anything else. In the words of the novelist John Barth, "The sum of history is no more than the stuff of metaphors." A chapter précis from one of his novels amplifies this point:

> The poet wonders whether the course of human history is Progress, a Drama, a Retrospect, a Cycle, an Undulation, a Vortex, a Right or Left handed Spiral, a mere Continuum or what have you. Certain evidence is brought forward but of an ambiguous and inconclusive nature.[14]

We no longer believe that history is determined by a class or a nation acting in its name. Even American politicians have stopped using the term the 'American Century'.

One of the main reasons the West was paralysed by indecision in Bosnia was that it could not interpret the present with reference to the future, only the past. *Everything is historical but nothing is historic.* We cannot determine what our present will mean to our descendants. As a result we cannot make the present significant for ourselves. We cannot determine what the future will find significant or not. We have no ground of action.

At least the Hegelian worldview served a serious intellectual purpose. It defined the grounds of history for the societies that employed it. It provided the Western world with a purpose and a sense of meaning. Today it has neither. It is characterised accordingly by historical fatigue.

The point is captured particularly vividly in Saul Bellow's novel *The Dean's December* (1982), a rather sad tale about a college dean, Albert Corde, who finds himself dangerously out of step with the times. As Corde is told by the "new man", Dewey Spengler, he "pushes poetry too hard". Spengler takes him to task for the language he continues to use. He criticises him for remaining true to a poetic vision, or rather one in keeping with the poetics of history. That world, he is told abruptly, is now far away. The postmodern world has no time for recitations from Eliot's 'The Waste Land', or discussions about Hegel, or disputes about "the will to power". "All that, old pal, was boyhood".

Later we learn that Corde had made his debut as a writer by writing about the Potsdam Conference for the *New Yorker.* He had won acclaim for his perspicacity in foreseeing the fall of Churchill, the rise of Truman and the onset of the Cold War. He had been rewarded for being in step with the times. But he had not kept up. He was incapable of "grasping the full implications of world transformation, the growth of a new technology for managing world affairs, the new factors, the analytical paradigms which guide the decisions of authority in all post-industrial societies." His particular brand of twentieth-century humanism was too feeble to prepare him for the twenty-first.[15] After reading his most recent writings, Spengler is reminded of certain passages from Ortega y Gasset's *Revolt of the Masses* and Malraux's conversations with de Gaulle. Their presence merely accentuates the absence of more contemporary voices.

Towards the end of the book, Corde himself begins to recognise that his own language of discourse no longer resonates with his readers. It no longer rings true. He is the first to confess that he does not know the new passwords or codes. He finds that contemporary writers have little to say about the great moral, emotional or imaginative issues of the hour. His fellow scholars are no longer willing to enunciate great certainties any longer, still less fight for them.

The Western Community cannot long survive in such an age. We deceive ourselves, of course, if like Dewey Spengler we think we can act without imagination or that we can live a life based on purely pragmatic rather than normative concerns. It is probably too late for the West to find new ground on which to stand, but it is not too late for the Western powers to engage with history on other terms.

Conclusion

It would be wrong, however, to end on a pessimistic note, for it is possible to see the future in less ironic terms. Indeed, it is possible to see it in a refreshingly new light. Let me conclude, then, by invoking another East European voice, not that of Cioran but of Václav Havel speaking at a conference in Aachen in May 1996.

As Havel reminded his audience, the word 'Europe' means sunset, as Asia means sunrise. The title of Spengler's book *The Decline of the West (Der Untergang des Abendlandes)*, meant "the land of the twilight". Cioran was writing with an historical consciousness that once dominated the Western Alliance. Havel is a postmodern man. In Cioran's day the word 'twilight' traditionally was linked with notions of end, ruin, defeat or approaching death. In Havel's mind it signifies the end of a phase or a cycle and the beginning of something new. It affords us time for reflection to look at the past in perspective and "to gain strength and resolve for the day to come".

Havel talks of a new Europe, a wider one in the sense that it still has a "metaphysically anchored sense of responsibility". A time of twilight is a good moment for Europe to rededicate itself to a different project, to admit clearly that there are values transcending Europe itself, that we are all accountable for humanity as a whole.

> Europe has one final possibility if it so desires: it can reclaim its finest spiritual and intellectual traditions and . . . look for what they have in common with other cultures and other spheres of civilisation and join forces with them in search for the common moral minimum necessary to guide us . . . so that we can confront jointly whatever threatens our lives together.[16]

As I have suggested, this is the great challenge that we all face, the Western world in particular. The West prevailed in its great struggle after 1870 to prevent its own future from being made for it by others. It ensured that the communication between cultures would not be monolingual. Together or separately, it must engage in a dialogue with others. That is the price it must pay if civilisation itself is to be secured.

Notes

Preface

1. See Leonard Woolf, *The Journey Not the Arrival Matters: an autobiography of the years 1939–1969* (London: Hogarth Press, 1969), p. 12. The English love of 'common sense' is not confined to philosophy. "The best Russian writer", claimed W. H. Auden, "is Checkov because he is the only one with the least bit of common sense". Cited in Aldo Buzzi, *Journey to the Land of the Flies and Other Travels* (New York: Random House, 1996), p. 19.

2. Karl Popper, *Unended Quest: an intellectual autobiography* (London: Routledge, 1992), p. 90.

Chapter One

1. Cited in Simon Schama, *Citizens: a chronicle of the French Revolution* (London: Penguin, 1989), p. 640. In *The Decline of the West* Spengler paid Goethe this compliment about his intuitive grasp of history: "No general, no diplomat let alone the philosophers ever so directly felt history 'becoming'. It is the deepest judgment that any man ever uttered about a great historical act in the moment of its accomplishment". See *The Decline of the West,* transl. Charles Atkinson (Oxford: Oxford University Press, 1991), pp. 20–21.

2. Louis Dumont, *German Ideology: from France to Germany and back* (Chicago: University of Chicago Press, 1994), p. 171.

3. Erich Heller, *The Disinherited Mind: essays in modern German literature and thought* (Cambridge: Bowes & Bowes, 1952), p. 83.

4. Cited in Robert Hutchins, 'Goethe and the unity of mankind', in Arnold Bergstrasser, ed., *Goethe and the Modern Age* (New York: Regnery, 1949), p. 390.

5. Ibid., p. 391.

6. Joachim Ritter, *Hegel and the French Revolution: essays on the Philosophy of Right* (Cambridge: MIT Press, 1982), p. 43.

7. Cited in V. R. Berghahn, *Modern Germany: society, economics, and politics in the twentieth century* (Cambridge: Cambridge University Press, 1982), p. 192.

8. See Barry Cooper, *The End of History: an essay on modern Hegelianism* (Toronto: University of Toronto Press, 1984), p. 205.

9. L. T. Hobhouse, *The Metaphysical Theory of the State* (London: Routledge, 1993), p. 6.

10. Ralf Dahrendorf, *Society and Democracy in Germany* (New York: Doubleday, 1969), p. 192.

11. Friedrich Nietzsche, *The Joyful Wisdom,* transl. Thomas Common, vol. 10 of *Complete Works of Nietzsche,* ed. Oscar Levy (London: T. N. Foulis, 1911), section 357.

12. M. A. Gillespie, *Nihilism Before Nietzsche* (Chicago: University of Chicago Press, 1995), p. 256.

13. See Shlomo Avineri, *Hegel's Theory of the Modern State* (Cambridge: Cambridge University Press, 1972), p. 237. For Walter Benjamin, see Susan Sontag,

179

Under the Sign of Saturn (New York: Vintage, 1996), p. 132. The scorn with which the Western world was held by the Soviet Union in the Stalinist years was summed up pithily in a conversation between two Red Army generals: "'Of course, we're not greatly interested in Western Europe as such', the general answered after a moment's thought. 'It'll probably be more difficult to plant communism in the Europeans than in any other peoples. They're too spoilt economically and culturally'. 'There you are! You yourself admit it's very difficult to make Europe communist,' Klykov expressed his thoughts aloud. 'If we intend to build communism seriously there we'll have to send half the population to Siberia and feed the other half at our expense'". Cited in Nikolai Tolstoy, *Stalin's Secret War* (London: Jonathan Cape, 1981), p. 361.

14. Wyndham Lewis, *The Art of Being Ruled* (Santa Rosa: Black Sparrow Press, 1989), pp. 360–361. Carlyle had similarly dismissed the United States in Hegelian terms. "The title to be a commonwealth or a nation at all . . . is still a thing they are but striving for". What they had was "cotton crops and Indian corn and dollars . . . and half a world of untilled land where populations that respect the constable can live, for the present, *without* government. . . ." From 'The present day' (1850), cited in Christopher Ricks and William L. Vance, eds., *The Faber Book of America* (London: Faber and Faber, 1992), pp. 176–177.

15. Cited in Paul Johnson, *The Birth of the Modern* (London: Weidenfeld & Nicholson, 1991), p. 61.

16. Bauer was not strictly accurate. In a letter to a Russian nobleman who had attended his lectures in Heidelberg Hegel congratulated him on the fact that his country already occupied "a conspicuous place in the realm of world history" and that it would have "an even higher vocation in the future." Other states had passed their peak. Russia, on the other hand, "which is already perhaps the strongest of all, carries in its womb an immense possibility of developing its intensive nature". Avineri, *Hegel's Theory of the Modern State, op. cit.*, p. 234.

17. Eric Voeglin, 'Nietzsche, the crisis, and the war', *Journal of Politics* 6 (1944), pp. 205–209.

18. Ibid.

19. For all references to Michelet and Martin, see Hans Kohn, *Pan Slavism: its history and ideology* (Chicago: University of Notre Dame Press, 1953), p. 113. For Herzen, see Arnold Toynbee, *A Study of History* (Oxford: Oxford University Press, 1954), vol. 8, pp. 701–703.

20. Octavio Paz, *Convergences: essays on art and literature* (London: Bloomsbury, 1987), p. 147.

21. Ronald Dore, 'Unity and diversity in world culture', in Hedley Bull and Adam Watson, eds., *The Expansion of International Society* (Oxford: Oxford University Press, 1984), p. 411.

22. W.J.F. Jenner, *The Tyranny of History: the roots of China's crisis* (London: Allen Lane, 1992), p. 225. Jenner discusses China in 'Pazian' terms. It is a self-contained civilisation because it has only one script. It is not an intercultural discourse. With the Qin tyranny local variations in script were abolished and uniform characters introduced as a centralising device. "The script, identical through space and time, permanent and absolute, inhibits the development of local linguistically defined loyalties because they cannot be written down. Imagine how China might have developed if Indian or Central Asian Buddhist missionaries in the fourth and fifth centuries A.D. had persuaded their less educated converts to use an Indian de-rived phonetic script. . . . Different written vernacular languages might have emerged that existed beside a high culture . . . like the European vernaculars along-side Latin. Would local nationalisms and local nation states have emerged with dif-

ferent local cultures . . . having to earn the loyalty of their subjects through constitutional compacts? These are, of course, improper questions, and like all historical what-ifs, not really answerable" (p. 226).

23. Cited in Christopher Thorne, *Border Crossings: studies in international history* (London: Hamish Hamilton, 1988), p. 67.

24. Cited in Hugo Ball, *Flight out of Time* (Berkeley: University of California Press, 1996), p. 118.

25. Dumont, *German Ideology, op. cit.*, p. 121.

26. Cited in Michael Hamburger, *A Proliferation of Prophets: essays on German writers from Nietzsche to Brecht* (Manchester: Carcanet Press, 1983), p. 45.

27. Ludwig Dehio, *Germany and World Politics in the Twentieth Century* (London: Chatto and Windus, 1959), p. 76.

28. Paul Gottfried, *Carl Schmitt: politics and theory* (London: Claridge Press, 1990), p. 43.

29. Thomas Mann, *Reflections of a Nonpolitical Man*, transl. W. D. Morris (New York: F. Unger, 1983), p. 377.

30. Keith Ansell-Persall, *An Introduction to Nietzsche as a Political Thinker* (Cambridge: Cambridge University Press, 1995), p. 96.

31. Cited in Ball, *Flight out of Time, op. cit.*, pp. 138–139.

32. Dumont, *German Ideology, op. cit.*, p. 54.

33. Cited in Dehio, *Germany and World Politics, op. cit.*, p. 76. Max Delruck called the Anglo-German arms race a "dry war"; Widenmann "a latent war".

34. David Beetham, *Max Weber and the Theory of Modern Politics* (Cambridge: Polity, 1985), pp. 142–143.

35. Hamburger, *A Proliferation of Prophets, op. cit.*, p. 77.

36. Ronald Hingley, *The Russian Mind* (London: Bodley Head, 1977), p. 123.

37. Cited in *The Prussian Spirit: a survey of German literature and politics, 1914–1940* (London: Faber and Faber, 1942), p. 62.

38. Cited in David Watson, *Hannah Arendt* (London: Fontana, 1992), p. 60.

39. See G. M. Hyde, 'Russian futurism', in Malcolm Bradbury, ed., *Modernism: a guide to European literature, 1890–1930* (London: Penguin, 1976), p. 261.

40. Georges Nivat, 'Man and the gulag', in Philip Windsor, ed., *Experiencing the Twentieth Century* (Tokyo: University of Tokyo Press, 1985), p. 227.

41. Arnold Toynbee, *Civilisation on Trial* (New York: Oxford University Press, 1948), pp. 7–8.

42. Cited in F. M. Turner, *The Greek Heritage in Victorian Britain* (London: Chatto and Windus, 1981), p. 187.

43. R. V. Jones, *Most Secret War: British scientific intelligence, 1939–1945* (London: Weidenfeld & Nicholson, 1978), pp. 109–110.

44. Cited in Peter Dickson, *Kissinger and the Meaning of History* (Cambridge: Cambridge University Press, 1978), p. 78.

45. Graham Parkes, ed., *Nietzsche and Asian Thought* (Chicago: University of Chicago Press, 1991), p. 19.

46. Friedrich Nietzsche, *Human, All Too Human: a book for free spirits*, transl. R. J. Hollingdale (Cambridge: Cambridge University Press, 1994), 1:616.

47. Eberhard Scheiffele, 'Questioning one's "own" from the perspective of the foreign', in Parkes, *Nietzsche and Asian Thought, op. cit.*, p. 44.

48. Ibid. The reference is to *Antichrist* (1888), section 43.

49. H. L. Stewart, *Nietzsche and the Ideas of Modern Germany* (London, 1915).

50. F. Hearnshaw, *Germany: the aggressor throughout the ages* (New York, 1941), p. 235.

51. Robin D. Butler, *The Roots of National Socialism, 1783–1933* (London: Faber and Faber, 1941).

52. Cited in Voeglin, 'Nietzsche, the crisis, and the war', *op. cit.*, pp. 185–186. The reference is to Hearnshaw's *Germany: the aggressor throughout the ages, op. cit.*

53. Ibid.

54. Søren Kierkegaard, *Papers and Journals: a selection,* transl. Alastair Hannay (London: Penguin, 1996), p. 180. Kierkegaard himself was not so lucky. "I was born in 1813, the wrong fiscal year, in which so many other bad banknotes were put in circulation, and my life seems best compared with one of them. There is something of greatness about me but because of the poor state of the market I am not worth much" (p. 179).

55. E. E. Sleinis, *Nietzsche's Revaluation of Values: a study in strategies* (Urbana: University of Illinois Press, 1994), pp. 13–14.

56. See Eric Stokes, 'The first century of British colonial rule in India', *Past and Present* 58 (February 1973), pp. 140–141.

57. Cited in David Low, *Eclipse of Empire* (Cambridge: Cambridge University Press, 1991), p. 22.

58. Friedrich Nietzsche, *Thus Spake Zarathustra,* transl. R. J. Hollingdale (London: Penguin, 1969), p. 216.

59. Cited in Sleinis, *Nietzsche's Revaluation of Values, op. cit.*, pp. 215–216, n17.

60. Ibid., p. 15.

61. T. E. Hulme, *Speculations: essays on humanism and the philosophy of art,* ed. Herbert Read (London: Routledge and Kegan Paul, 1924).

62. Cited in Mark Warren, *Nietzsche and Political Thought* (Cambridge, Mass.: MIT Press, 1991), p. 162.

63. Richard Kearney, *Dialogues with Continental Thinkers* (Manchester: Manchester University Press, 1994), pp. 27–28.

64. Donald Mitchell, *The Language of Modern Music* (London: Faber and Faber, 1963), p. 106.

65. Cited in Dennis Washburn, *The Dilemma of the Modern in Japanese Fiction* (New Haven: Yale University Press, 1995), p. 4.

66. Cited in Christopher Thorne, *The Far Eastern War: states and societies, 1941–1945* (London: Counterpoint, 1989), p. 69.

67. Cited in Michael Walzer, *Interpretation and Social Criticism* (Cambridge, Mass.: Harvard University Press, 1987), pp. 62–63.

68. See the discussion in Arnold Toynbee, *A Study of History* (New York: Oxford University Press, 1964), vol. 1, pp. 670–674.

69. See Arthur Danto, 'Some remarks on the *Genealogy of Morals*', in Robert Solomon, ed., *Reading Nietzsche* (New York: Oxford University Press, 1988), p. 17.

70. George Steiner, *Language and Silence: essays on language, literature, and the inhuman* (New York: Atheneum, 1982), pp. 381–383.

71. Friedrich Nietzsche, *Daybreak: thoughts on the prejudices of morality,* transl. R. J. Hollingdale (Cambridge: Cambridge University Press, 1992), 1:631.

72. Nietzsche, *Thus Spake Zarathustra, op. cit.*, 3:12.

73. Ibid., p. 224.

74. Gillespie, *Nihilism Before Nietzsche, op. cit.*, p. 256.

Chapter Two

1. Cited in Robert Holland, *The Pursuit of Greatness: Britain and the world, 1900–1970* (London: Fontana, 1991), p. 92.

2. Joseph P. Lash, *Roosevelt and Churchill, 1939–1941: the partnership that saved the West* (London: Andre Deutsch, 1977), pp. 391–400.

3. Ibid.

4. Ibid.

5. For a critical view of the Atlantic Charter, see John Charmley, *Churchill: the end of glory* (London: Sceptre, 1993), p. 460.

6. Richard Mayne, *Post-war: the dawn of today's Europe* (London: Thames and Hudson, 1983), pp. 180–181.

7. J. L. Borges, 'The modesty of history', in *Other Inquisitions, 1937–1952* (Austin: University of Texas Press, 1964), p. 167.

8. Cited in Patrick Devlin, *Too Proud to Fight: Woodrow Wilson's neutrality* (Oxford: Oxford University Press, 1974), p. 379.

9. D. Harvey, *Collision of Empires: Britain in three world wars, 1793–1945* (London: Phoenix, 1992), p. 242.

10. Henry Kissinger, *Diplomacy* (New York: Simon and Schuster, 1994), p. 51.

11. Cited in Robert Strausz-Hupé, *Building the Atlantic Wall* (New York: Harper & Row, 1963), pp. 16–17.

12. Corelli Barnett, *The Collapse of British Power* (London: Eyre Methuen, 1972), p. 126.

13. Bernard Bosanquet, *The Philosophical Theory of the State* (London: Macmillan, 1965), p. lix.

14. Cited in Thomas Pangle, *The Ennobling of Democracy: the challenge of the postmodern age* (Baltimore: Johns Hopkins University Press, 1992), pp. 83–84.

15. Karl Mannheim, *The Diagnosis of Our Time* (London: Kegan Paul, 1943), p. 7.

16. Cited in Mayne, *Post-war, op. cit.*, p. 10.

17. Neal Ascherson, *Black Sea* (London: Jonathan Cape, 1995), pp. 108–109.

18. Cited in Georges Nivat, 'The crumbling of communism', in *The End of the Century: the future in the past,* ed. The Japan Foundation Center for Global Partnership (Tokyo: Kodansha International, 1995), p. 25. During the Second World War Churchill often thundered against the threat of "Russian barbarism . . . swamping the cultural independence of the old European states". Ernst Topitsch, *Stalin's War: a radical new theory of the origin of the Second World War* (London: Fourth Estate, 1987), p. 125. In the First World War the barbarians had been the Germans not the Russians. See Paul Fussell, *The Great War and Modern Memory* (London: Oxford University Press, 1973), pp. 40–41, for the impact that the German destruction of Ypres had on the English imagination. By comparison, the Germans have never forgotten the Soviet invasion of East Prussia in 1945. Looking back on the event in his narrative poem *Prussian Nights,* Solzhenitsyn records the rapes, the mindless violence and the devastation that the Red Army carried out. In his account only a clock "surviving through it all" measures time "honourably between the others and ourselves".

19. Cited in Owen Harries, 'The collapse of the West', *Foreign Affairs* 72:4 (September/October 1993), p. 42.

20. Roger Louis, 'Empire preserved', *Times Literary Supplement,* 5 May 1995.

21. Cited in Mayne, *Post-war, op. cit.*, p. 109.

22. Felipe Fernandez-Armesto, *Millennium: a history of the last thousand years* (London: Bantam Press, 1995), p. 377.

23. See my 'Dunkirk and other British myths of 1940', *National Interest* 22 (Winter 1990/1991).

24. Ibid.

25. Ibid.

26. Clarence Streit, *Union Now: a proposal for an Atlantic Union of the future* (New York: Harper & Row, 1940).

27. Cited in Wesley T. Wooley, *Alternatives to Anarchy: American supranationalism since World War II* (Bloomington: Indiana University Press, 1988), p. 129.

28. George Catlin, *Anglo American Union as a Nucleus of World Federation* (1943). For Anglo-Saxony, see *One Anglo-American Nation* (London: Phoenix House, 1957), p. 262.

29. Octavio Paz, *The Siren and the Seashell, and Other Essays on Poets and Poetry* (Austin: University of Texas Press, 1991), p. 46.

30. J. Gerald Kennedy, *Imagining Paris: exile, writing, and American identity* (New Haven: Yale University Press, 1993), p. 242.

31. Joseph Brodsky, *Less Than One: selected essays* (London: Penguin, 1987), p. 310.

32. Malcolm Bradbury, *Dangerous Pilgrimages: trans-Atlantic mythologies and the novel* (London: Secker and Warburg, 1995), p. 242.

33. Cited in Michael North, *The Political Aesthetic of Yeats, Eliot, and Pound* (Cambridge: Cambridge University Press, 1991), pp. 124–125.

34. Kerry H. Whiteside, *Merleau-Ponty and the Foundation of an Existential Politics* (Princeton: Princeton University Press, 1988), pp. 149–150.

35. Cited in John Lukacs, *The Last European War: September 1939–December 1941* (London: Routledge and Kegan Paul, 1976), p. 515.

36. Ibid.

37. Saul Bellow, *Mosby's Memoirs and Other Stories* (London: Penguin, 1971), p. 160. Burnham is not much remembered today, but his book was one of the most widely read of the century. The late Ernest Gellner wrote: "The toolbox of the half track I drove to Prague for the victory parade in May 1945 contained four books: Koestler's *Darkness at Noon,* Orwell's *Animal Farm,* the now forgotten but then widely discussed *Managerial Revolution* by James Burnham and Cyril Connolly's *Unquiet Grave*". 'The rest is history', *Prospect,* May 1996, p. 34.

38. For a good discussion, see William Myers, *Evelyn Waugh and the Problem of Evil* (London: Faber and Faber, 1992), pp. 129–131.

39. See Lionel Grossman, 'Cultural history and crisis: Burckhardt's *Civilisation of the Renaissance in Italy'*, in Michael S. Roth, ed., *Rediscovering History: culture, politics, and the psyche* (Stanford: Stanford University Press, 1994), pp. 404–431.

40. José Ortega y Gasset, *History as a System and Other Essays Toward a Philosophy of History* (New York: Norton, 1962), pp. 82–83. Interestingly, François Guizot made a similar point when writing of Britain in his *History of the Civilisation of Europe* (London: Penguin, 1996). What distinguished Europe was that it never fell under the domination of an exclusive principle. Of all European countries this was the most notable feature of England: "Never has any ancient element completely perished; never has any new element wholly triumphed or any special principle attained to an exclusive preponderance. There has always been a simultaneous development of different forces" (p. 229). It has become an article of faith that Britain was less modern than Germany in terms of its interest in science and industry. See Martin Wiener, *English Culture and the Decline of the Industrial Spirit, 1850–1980* (Cambridge: Cambridge University Press, 1981). But even this is not true. David Edgerton, in *Science, Technology, and the British Industrial 'Decline', 1870–1970* (Cambridge: Cambridge University Press, 1996), challenges such views quite trenchantly. "British higher education, the British state and British industry were, if anything, peculiarly scientific and technological". Britain produced more scientists and engineers per capita than any other major capitalist country during the 1950s and 1960s. British in-

dustry spent more of its own money on research and development than German and Japanese industry well into the late 1960s, and Britain patented more technologies in the United States than Germany until the late 1950s. As for the boardroom's being bereft of engineers, this too is a myth. By 1950 some 20 percent of the senior men in British manufacturing had university-level scientific or technical education. As for spending on research and development, Britain spent more than its competitors, Germany and France, well into the 1960s.

41. Cited in William Roger Louis, *British Strategy in the Far East, 1919–1939* (Oxford: Clarendon Press, 1971), p. 73.

42. Wyndham Lewis, *America and Cosmic Man* (New York: Doubleday, 1949), p. 169.

43. Ritchie Ovendale, *The English-Speaking Alliance: Britain, the United States, the Dominions and the Cold War, 1945–1951* (London: Allen and Unwin, 1985), p. 274.

44. Malcolm Bradbury, 'The name and nature of Modernism', in Bradbury, *Modernism: a guide to European literature, 1890–1930* (London: Penguin, 1976), p. 48.

45. *The Table Talk of W. H. Auden*, ed. Nicholas Jenkins (London: Faber and Faber, 1990), p. 23.

46. Cited in *Collected Essays: journalism and letters of George Orwell*, vol. 3 (London: Penguin, 1970), p. 180.

47. Thomas Mann, *Doctor Faustus* (London: Everyman, 1992), p. 306.

48. Ilya Ehrenburg, *The War, 1941–1945* (London: MacGibbon and Kee, 1964), p. 192.

49. John Hersey, *Life Sketches* (New York: Vintage, 1991), p. 35. Luce was not always a good prophet. For some highly inaccurate predictions, see Henry Luce, 'A speculation about the year 1980', in *The Fabulous Future: America in the 1980s* (New York: Dutton and Co., 1955), p. 192.

50. See James McFarlane, 'The mind of modernism', in Malcolm Bradbury, ed., *The Modernist Novel* (London: Penguin, 1976), p. 73.

51. See Henry Adams, *The Education of Henry Adams*, ed. Ernest Samuels (New York: Library of America, 1983), p. 1153.

52. Le Corbusier, *When the Cathedrals Were White: a journey to the country of timid people* (New York: Reynal and Hitchcock, 1947), p. 78.

53. Cited in Mayne, *Post-war, op. cit.*, p. 109.

54. George Steiner, 'Proofs' in *The Deeps of the Sea, and Other Fiction* (London: Faber and Faber, 1996), p. 67.

55. José Ortega y Gasset, *The Revolt of the Masses* (Chicago: University of Chicago Press, 1986), pp. 14–15.

56. Carlo Levi, *Christ Stopped at Eboli* (New York: Farrar, Straus and Giroux, 1991), pp. 123–125.

57. Robert Park, *Race and Culture* (Boston, 1945), p. 144.

58. Octavio Paz, *Children of the Mire: modern poetry from Romanticism to the avant-garde* (Cambridge, Mass.: Harvard University Press, 1974), p. 29.

59. Cited in Geoffrey Perrett, *Days of Sadness, Years of Triumph: the American people, 1939–1945* (New York: Coward, McCann and Geoghegan, 1973), p. 417.

60. Gordon Craig, 'The Mann nobody knew', *New York Review of Books*, 29 February 1996, p. 38. The situation for less established cultures, of course, was more serious still. Writing of his own country, Nigeria, the novelist Chinua Achebe speaks of African time becoming American time. Because of their servility to all things American the intellectuals have no time of their own; they only have an American future. Africa has been distanced, he writes, from its traditions, which

have been devalued; distanced from the masses because the intellectuals have been Westernised; and distanced from its own language because they speak American English. Africa has been spatialised by history. It is a continent without a past. All that it has is a future lived not on its terms, but America's. Cited in Abdulrazak Gurnah, ed., *Essays on African Writing* (London: Heinemann, 1993), p. 3.

61. George Lichtheim, *The New Europe* (New York, 1963), p. 224.

Chapter Three

1. William McNeil, *Arnold Toynbee: a life* (Oxford: Oxford University Press, 1989), pp. 213–216.

2. C. B. Macpherson, *Burke* (Oxford: Oxford University Press, 1980), p. 4.

3. François Furet, *Interpreting the French Revolution* (Cambridge: Cambridge University Press, 1981), p. 6.

4. See Robert Palmer, *The Age of the Democratic Revolution: a political history of Europe and America, 1760–1800*, vol. 1, *The Challenge* (Princeton: Princeton University Press, 1969), pp. 187–188.

5. All Burke quotations are from Jennifer Welsh, *Edmund Burke and International Relations* (London: Macmillan, 1995), this one from p. 142.

6. Gary Wills, 'Total war', in Christopher Ricks and William L. Vance, eds., *The Faber Book of America* (London: Faber and Faber, 1992), pp. 422–426.

7. Dean Acheson, *This Vast Eternal Realm* (New York: W. W. Norton, 1973), p. 172.

8. Welsh, *Edmund Burke and International Relations, op. cit.*, p. 142.

9. Ibid., p. 89.

10. Ibid., p. 96.

11. Cited in Raymond Aron, *The Imperial Republic: The United States and the world, 1945–1973* (London: Weidenfeld & Nicholson, 1974), p. 17.

12. Writing at the height of U.S.-Soviet cooperation—in the closing stages of World War Two—Pitirin Sorokin (a Russian-American) was equally hopeful of the future. The "chances for . . . cooperation between Russia and the United States are better than those of an armed conflict in the respective relations of either of these countries than any other great power". Cited in Christer Jonsson, *Superpower: comparing America and Soviet foreign policy* (London: Pinter Publishing, 1984), p. 40.

13. John R. Deane, *The Strange Alliance* (New York: Viking, 1947).

14. John Baylis, *Anglo-American Defence Relations, 1939–1980: the special relationship* (London: Macmillan, 1981), pp. 32–37.

15. Cited in Hans Kohn, *Twentieth Century: a midway account of the Western world* (London: Victor Gollancz, 1950), pp. 232–234.

16. Cited in Frank Munk, *Atlantic Dilemma: partnership or community* (New York: Dobbs Ferry, 1964), p. 5.

17. Cited in ibid.

18. Henry Kissinger, *A World Restored* (Cambridge, Mass.: Harvard University Press, 1957), p. 211.

19. Clarence Streit, *Freedom's Frontier: Atlantic union now* (New York, 1961).

20. Cited in Munk, *Atlantic Dilemma, op. cit.*, p. 61.

21. Jean Monnet, *Memoirs* (Garden City, N.Y.: Doubleday, 1978), pp. 309–311, 324.

22. Cited in Akira Iriye, 'War as peace, peace as war', in Philip Windsor and Akira Iriye, eds., *Experiencing the Twentieth Century* (Tokyo: University of Tokyo Press, 1985), p. 44.

23. See my *The Future of the Atlantic Alliance* (London: Macmillan, 1984), p. 4.

24. Ibid.

25. Samuel P. Huntington, *The Clash of Civilizations and the Remaking of World Order* (New York: Simon and Schuster, 1996), p. 55.

26. For Grey, see Andrew Williams, 'Meaning and the new world order', paper presented at a seminar on 'Meaning and International Relations', Oxford, Maison Française, 6–7 December 1996; for Roosevelt, see John Gerard Ruggie, *Winning the Peace: America and world order in the new era* (New York: Columbia University Press, 1996), p. 19.

27. See my *A Nation in Retreat: Britain's defence commitment* (London: Brassey's, 1985), p. 114.

28. Ibid.

29. Ibid.

30. Robert Gates, 'Address to the American Newspaper Publishers Association', Vancouver, British Columbia, 7 May 1991, in *American Leadership and the New World Order* (Washington, D.C.: Department of State Bureau of Public Affairs, 1991).

31. *Observer*, 1 January 1993.

32. *Washington Post*, 26 February 1993.

33. Address by Secretary of State James Baker to the Berlin Press Club, 12 December 1984, reprinted in *Berlin Speeches of Secretary of State James Baker* (Washington, D.C.: U.S. Information Agency, 1991).

34. See my 'The New World Order and the special relationship in the 1990s', *International Affairs* 68:3 (1992), pp. 407–421.

35. Malcolm Rifkind, 'Need for an Atlantic community to better reflect US-Euro relations', *Nato Review*, March 1995, pp. 11–15.

Chapter Four

1. Octavio Paz, *Convergences: essays on art and literature* (London: Bloomsbury, 1987), p. 146.

2. William Pfaff, *Barbarian Sentiments: how the American Century ends* (New York: Hill and Wang, 1989), p. 66.

3. John Lukacs, *The Last European War: September 1939–December 1941* (London: Routledge and Kegan Paul, 1976), p. 496.

4. Ibid.

5. Max Beloff, *Europe and the Europeans* (London: Chatto & Windus, 1957), p. 10.

6. Kerry Whitehead, *Merleau-Ponty and the Foundation of Existential Politics* (Princeton: Princeton University Press, 1988), pp. 40–42.

7. Ibid.

8. Cited in Barry Cooper, *Merleau-Ponty and Marxism: from terror to reform* (Toronto: University of Toronto Press, 1979), p. 83.

9. Ibid.

10. Cited in Mary Jean Green, *Fiction in the Historical Present: French writers in the thirties* (Hanover, N.H.: University Press of New England, 1986), p. 6.

11. Ibid.

12. Whitehead, *Merleau-Ponty and the Foundation of Existential Politics, op. cit.*, pp. 40–42.

13. See Walter Biemel, 'The decisive phase in the development of Husserl's phenomenology', in R. O. Elveton, ed., *The Phenomenology of Husserl: selected critical readings* (Chicago: Quadrangle Books, 1970).

14. See introduction by Elizabeth Young-Bruehl in Albert Camus, *Between Hell and Reason: essays from the Resistance newspaper 'Combat', 1944–1947,* ed. Alexandre de Gramont (Hanover, N.H.: University Press of New England, 1991), p. 7.

15. Ibid.

16. Germaine Breé, *Camus and Sartre: crisis and commitment* (London: Calder and Boyars, 1974), p. 161.

17. Ibid., p. 164.

18. Louis Dumont, *German Ideology: from France to Germany and back* (Chicago: University of Chicago Press, 1994), pp. 230–234.

19. Maurice Merleau-Ponty, *The Phenomenology of Perception* (London: Routledge and Kegan Paul, 1962), pp. viii, xxi.

20. Michel Tournier, *The Wind Spirit* (London: Collins, 1989), p. 71.

21. Raymond Aron, *Memoirs: fifty years of political reflection* (New York: Holmes & Meier, 1990), p. 40. See also Jean-François Lyotard, who records: "I come here with the assurance that we will speak freely about everything like last year (the events of 1989). But what everything? Everything that is attached to the name of Germany for the French philosopher of my age: a language, a way of being and thinking, acquired as well as can be expected as a child, from Schiller, Heine, Rilke, as an adolescent through Hofmannsthal and Storm; spat out, interrupted by the occupying forces; the moan of a young dying soldier, "Mutter", on a stretcher in the aid station of the Passage Saint André des Arts, 1944, Paris: taken up again as a dead language from Husserl, Marx (1844 Manuscripts, '44 once again, my twenties) from Hegel, Freud, Frege, Nietzsche, Kant, Wittgenstein, Heidegger, Adorno. Throughout my life. Germans on my bedside table." *Political Writings* (London: University College London Press, 1993), p. 77.

22. Fernand Braudel, *A History of Civilisations* (London: Allen Lane, 1994), pp. 27–28.

23. Ibid.

24. Fernand Braudel, *The Mediterranean and the Mediterranean World in the Age of Philip II* (London: Collins, 1973), vol. 2, p. 1244.

25. Ibid.

26. Edwin Plowden, *An Industrialist in the Treasury: the post-war years* (London: Andre Deutsch, 1989), p. 73.

27. Cited in Braudel, *History of Civilisations, op. cit.,* p. 9.

28. Edmund Husserl, *Phenomenology and the Crisis of Philosophy* (New York: Harper & Row, 1965), p. 17.

29. Samuel Hynes, *The Auden Generation: literature and politics in England in the 1930s* (London: Bodley Head, 1976), pp. 11–12.

30. Cited in Detlev Peukert, *The Weimar Republic: the crisis of classical modernity* (London: Allen Lane, 1991), pp. 180–181.

31. Cited in Hans Kohn, 'Toynbee and Russia', in Edward T. Gargan, ed., *The Intent of Toynbee's History* (Chicago: Loyola University Press, 1961), p. 130.

32. Cited in Carl H. Pegg, *Evolution of the European Idea, 1914–1932* (Chapel Hill: University of North Carolina Press, 1983), p. 44.

33. Cited in Peukert, *The Weimar Republic, op. cit.,* p. 181.

34. Cited in Eric C. Hansen, *Disaffection and Decadence: a crisis in French intellectual thought, 1848–1898* (Washington, D.C.: University Press of America, 1982), p. 20.

35. Victor Farias, *Heidegger and Nazism* (Philadelphia: Temple University Press, 1989), p. 68.

36. Cited in Pegg, *Evolution of the European Idea, op. cit.,* p. 108.

37. Cited in Jacques Derrida, *The Other Heading: reflections on today's Europe* (Bloomington: University of Indiana Press, 1992), p. 126.

38. Cited in Alan Stoekl, *Agonies of the Intellectual: commitment, subjectivity, and the performative in the twentieth-century French tradition* (Lincoln: University of Nebraska Press, 1992), p. 72.

39. Cited in J. Améry, *Preface to the Future: culture in a consumer society* (London: Constable, 1974), p. 151.

40. *The Times* (London), 22 June 1993.

41. Ibid.

42. *The Times* (London), 29 September 1993.

43. Lukacs, *The Last European War, op. cit.*, p. 221.

44. H. R. Kedward, *Resistance in Vichy France: a study of ideas and motivation in the Southern Zone, 1940–1942* (Oxford: Oxford University Press, 1978), p. 243.

45. Cited in Zeev Sternhell, *Neither Right Nor Left: fascist ideology in France* (Berkeley: University of California Press, 1986), p. 279.

46. Cited in Frederic J. Grover, *Drieu La Rochelle and the Fiction of Testimony* (Berkeley: University of California Press, 1958), p. 57.

47. Patrick T. Pasture, 'The April 1944 "Social Pact" in Belgium and its significance for the post-war welfare state', *Journal of Contemporary History* 28 (1993), pp. 695–714.

48. Detlev Peukert, *Inside Nazi Germany: conformity, opposition, and racism in everyday life* (London: Penguin, 1993), p. 242.

49. Robert Marjolin, *Architect of European Unity: memoirs, 1911–1986* (London: Weidenfeld & Nicholson, 1989), p. 286.

50. Lester C. Thurow, *Head to Head: the coming economic battle among Japan, Europe, and America* (London: Nicholas Breasley, 1992), p. 86.

51. During the hard negotiations between Europeans and Americans over free trade in the 1980s the Reagan and Bush administrations' trade negotiators were frequently very critical of their predecessors in the 1960s and 1970s for allowing the Europeans to break so many agreements on agricultural trade. What they had in mind was the doubtful applicability to GATT of the Common Agricultural Policy (conceded in the Uruguay Round), EC efforts to evade the Dillon Round binding on soya beans, the 1960s chicken war, preferential EC arrangements for Mediterranean countries and so on. For a good summary of trade rivalry between the United States and Europe, see Ernest Preeg, 'The US Leadership Role in World Trade', *Washington Quarterly*, Spring 1992.

52. John Rupert Colville, *The Fringes of Power: Downing Street diaries, 1939–1955* (New York: Norton, 1985), p. 188.

53. Lukacs, *The Last European War, op. cit.*, p. 493.

54. Ibid., p. 495.

55. John Laughland, 'The thousand-year Reich', *Spectator*, 22 June 1991. For Ribbentrop's ideas on European union, see Michael Bloch, *Ribbentrop* (London: Bantam, 1992).

56. Colville, *Fringes of Power, op. cit.*, p. 188.

57. A. W. DePorte, *Europe Between the Superpowers: the enduring balance* (New Haven: Yale University Press, 1979), p. 201.

58. Jean Monnet, *Memoirs* (Garden City, N.Y.: Doubleday, 1978), p. 212.

59. Raymond Poidevin, *Robert Schuman: homme d'état, 1886–1963* (Paris: Imprimerie Nationale, 1986), pp. 265ff.

60. Robert Schuman, 'The Atlantic Community and Europe', *Orbis*, Winter 1958, pp. 408–411.

61. DePorte, *Europe Between the Superpowers, op. cit.*, p. 203.

62. Michael J. Hogan, *The Marshall Plan: America, Britain, and the reconstruction of Western Europe, 1947–1952* (Cambridge: Cambridge University Press, 1987), p. 440.

63. Alan Milward, 'The Great Fixer of modern Europe', *Sunday Telegraph*, January 15 1995.

64. Frank Munk, *Atlantic Dilemma: partnership or community* (New York: Dobbs Ferry, 1964), p. 60.

65. Werner Feld, *The European Community in World Affairs: economic power and political influence* (Boulder: Westview Press, 1983), p. 262.

66. Cited in ibid., pp. 190–191.

67. Cited in Anthony Hartley, 'Translating frivolity: the United States versus Europe', *Encounter* 40:40 (April 1973), p. 45 (my emphasis).

68. Henry Kissinger, *The Troubled Partnership: a reappraisal of the Atlantic Alliance* (New York: McGraw Hill, 1975), p. 245.

69. Henry Kissinger, 'The Atlantic Alliance needs renewal in a challenging world', *International Herald Tribune*, 2 March 1992.

70. Thurow, *Head to Head, op. cit.*, p. 86.

71. Cited in Julius Friend, *The Linchpin: French-German relations, 1950–1990* (New York: Praeger, 1991).

72. Cited in John Laughland, *The Death of Politics: France under Mitterrand* (London: Michael Joseph, 1994), p. 226.

73. *The Times* (London), 9 February 1990.

Chapter Five

1. Martin Heidegger, *On the Way to Language* (New York: Harper & Row, 1971), p. 15.

2. Cited in Peter Ackroyd, *Notes for a New Culture* (London: Alkin, 1993), pp. 70–73.

3. Cited in Walter Biemel, 'The decisive phase in the development of Husserl's philosophy', in R. O. Elveton, ed., *The Phenomenology of Husserl: selected critical readings* (Chicago: Quadrangle Books, 1970), p. 168.

4. Edmund Husserl, *The Crisis of European Sciences and Transcendental Phenomenology* (Evanston: Northwestern University Press, 1970), p. 17.

5. Cited in Jacques Derrida, *The Other Heading: reflections on today's Europe* (Bloomington: University of Indiana Press, 1992), p. 8.

6. See Albert Camus, 'The new Mediterranean culture', in Camus, *Lyrical and Critical Essays*, ed. Philip Thody (New York: Vintage, 1968), pp. 189–198. What made Camus's vision very different from that of his contemporaries was its interracial mix. Compare Le Corbusier's grand scheme for the division of Europe along racial lines. In that plan Europe was to be divided into three racial groupings: the Mediterranean for the Latin Federation; Central Europe for the Germanic people; and a Slavic USSR. See Mark Antliff, *Inventing Bergson: cultural politics and the Parisian avant-garde* (Princeton: Princeton University Press, 1993), pp. 183–184.

7. Cited in Z.A.B. Zeman, *Pursued by a Bear: the making of Eastern Europe* (London: Chatto and Windus, 1989), p. 13.

8. Norman Davies, *Europe: a history* (Oxford: Oxford University Press, 1996), pp. 39–42.

9. Václav Havel, 'A call for sacrifice', *Foreign Affairs* 73 (March/April 1994), p. 4.

10. G.W.F. Hegel, *Lectures on the Philosophy of History* (New York: Oxford University Press, 1979), p. 103.

11. Zsigmond Moricz, *Be Faithful unto Death,* transl. Stephen Vizinczey (Prague: Central European University Press, 1995), p. 177.

12. John Lukacs, *The Last European War: September 1939–December 1941* (London: Routledge and Kegan Paul, 1976), p. 171.

13. Danilo Kis, 'Variations on Central European themes', in *Homo Poeticus: essays and interviews* (Manchester: Carcanet, 1996), p. 98.

14. Ibid., p. 101.

15. Cited in Fritz Ernst, *The Germans and Their Modern History* (New York: Columbia University Press, 1966), p. 125.

16. *German Comments,* no. 34 (April 1994), pp. 92–93.

17. Cited in Timothy Garton Ash, *In Europe's Name: Germany and the divided continent* (New York: Vintage, 1994), p. 21.

18. David Watson, *Hannah Arendt* (London: Fontana, 1992), pp. 49–51.

19. Timothy Garton Ash, 'Germany's choice', *Foreign Affairs* 73:4 (July/August 1994), p. 67.

20. *International Herald Tribune,* 2 May 1994.

21. Garton Ash, 'Germany's choice', *op. cit.,* p. 79.

22. Josef Joffe, 'Deutsche Aussenpolitik—Postmodern', *Internationale Politik,* 1995:1, p. 45.

23. Cited in Giles Radice, *The New Germans* (London: Michael Joseph, 1994), p. 24.

24. Cited in Kim Holmes, *The West German Peace Movement and the National Question* (Austin: Institute for Foreign Policy Analysis, March 1984), p. 11.

25. Ibid., p. 19.

26. See Bernard Willms, *The German Nation* (Cologne: Mashkre, 1982), pp. 207–208.

27. Philippe Lacoue-Labarthe, *Heidegger, Art, and Politics* (Oxford: Basil Blackwell, 1990), p. 80.

28. Holmes, *The West German Peace Movement, op. cit.,* p. 23.

29. Botho Strauss, *Beginnlosigkeit: Reflexionen über Fleck und Linie* (Munich: Carl Hanser Verlag, 1992), p. 261.

30. Cited in Rainer Zitelman, K. Weissman, and M. Grossheim, eds., *Westbindung: Chancen und Risken für Deutschland* (Berlin: Propylaen, 1993), p. 31.

31. David Calleo, *The German Problem Reconsidered* (Cambridge: Cambridge University Press, 1978), p. 202.

Chapter Six

1. Mark Twain, *The Innocents Abroad* (New York: Signet, 1966), p. 457.

2. *Wall Street Journal,* 3 February 1997.

3. Cited in Fernand Braudel, *The Identity of France,* vol. 1, *History and Environment* (London: Collins, 1988), p. 18.

4. See Edward Luttwak, *The Endangered American Dream* (New York: Simon and Schuster, 1993).

5. Address by Secretary of State James Baker to the Berlin Press Club, 12 December 1989, in *Berlin Speeches of Secretary of State James Baker* (Washington, D.C.: U.S. Information Agency, 1991).

6. See G. K. Chesterton, *What I Saw in America* (New York: Dodd, Mead, 1922), p. 296.

7. Charles Weiner, 'The new site for the seminar: the refugees and American physics in the 1930s', in Donald Fleming, ed., *The Intellectual Migration: Europe*

and America, 1930–1960 (Cambridge, Mass.: Belknap Press of Harvard University Press, 1969), p. 227.

8. Cited in Michael Hamburger, *A Proliferation of Prophets: essays on German writers from Nietzsche to Brecht* (Manchester: Carcanet Press, 1983), p. 240.

9. Martin Jay, *Permanent Exiles: essays on the intellectual migration from Germany to America* (New York: Columbia University Press, 1985), p. 28.

10. Cited in Lewis Coser, *Refugee Scholars in America* (New Haven: Yale University Press, 1984), p. 86.

11. Theodor W. Adorno, *Minima Moralia* (London: New Left Books, 1974), p. 102.

12. Alfred Kazin, *New York Jew* (London: Secker and Warburg, 1978), p. 191.

13. Cited in Paul Johnson, 'Hitler's gift to Britain', *Sunday Telegraph*, 29 January 1995.

14. D. B. Fleming, 'Foreign policy issues and social studies textbooks in the United States', in R. Berghahn, ed., *Perception of History* (Oxford: Berg Publishers, 1987), p. 117.

15. Cited in Hedley Donovan, *Roosevelt to Reagan: a reporter's encounters with nine presidents* (New York: Harper and Row, 1985), pp. 233–235.

16. William McNeil, 'Myth, history, or truth: myth, history, and historians', *American Historical Review* 91:1 (February 1986), p. 6.

17. Richard Aldyce, 'The rise and fall of civilisation courses', *American Historical Review* 87 (1982), p. 717.

18. Cited in Peter Novick, *That Noble Dream: the 'objectivity question' and the American historical profession* (Cambridge: Cambridge University Press, 1988), p. 311.

19. Russell A. Kazan, 'Revisiting assimilation: the rise, fall, and the appraisal of the concept of American ethnic history', *American Historical Review* 100:2 (April 1995), p. 470.

20. Novick, *That Noble Dream, op. cit.*, p. 310.

21. Daniel Boorstin, *The Image: or, what happened to the American Dream* (New York: Atheneum, 1962), p. 6.

22. Susan Sontag, *On Photography* (London: Penguin, 1986), p. 73.

23. Cited in Paul Ricoeur, *Time and Narrative*, vol. 1 (Chicago: University of Chicago Press, 1983), p. 171.

24. Gerda Bikales and Gary Imhoff, 'A kind of discordant harmony: issues in assimilation', in David Simcox, ed., *U.S. Immigration in the 1980s* (Boulder: Westview Press; and Washington, D.C.: Center for Immigration Studies, 1988), p. 143.

25. Karen I. Blu, *The Lumbee Problem* (New York: Cambridge University Press, 1980), cited in Sylvia Junko Yanagisako, *Transforming the Past: tradition and kinship among the Japanese Americans* (Stanford: Stanford University Press, 1985), pp. 254, 260.

26. Cited in David Lehman, *Signs of the Times: deconstruction and the fall of Paul de Man* (London: Poseidon Press, 1990), p. 23.

27. Cited in ibid.

28. Theodore H. White, *In Search of History: a personal adventure* (New York: Harper & Row, 1978), p. 538.

29. *The Complete Works of J. Russell Lowell*, vol. 6, *Literary and Political Addresses* (Boston, 1919), p. 219.

30. Cited in Anne Morrow Lindbergh, *Gift from the Sea* (New York: Harper & Row, 1955), p. 61.

31. Sacvan Bercovich, 'Rights of assent: rhetoric, ritual, and the ideology of American consensus', in Sam B. Girgus, ed., *The American Self: myth, ideology, and popular culture* (Albuquerque: University of New Mexico Press, 1981), pp. 5–6.

32. U.S. Bureau of the Census, *Statistical Abstracts of the United States* (Washington, D.C., 1993), p. 18. See also Linda Chavez, 'What to do about immigration?' *Commentary* 79:3 (March 1995).

33. *The Times* (London), 15 March 1996.

34. Cited in *The Times* (London), 24 July 1994.

35. Horace M. Kallen, 'National solidarity in the Jewish minority', *Annals of the American Academy of Political and Social Science*, September 1942, p. 17.

36. Cited in Kazan, 'Revisiting assimilation', *op. cit.*, p. 443.

37. Cited in Casey Nelson Blake, *Beloved Community: the cultural criticism of Randolph Bourne, Van Wyck Brooks, Waldo Frank, and Lewis Mumford* (Chapel Hill: University of North Carolina Press, 1990), p. 115.

38. Ibid., p. 119. See also Leslie Vaughan, 'Cosmopolitanism, ethnicity of American identity: Randolph Bourne's transnational America', *Journal of American Studies* 25 (1991).

39. Cited in John Lukacs, *America* (New York: Scribner, 1982), p. 135.

40. Cited in G. Pierson, 'The migrant factor in American history', in Michael McGiffert, ed., *The Character of Americans: a book of readings* (Homewood, Ill.: Dorsey Press, 1964), p. 122.

41. Maxine Seller, *To Seek America: a history of ethnic life in the United States* (New York: Jerome S. Ozer, 1977), p. 104.

42. John Buenker, 'Mainstream America and the immigrant experience', in Stanley Coben, ed., *The Development of an American Culture* (New York: St. Martin's Press, 1983), pp. 331–332.

43. Henry James, *The American Scene*, cited in William Boelhower, *Through a Glass Darkly: ethnic semiosis in American literature* (New York: Oxford University Press, 1987), p. 18.

44. William Barrett, 'Introspective America', *Confluence* 1:1 (March 1952), p. 44.

45. Waldo Frank, *Our America* (New York: Charles Scribner, 1919), pp. 231–232.

46. Paul J. Carter, *Waldo Frank* (New York: Twayne Publishers, 1967), p. 135. See also Waldo Frank, *The Rediscovery of America: an introduction to the philosophy of the American mind* (New York: Charles Scribner, 1929), p. 60.

47. Cited in Carlos Fuentes, *The Buried Mirror: reflections on Spain and the New World* (Boston: Houghton Mifflin, 1992), pp. 346–347.

48. Octavio Paz, *The Other Mexico: critique of the pyramid* (New York: Grove Press, 1972), p. 23.

49. Waldo Frank, *The Rediscovery of America, op. cit.*, p. 176.

50. John Dewey, 'Reconstruction in Philosophy', in *John Dewey: middle works, 1899–1924*, vol. 12, ed. Jo Ann Boydston (Carbondale: Southern Illinois University Press, 1982), p. 191.

51. Ibid., p. 201. See also Le Corbusier, *When the Cathedrals Were White: a journey to the country of timid people* (New York: Reynal and Hitchcock, 1947): "The colonists—for there actually are colonists and the American spirit itself is strongly marked by the disciplines and irruptions of a society which in a sense has just disembarked, attracted violently opposed motives: some wishing to save and maintain their faith, their religion and their ethical attitude; others eager for adventures for deeds, for money making. The colonists are renewed every day" (p. 107).

52. William Pfaff, *Barbarian Sentiments: how the American Century ends* (New York: Hill and Wang, 1989), p. 23.

53. Tony Judt, 'Austria and the ghost of the new Europe', *New York Review of Books*, 15 February 1996, p. 25.

54. Cited in Peter C. Carafiol, *The American Ideal* (Oxford: Oxford University Press, 1991), pp. 71–72.

55. Cited in John Ney, *The European Surrender: a descriptive study of the American social and economic conquest* (Boston: Little, Brown, 1970), pp. 488–489.

56. Ibid.

57. Gilbert Adair, 'No time like the future', *Sunday Times*, 6 February 1994.

Chapter Seven

1. Robert Pippin, *Modernism as a Philosophical Problem: on the dissatisfactions of European high culture* (Oxford: Basil Blackwell, 1991), p. 166.

2. See Michael Gillespie, *Hegel, Heidegger, and the Ground of History* (Chicago: University of Chicago Press, 1984), p. 157.

3. Cited in Richard Kearney, ed., *Dialogues with Contemporary Continental Thinkers* (Manchester: Manchester University Press, 1984), p. 130.

4. Cited in Christopher Thorne, *The Issue of War: states, societies, and the Far Eastern conflict, 1941–1945* (London: Hamish Hamilton, 1985), p. 198.

5. Cited in Frank Field, *British and French Writers of the First World War: comparative studies in cultural history* (Cambridge: Cambridge University Press, 1991), p. 189.

6. Michael Hamburger, *A Proliferation of Prophets: essays on German writers from Nietzsche to Brecht* (Manchester: Carcanet Press, 1983), p. 240.

7. Cited in David Rieff, *Los Angeles: capital of the Third World* (London: Jonathan Cape, 1991), p. 74.

8. Geoffrey Barraclough, *An Introduction to Contemporary History* (London: Penguin, 1970), p. 76.

9. Cited in Donald White, 'The American Century in world history', *Journal of World History* 3:1 (Spring 1992), pp. 114–115.

10. Samuel Huntington, *The Clash of Civilizations and the Remaking of World Order* (New York: Simon and Schuster, 1996), p. 218.

11. William Dray, *Perspectives on History* (London: Routledge and Kegan Paul, 1980), p. 124.

12. Cited in E. H. Gombrich, *Meditations on a Hobby Horse and Other Essays on the Theory of Art* (London: Phaidon, 1994), p. 82.

13. Cited in Ben-Ami Shillony, *Politics and Culture in Wartime Japan* (Oxford: Clarendon Press, 1981), pp. 134–135.

14. Mahathir Mohamad and Shintaro Ishihara, *The Voice of Asia: two leaders discuss the coming century* (Tokyo: Kodansha International, 1995), p. 80.

15. Michael Vatikiotis, 'Family matters: modern-day tensions strain Southeast Asia's social fabric', *Far Eastern Review*, 1 January 1996, pp. 38–41.

16. See H. D. Harootunian, 'Foucault, genealogy, history: the pursuit of otherness', in Jonathan Arac, ed., *After Foucault: humanistic knowledge, postmodern challenges* (New Brunswick: Rutgers University Press, 1988), p. 131.

17. Cited in Gianni Vattimo, *The Adventure of Difference: philosophy after Nietzsche and Heidegger* (Cambridge: Polity, 1993), p. 33.

18. Harootunian, 'Foucault, genealogy, history', *op. cit.*, p. 131.

19. See Dennis C. Washburn, *The Dilemma of the Modern in Japanese Fiction* (New Haven: Yale University Press, 1995), p. 7.

20. Stefan Tanaka, *Japan's Orient: rendering pasts into history* (Berkeley: University of California Press, 1993), p. 277.

21. Robert Bellah, 'Japan's cultural identity: some reflections on the work of Watsuji Tetsuro', *Journal of Asian Studies* 24:4 (August 1965), pp. 581–583.

22. Ibid., p. 587.

23. See the introduction by Masao Abe, Kitaro Nishida, *An Inquiry into the Good* (New Haven: Yale University Press, 1990). See also Keiji Nishitani, *Nishida Kitaro* (Berkeley: University of California Press, 1991).

24. See T. Kasulis, 'The Kyoto School and the West', *Eastern Buddhist* 15:2 (1982), pp. 125–144.

25. Cited in Graham Parkes, *Nietzsche and Asian Thought* (Chicago: University of Chicago Press, 1991), p. 15.

26. See Gary Zukav, *The Dancing Wu Li Masters: an overview of the new physics* (London: Rider, 1979), pp. 326–328. See also Fritjov Capra, *The Turning Point: science, society, and the rising culture* (New York: Simon and Schuster, 1985).

27. Cited in Parkes, *Nietzsche and Asian Thought, op. cit.*, p. 209.

28. Robert Bellah, *Tokugawa Religion: the values of pre-industrial Japan* (Glencoe, Ill.: Free Press, 1957), p. 19.

29. D. Harvey, *Collision of Empires: Britain in three world wars, 1793–1945* (London: Phoenix, 1992), pp. 511–512.

30. Patrick Smith, *Japan: a reinterpretation* (New York: Pantheon, 1996), pp. 320–322.

31. Mohamad and Ishihara, *The Voice of Asia, op. cit.*, p. 83.

32. Nicholas D. Kristof and Sheryl WuDunn, *China Wakes: the struggle for the soul of a rising power* (New York: Random House, 1995). For an excellent account of the political importance of the scientific spirit in modern China see H. Lyman Miller, *Science and Dissent in Post-Mao China: the politics of knowledge* (Seattle: University of Washington Press, 1996).

33. Youssef Choueiri, *Islamic Fundamentalism* (London: Pinter Publishers, 1990), p. 82.

34. Cited in David Pryce-Jones, *The Closed Circle: an interpretation of the Arabs* (London: Paladin, 1990), p. 89.

35. Choueiri, *Islamic Fundamentalism, op. cit.*, p. 133.

36. Cited in Bassam Tibi, *The Crisis of Modern Islam* (Salt Lake City: Utah University Press, 1988), p. 5.

37. Ibid.

38. See the excellent study on which I have relied very heavily by Asaf Hussain, *Beyond Islamic Fundamentalism: the society of faith and action* (London: Volcano Press, 1992), pp. 28–34.

39. For this historical interpretation, see the discussion by John Esposito, *The Islamic Threat: myth or reality?* (Oxford: Oxford University Press, 1992), pp. 175–181.

40. Cited in ibid.

41. Albert Camus, *The Rebel* (London: Hamish Hamilton, 1953), p. 188.

42. Information derived from the Nixon Library, provided to me by Lee Peterson, to whom I am grateful.

43. See Uriel Tal, 'On structures of political theology and myth in Germany prior to the Holocaust', in Yehuda Bauer and Nathan Rotenstreich, *The Holocaust as Historical Experience* (New York: Holmes & Meier, 1981), pp. 43–77.

44. The Western Alliance was never a religious construct, although in 1948 Ernest Bevin did call for a "spiritual federation" of the Western democracies. See

Ritchie Ovendale, *The English-Speaking Alliance: Britain, the United States, the Dominions and the Cold War, 1945–1951* (London: Allen and Unwin, 1985), p. 66. Some theologians, however, have seen it in religious terms. See Ernst Troeltsch, *The Absoluteness of Christianity and the History of Religions* (Richmond: John Knox Press, 1971), and Lamin Sanneh, *Encountering the West: Christianity and the global cultural process* (London: Harper Collins, 1993). For the contemporary importance of religion in political life, see John Milbank, *Theology and Social Theory: beyond secular reason* (Oxford: Basil Blackwell, 1990).

45. Edward T. Gargan, *The Intent of Toynbee's History* (Chicago: Loyola University Press, 1961), p. 67.

46. Ernest Gellner, *Postmodernism, Reason, and Religion* (London: Routledge, 1992), p. 22.

47. Ronald Hingley, *The Russian Mind* (London: Bodley Head, 1977), p. 77.

48. Ernst Neizvestnyi, *Space, Time, and Synthesis in Art: essays on art, literature, and philosophy* (London: Mosaic, 1990), p. 45.

49. See Marshall Berman, *All That Is Solid Melts into Air: the experience of modernity* (London: Verso, 1982), pp. 195–206.

50. Alexander Hertzen, 'The Russian people and socialism: an open letter to Jules Michelet', in *From the Other Shore,* transl. Moira Budberg (Oxford: Oxford University Press, 1979), p. 199.

51. Joseph Brodsky, '"The post-communist nightmare": an exchange', *New York Review of Books,* 17 February 1994, p. 29. Reprinted in *On Grief and Reason: essays* (London: Hamish Hamilton, 1996), pp. 212–223.

52. Ibid., p. 30.

53. Cited in Tony Smith, *America's Mission: the United States and the worldwide struggle for democracy in the twentieth century* (Princeton: Princeton University Press, 1994), p. 322.

54. Ibid.

55. Cited in Miroslav Holub, *The Dimension of the Present Moment* (London: Faber and Faber, 1990), p. 105.

56. Cited in Fernand Braudel, *A History of Civilisations* (London: Allen Lane, 1994), p. 8.

Chapter Eight

1. The best edition of Spengler's *Decline of the West* is the abridged edition of Helmut Werner (Oxford: Oxford University Press, 1991).

2. Cited in William Dray, *Perspectives on History* (London: Routledge and Kegan Paul, 1980), p. 110.

3. Erich Heller, *The Disinherited Mind: essays in modern German literature and thought* (Cambridge: Bowes & Bowes, 1952), p. 182.

4. Walter Isaacson, *Kissinger: a biography* (London: Faber and Faber, 1992), p. 761. For the best account of Spengler's influence on Kissinger, see Peter Dickson, *Kissinger and the Meaning of History* (Cambridge: Cambridge University Press, 1978).

5. Henry Kissinger, *The Troubled Partnership* (New York: McGraw Hill, 1965), p. 249.

6. Raymond Aron, *In Defense of Decadent Europe* (South Bend, Ind.: Regnery, 1979), p. 263.

7. Jean-François Revel, *The Totalitarian Temptation* (London: Penguin, 1978).

8. *Daily Telegraph,* 20 July 1994.

9. A.J.P. Taylor, *Europe: grandeur and decline* (London: Penguin, 1969), p. 77.

10. E. M. Cioran, *The Temptation to Exist* (London: Quartet, 1987), p. 59.

11. Cited in Michael S. Roth, *The Ironist's Cage: memory, trauma, and the construction of history* (New York: Columbia University Press, 1995), p. 149.

12. Paul Ricoeur, *Time and Narrative,* vol. 2 (Chicago: Chicago University Press, 1984), p. 202.

13. Jean-Luc Nancy, *The Birth to Presence* (Stanford: Stanford University Press, 1993), p. 144.

14. John Barth, *The Sot-weed Factor* (New York: Doubleday, 1960), p. 134.

15. Saul Bellow, *The Dean's December* (London: Penguin, 1982), pp. 294–298.

16. Václav Havel, 'The hope for Europe,' Address in Aachen, 15 May 1996, reprinted in *New York Review of Books,* 20 June 1996, p. 38.

Index

9 780813 333687